THE ESSENTIAL O'CASEY

S0-AIL-577

INTERNATIONAL PUBLISHERS
381 Park Avenue South NEW YORK, N. Y. 10016

THE ESSENTIAL
O'CASEY

By Jack Mitchell

"A feeling for life rather than a sense of the theatre is the first thing a man must have if he wishes to become a dramatist . . ."

Sean O'Casey

"The weather, like the inhabitants, has a more acute character, it moves in sharper, more sudden contrasts; the sky is like an Irish woman's face: here also rain and sunshine succeed each other suddenly and unexpectedly and there is none of the grey English boredom."

Frederick Engels

R
929
33
768

THE ESSENTIAL O'CASEY

A Study of the
Twelve Major Plays of
Sean O'Casey

Jack Mitchell

BIP 88

International Publishers
New York

GOSHEN COLLEGE LIBRARY
GOSHEN, INDIANA

This edition is published simultaneously by
International Publishers, New York and
Seven Seas Books, Berlin, 1980

*For Eric and Niall and all their friends in the South and
in the North. They know where they're going and O'Casey's
dream goes with them.*

ACKNOWLEDGEMENTS
The extracts of quotations from the works and plays by Sean
O'Casey, (*Purple Dust, Red Roses for Me, The Bishop's Bon-
fire, The Shadow of a Gunman, Juno and the Paycock, The
Plough and the Stars, The Silver Tassie, Within the Gates, The
Star Turns Red, Cock-a-doodle Dandy, Behind the Green Cur-
tains, Figuro in the Night*) are used with the kind permission of
Macmillan, London and Basingstoke. Permission for the U.S.A.
and the Philippines of quotations from *Purple Dust* (Copyright
1940 by Sean O'Casey, renewed 1968 by Eileen O'Casey); from
Red Roses for Me (Copyright 1943, 1944 by Sean O'Casey,
renewed 1971, 1972 by Eileen O'Casey, Breon O'Casey and
Shivaun Kenig); from *The Bishop's Bonfire* (Copyright 1955 by
Sean O'Casey) are used with the kind permission of Macmillan
Publishing Co., Inc., New York.

**Library of Congress Cataloging in Publication
Data**

Mitchell, Jack, 1932-
The essential O'Casey.

1. O'Casey, Sean, 1880-1964 –
Criticism and interpretation. I. Title.
PR6029.C33Z768   822'.914   80-13284
ISBN 0-7178-0557-3 (pbk.)

Copyright © Seven Seas Books, Berlin, 1980
Cover Design by Klaus Krüger
Printed in the German Democratic Republic

All quotations from the twelve plays by Sean O'Casey are taken from the following books published by Macmillan, London:

Three Plays (1967): The Shadow of a Gunman; Juno and the Paycock; The Plough and the Stars. *Three More Plays* (1969): The Silver Tassie; Purple Dust; Red Roses for Me. *Collected Plays:* The Star Turns Red (Vol. II, 1952); Within the Gates (Vol. II, 1952); Cock-a-doodle Dandy (Vol. IV, 1951). *The Bishop's Bonfire* (1955). *Behind the Green Curtains, Figuro in the Night, The Moon Shines on Kylenamoe* (1961): Behind the Green Curtains; Figuro in the Night.

CONTENTS

INTRODUCTION

Sean O'Casey first turned seriously to writing plays around the year 1920, when he was approaching the age of forty. This had been preceded by two decades of intense participation in the national and class struggles of his native Ireland—as a champion of Gaelic culture, militant trade-unionist and socialist activist. From the early twenties to his death in 1964 playwriting became his chief occupation. He was the first English-speaking dramatist of proletarian background to enter the arena of world theatre. This is a book about his plays.

These plays he regarded as weapons, a continuation of the same struggle with different means—the struggle for the emancipation of the Irish people and all working people from poverty, ignorance and exploitation, for the creation of a new society in which men and women would be free to develop all their capacities as harmonious human beings. Alongside his playwriting he continued to express this standpoint in direct political activity—in his connection with London Unity Theatre in the late thirties, his work on the Advisory Board of the *Daily Worker*, his call to support the World Peace Council's Stockholm Appeal against nuclear weapons in the early fifties, his solidarity with Republican Spain and the Soviet Union, and so on.

How did O'Casey use the drama as a weapon? Does his use of it in this way bear out the view that politics (usually meaning left-wing political partisanship) are best kept out of art, for art's sake? Or was he able to get away with combining the two because—as some critics have proposed—his Communism was of an "unorthodox" or "Christian" brand?[1] Or can we appreciate O'Casey and ignore his Communism, as the U.S. critic John Gassner advocates?[2] Or does O'Casey's work demonstrate that in the modern world only a preoccupation with these things can lead to enduring artistic achievement, true realism? I hope that this book will throw some light on these questions.

In the case of Bertolt Brecht this revolutionary political preoccupation has been no obstacle to his becoming a pre-eminent figure and influence in the world theatre of our epoch. If this influence has often been superficial it has been widespread. The English-speaking theatre has been no exception. This has not been so with O'Casey. In those countries culturally and linguistically nearest to him his work has been persistently under-performed and his influence on the drama and theatre there has remained slight—though his name was something of a household word. It is mainly in the socialist countries—perhaps above all in the German Democratic Republic—that real headway has been made in establishing O'Casey as part of the classical repertoire.

Where do the reasons lie for this neglect on his own "native grounds?" In weaknesses inherent in the plays themselves? Or perhaps in their inherent strengths which do not correspond to the needs of the commercial theatre? Or in the inadequacies of much O'Casey criticism?

Or is O'Casey's drama, for all its charm and novelty, perhaps too Irish to open up perspectives for world revolutionary theatre as a whole, while Brecht with his "epic theatre" was able to map out the main line of advance? Or does the new theatre need both Brecht and O'Casey, a synthesis of the two approaches, as the French dramatist Arthur Adamov advocates?[3] Are the two playwrights, in their differences, always so different? Must O'Casey be seen as the junior partner in this suggested pair, or must the Irish playwright be established as the creator of a revolutionary drama on a par with Brecht? I hope to provide some tentative answers to these questions in the course of this study.

The urge to experiment is as strong in O'Casey as in the German playwright. In fact, from the point of view of the modifications in approach and technique made from one play to another, it is O'Casey who is perhaps the more volatile of the two.

What does O'Casey's increasing use of symbol, parable and fantasy signify? Is it, as many have suggested, a steady falling away from a high point reached in the seemingly more traditional early "Dublin trilogy?" Was it an urge to experiment for its own sake, an urge which tempted him away from his true vein–creating "character"–into a style where character was subordinated to the reigning theme and statement. This has become something of a maxim in traditional O'Casey criticism. Some scholars, for instance the West-German Heinz Kosok,[4] maintain that it was a systematic move away from "realism" to an art of the imagination and fantasy, which is, by its very nature, supposedly anti-realistic. Another view is that O'Casey's mature and particular genius lies in the combination of individualised, close-to-reality images with those of a more symbolic and fantastic nature, direct statement and parable, as is more and more the case in the later plays.[5] Then there are those who place the peak of his achievement in the "middle period" from 1939 to 1943, when revolutionary events and figures appear most directly in his work. In how far can one speak of an artistic advance or decline in O'Casey's career? Or do the changes in his technique represent a difference of kind, but not of quality?

In trying to answer some of these questions I have chosen the method of detailed play-by-play analyses as the most suitable. In this way I analyse all the major longer plays. I have left out two long plays which I feel do not represent O'Casey's art at its best–*Oak Leaves and Lavender* and *The Drums of Father Ned*. The one-acters deserve more space than could have been devoted to them here.

On the basis of my analyses I try to work out a practical and all-embracing interpretation in each case, regarding each play as a relatively autonomous artistic model of reality, with its own specific and irrepeatable relationship to the latter.

Despite the respectable number of works already written on O'Casey's plays a great deal of groundwork still remained to be done. A mass of distortion and misinterpretation still had to be put right. My form of analysis and interpretation is aimed at helping to improve both the production and reception of O'Casey's plays. The interpretations are conceived as an encouragement and guide line for both the theatre worker and the member of the audience. But at the same time they are addressed to that far larger number of people who have read or are interested in reading the plays on the printed page.

In some instances my interpretations have been influenced by seeing stage or television productions, but in every case my main point of departure and reference has been the printed text backed by general knowledge of O'Casey's artistic and political personality.

Am I not running the risk of reading too much into the texts? Are my interpretations, singly and as a whole, not too consistent within themselves? Is it not rather presumptuous to base such complete interpretations on the text-on-the-page? Is the play on the page rather a kind of raw material, a fund of stimulating possibilities to be moulded at will by the production team? This is a point of view very much in favour with a certain school of theatre writers and producers at the moment. It was not O'Casey's view. For him the written play, as it came from the mind of the dramatist, was the basis and determinant of the whole theatrical process. The production was there to bring out the play, more or less as the musicians are there to interpret the scores of a Mozart or Beethoven. His detailed and frequent stage instructions bear this out. So do pronouncements like "A good acting play that is not also good enough to be enjoyed in the study is not worth a dying tinker's damn"[6] or "I learned more from reading plays than seeing them on the stage."[7]

So the main thing was already embedded in the text. What was the "main thing"? For O'Casey the purpose of a play was never the creation of "character" for its own sake or the stringing together of comic and tragic episodes. The main thing for him was the impulses it contained, its "message": "Indeed the very first glimmer of the conception for a play is an idea. There is hardly a thing written as a play, a novel, or a poem, that hasn't an idea under it, hovering over it, or in its very core."[8] Of his great mentor he says, "Ay, and Shakespeare, too; although not deliber-

14

ately 'propagandist', for that time had not yet come [. . .] his plays twinkle with messages [. . .] [He] even tried to make England look at her history in his way."[9] However, "it is one thing to have an idea in a head and quite another to place it in a play. It takes a master-mind to do that so that it will appeal to the imagination of an audience. Shaw and Ibsen are masters of this fancy."[10]

The aim of this book is to find out if and how O'Casey sets about doing this, to find out what he means, what the plays are about, to investigate the dialectical, mutually determining relationship between the particular themes of each play and its structure and characters.

After a bad experience at the beginning of his career O'Casey vowed that "never again would he reveal to anyone what he was trying to do; never again, except under curious circumstances, would he speak of work in progress. If he spoke at all, he would talk of something he but faintly intended to do."[11] And he stuck to this.

I have endeavoured to base my interpretations on the totality of the evidence and so get as near as possible to the core of O'Casey's meaning for our time. Is O'Casey's art deeply enough rooted in his time (which is ours) to live beyond a particular epoch? This is really the question of the quality of his realism, a question to which I try to suggest some preliminary answers.

Notes

1. For instance Saros Cowasjee in *Sean O'Casey* (Writers and Critics), Edinburgh and London, 1966, ch. IV; and Maureen Malone in *The Plays of Sean O'Casey*, Southern Illinois University Press, 1969, p. 67

2. In "The Prodigality of Sean O'Casey" in *Sean O'Casey, Modern Judgements*, ed. Ronald Ayling, London, 1969, p. 112

3. Arthur Adamov, Roger Planchon, René Allio, "Wie stehen wir zu Brecht?" in *Sinn und Form*, No. 5/6, Berlin, 1961, p. 939

4. Heinz Kosok, *Sean O'Casey, das dramatische Werk*, Berlin (West), 1972, pp. 12 and 335
5. Manfred Pauli, *Sean O'Casey, Drama, Poesie, Wirklichkeit*, Berlin, 1977
6. Sean O'Casey, *The Flying Wasp*, London, 1937, p. 94
7. Letter to Horace Reynolds, Feb. 11, 1938, in *The Letters of Sean O'Casey*, Vol. 1, ed. David Krause, London, 1975, p. 701
8. Sean O'Casey, "The Play of Ideas" in *Blasts and Benedictions*, ed. Ronald Ayling, London and New York, 1967, p. 24
9. Sean O'Casey, "Out Damned Spot" in *Under a Colored Cap*, London and New York, 1964, p. 257
10. "The Play of Ideas," op. cit., p. 24
11. Sean O'Casey, *Inishfallen, Fare Thee Well* in *Autobiographies II*, London, 1963, p. 148

PART ONE THE REVOLUTION THAT WAS AND WAS NOT

Sean O'Casey's first and last love was Ireland and her working people. At first this love took the form of an ardent nationalism in the traditional revolutionary-republican vein. Some time before the great Dublin Lockout of 1913 this passionate proletarian came under the influence of the man who was to remain his hero throughout his life–Jim Larkin, the legendary labour leader and the dynamo behind the Dublin class war of 1913. O'Casey threw himself heart and soul into this conflict and from that point on can be traced his maturity as a class-conscious socialist and Communist internationalist. At the same time he remained true to the best traditions of Irish republican nationalism.

In the period after the inconclusive ending of that terrible eight-month battle and Larkin's departure for the U.S.A., O'Casey came more and more into conflict with certain tendencies within the Irish Labour movement. In the years leading up to the Rising of 1916 he quarrelled with the man who took over the leadership of the left wing of the movement from Larkin–James Connolly, and the latter's policy of allying militant labour with the patriotic bourgeois nationalists who had often been their class enemies in the 1913 struggle. It was not, as has often been implied, that O'Casey wanted the workers to keep themselves to themselves and go it alone as far as the revolution was concerned. He makes this clear in a letter to the *Dublin Saturday Post* of September 22, 1917:

"What I think the Labour movement ought to do is to make the workers, by education and propaganda, a power in all these organisations, particularly in those that appeal to the national sentiments of the people [. . .] So far from neglecting to interfere with any organisation we must interfere with them all."[1]

As O'Casey saw it the interference was more and more in the other direction. Not fully understanding Connolly's anti-imperialist strategy he held him responsible for leading the workers into the overpowering embrace of the bourgeois nationalists. This is why O'Casey did not take a direct part in the Easter Rising of 1916. Objectively the working class was certainly the junior partner in it, and this O'Casey could not stomach. After the 1916 defeat and the death of Connolly, the Labour movement fell into the hands of reformists who were willing to accept a socially subservient position for their class. The workers had had the historical initiative wrested from their grasp. O'Casey could find no place for himself now within this organised movement. He felt the workers were being misled by it, and misused for alien ends.

More and more he takes on the role of commentator on and analyst of contemporary developments—a publicist from revolutionary proletarian positions, while still earning his living as a labourer.

But what made him turn playwright around 1920, at the age of forty? O'Casey did not suddenly transform himself into a literary and dramatic artist. He had put himself through an almost twenty-year literary apprenticeship, mainly in the operative or tactical genres such as articles, polemics, poems, historical essays, political songs—but also in writing short dramatic pieces. Nevertheless, he seems to have taken the conscious decision in the period 1920–2 to throw the main weight of his activity into the drama and to continue his contribution to the class struggle in this form from now on.

It was at this point in history that he saw his growing fears for the fate of the Irish revolution being tragically borne out. Ireland, in the decade from 1911 to 1921, had been—despite all reservations and set-backs—one of the storm-centres of world revolution. But this revolution, which could have been a beacon to the oppressed masses everywhere, as was the Russian revolution, had been betrayed and the people defeated for the time being. It was time to take stock, to analyse in depth what had gone wrong. The drama, as a strategic art-form, was well suited to this purpose. It had a strong and progressive tradition in the writing of Irish men of letters (almost every "English" playwright since the end of the Elizabethan era had been of Irish extraction). And of course O'Casey's personal talents went in this direction too. In addition there was that exception among bourgeois theatre institutions, the Abbey Theatre in Dublin, which at that time both encouraged writers from the people and provided a platform for the dissemination of progressive ideas via the stage.

The year 1913 had been the coming-of-age not only of O'Casey (it remained the definitive experience of his life) but of the Irish workers as a class, conscious of itself. They had demonstrated that the future of the nation must lie with them. They alone were capable of bringing the seven-hundred-year Irish struggle for national independence and social liberty to a triumphant conclusion. Writing immediately after the end of the lockout strike O'Casey shows that this perspective had become his own. "Personally, I hold the workers are beside themselves with foolishness to support any movement that does not stand to make the workers supreme, for these are the people, and without them there can be no life nor power." [2]

And now, in 1922, these people, the salt of the earth, had "won," as the product of all their sufferings and their exploits, that sorry abortion midwifed by the British government and the Irish bourgeoisie—the "Irish Free State." The real promise of revolution had degenerated into tragic and bloody civil war between factions of erstwhile comrades-in-arms. O'Casey was full of indignation and disappointment—and the birth of a new hope. Playing on the poet Yeats' famous line on the Easter Rising (A terrible beauty is born) he writes in his autobiography,

A TERRIBLE BEAUTY IS BORNEO. Here it was at last—The Irish Free State; or, as it was written down officially, Saorstat na hEireann. A discordant symphony in green." [3] "It won't be long till the gold harp's taken out of the green flag, and a bright, black tall-hat put in its place. The terrible beauty of a tall-hat is born to Ireland. [4]

In the same place he relates how he would wander through the slums and be filled with rage and astonishment that the poor wretches who cowered there did not rise up in furious action and rip the guts out of those who kept them in such straits.

"But Sean had more than hope now. He had had letters from a Raissa Lomonovska telling him about what was going on in the Soviet Union [...] In the spirit, Sean stood with these children, with these workers, with these Red Army Men pushing away with them the ruin they were rising from, the ruin from which all the people would one day rise, sharing the firmness of their unafraid hearts, adding his cheer to the cheers of the Soviet People.

"The terrible beauty had been born there, and not in Ireland. The cause of the Easter Rising had been betrayed by the commonplace bourgeois class, who laid low the concept of the common good and the common task, and were now decorating themselves with the privileges and powers dropped in their flight by those defeated by the dear, dead men."[5]

In the so-called "Dublin" or "Abbey" plays (*The Shadow of a Gunman,* 1923; *Juno and the Paycock,* 1924; *The Plough and the Stars,* 1926) O'Casey sets out to make the Irish working people plain to themselves, warts and all, to cut away without anaesthetic the tangle of myths, false and worn-out heroics, illusions, prejudices, weaknesses and self-comforters which had contributed to their defeat. He goes for precisely those characteristics of his working people which had been produced by centuries of colonial yoke and denial of national self-realisation on the one hand, and, on the other, by the inhuman conditions of poverty and ignorance in which they, as workers, were obliged to exist.

He emerges as the master myth-breaker in the period after a failed revolution, preparing the people for a future and better offensive. The historical tension between the fact of the workers' defeat in Ireland and the victory of their revolution in Russia accounts for the urgency, mercilessness and courage of this "self-criticism" by the Irish proletariat in the person of O'Casey. It is this basic tension which helps generate in O'Casey the historical optimism which enables him to look the degradation of his people full in the face and recognise the potentially world-changing human qualities through it—and so establish the equivalent of that tension within the plays, between the actual and the potential. It is this latter tension that lies at the very core of his dynamic, contradictory and deeply realistic image of the working people. What is generated is a deep conviction of the inexhaustibility of the people's sources of creative energy and their ultimate ability to revolutionise reality. The brilliant use of the comic element in these fundamentally tragic plays (O'Casey calls them tragedies, not tragi-comedies) provides us with a way in to this "double" nature of the people and to a full appreciation of the tragedy.

In these "Dublin" plays O'Casey does not, on the whole, indulge his penchant for the outspokenly symbolic, parabolic, and fantastic. In order to persuade his people that *this* was how things really stood with them it was necessary to avoid all "theatrical" devices which might provide an excuse for saying that he was tampering with reality. These plays had to appear not so much as a constructed model, but rather as a "mere" mirror, forcing people to accept its image as a true and exact likeness. Furthermore, if one wishes to make it clear that "outside help" in the form of miracles is not on the agenda, then it is better for the time being to keep fantastic figures and happenings off the stage.

These three plays analyse the state of the people at three crucial points in the process of their defeat—the Easter Rising, the "Black-and-Tan War" and the Civil War (not in that order). Always the overriding concern is with the state and fate of the people—the nation. For a similar *national* concern of such proportions and sense of responsibility one has to go back, as so often when seeking a comparison for this our first proletarian dramatist, to Shakespeare. Shakespeare is writing from a different perspective, it is true—from that of *achieved* national unity and from a historically still progressive social context. Nevertheless, he is largely preoccupied with the same thing–directly in the History plays, indirectly in *Macbeth*, *Lear*, etc.: with the theme of the paramount necessity of achieving national unity and overcoming feuding factionalism. Shakespeare judges his characters and social forces according to their role in this struggle. So does O'Casey.

Notes

1. *Letters*, Vol. 1, p. 62
2. Letter to the *Irish Worker*, Feb. 21, 1914. ibid., p. 40
3. *Inishfallen Fare Thee Well*, op.cit., p. 125
4. Ibid., p. 130
5. Ibid., pp. 137–138

1 THE SHADOW OF A GUNMAN

Written 1922; produced 1923 (Abbey Theatre, Dublin);
published 1925

> "...you can't always go be looks nowadays –"
> the Landlord

The time is May 1920 at the height of the hit-and-run war
between the Irish Republican Army and the irregular British occupation forces ("Black-and-Tans" and Auxiliaries).
Donal Davoren, thirty years old, writer of romantic verses,
shares a room in a Dublin slum with Seumas Shields, a
heavy thirty-five, pedlar and one-time patriot, now retired
into religion, superstition and bed. Assuming Davoren is an
I.R.A. gunman on the run, the tenement-dwellers assure
him of their support; flattered, he does not disillusion them,
especially when pretty young Minnie Powell, ardent Irish
patriot, falls in love with him.

The slum-dwellers: Tommy Owens, a broken-down young
man, forever declaring himself ready to die for Ireland;
Mrs Henderson, a soft-hearted gossip and admirer of the
literary powers of Mr Gallogher, a weedy little clerk;
Mr Grigson, alcoholic blow-hard Orangeman, coddled and
admired by his wife, Mrs Grigson. They seek a little reassurance and borrowed glory by dropping in on the morose
Donal.

Maguire, a friend of Seumas', breezes in and leaves a
bag, purportedly containing pedlar's wares, for Seumas to
look after till he returns. After a time when news arrives
that Maguire has been killed in an ambush they realise he
had been a "real" I.R.A. gunman.

British Auxiliaries raid the tenement. The two room-
mates look into the bag and discover to their horror that it
contains bombs. Minnie hides it in her room. Davoren and
Shields do nothing to hinder her. The "Auxies" terrorise
the inhabitants and discover the bombs. Minnie is arrested
and is accidentally shot dead, presumably by the I.R.A.
when the latter ambush the British while they are taking
her away. The women, especially Mrs Henderson, stand up

to the invaders; the brave-mouthed "menfolk" grovel before them. After the catastrophe Davoren pours bitter scorn on his own and Seumas' spinelessness. Seumas has the last word—he knew something would come of the tapping he'd heard on the wall.

Poverty, ignorance, lack of privacy and perspective, harassment, war, terror and violent death. Such is the general picture O'Casey gives of life in the Dublin slums. They do not behave like people involved in a mass struggle to emancipate themselves. The actual "liberation fighter" (Maguire) flits through them unrecognised, and dies at a distance. They only read about it in the papers. On the other hand, the forces of oppression are massively present, invading every room and tearing through the whole house like a whirlwind. In contrast to the romantic nationalist picture of a united heroic people, they are depicted as crippled by disunity, internal bickering, lack of mental discipline and leadership, by escapism, disillusionment on the one hand and illusions on the other, and by an inability to grapple responsibly with their situation as it really is.

The general reasons for this state of affairs are shown to be physical and mental deprivation plus religious mumbo-jumbo. Even Minnie, the best of them, is "like all of her class [...] not able to converse very long on the one subject, and her thoughts spring from one thing to another." (90) Davoren, we are told, has had a hard struggle through life, and it would drive him mad if it were not for the fact that he has known no other.

These are the general concerns of the play, but in particular it is about one overriding aspect of this *misère*. What is this specific theme which unites all the apparently heterogeneous parts into one artistic unity?

The scene with Mr Gallogher's letter, set near the beginning, brings it sharply into focus. Mr Gallogher, aided and abetted by Mrs Henderson, reads his letter to an appreciative audience of the tenement-dwellers. It is a complaint against his rowdy neighbours, appealing to the I.R.A. to come with their guns and sort them out. The letter has several implications. Here is a man from the people appealing to the revolutionary authorities (the new state in embryo) to take violent action against his fellow sufferers for some supposed petty injuries. The significant thing is that for Mr Gallogher and Mrs Henderson the real persecution lies in the "name calling and the language." (99) Great believers all in the power of the word, of the letter, to make and break. (Mr Gallogher's "rebellion" takes the form of a letter.) And it is a letter in which the meaning gets lost in a tangle of quasi-legal phrases and conventions—"in respect of and appertaining to [. . .] Deeming it disrespectable [. . .] as aforesaid specified [. . .] The name of the resident-tenant who is giving all this trouble and who, pursuant to the facts of the case aforesaid, mentioned, will be the defendant, is Dwyer . . ." (98–101) Poor Gallogher, when all is said and done, has a real problem—misery and overcrowding are driving him mad, but his real complaint is lost in formal ritual into which he is constantly being side-tracked. His flowery address to the Gentlemen of the Irish Republican Army elicits admiration from all except Davoren. "That's some swank." (Minnie, 98) Tommy Owens considers it a saying that will send the British Empire reeling. With unconscious irony Mrs Henderson singles out the word "precise" for special praise—"it cuts the ground from under their feet—so to speak." (99)

What emerges here is a belief in the word Almighty, ruler of heaven and earth. Behind it stands a more general fascination with the magic power and primacy of form, conventions, signs, myths and rituals. This confounding of their ability to get to grips with the essence of things, through a fatal fascination with form, is not indigenous to them but has been inculcated into them from above, through religion, through their smattering of schooling, through their work (Mr Gallogher is a solicitor's clerk).

It prevents them from seeing where their real oppression lies. Mrs Henderson is driven to fury at the injury done to Seumas by the children calling him "oul' hairpins." Minnie believes that the future of her love for Davoren is magically ensured by having him type her name, coupled with his, on a sheet of paper which she puts against her breast.

Often a felicitous word-formulation of their own enchants them so much that they seem loth to part with it, the result amounting almost to a speech impediment: "I suppose I could call meself as good a Gael as some of those that are knocking about now—knocking about now—as good a Gael as some that are knocking about now . . ." (Seumas, 84)

A high point in their fascination with conventional word-patterns as a magic ritual with power to master reality is represented by the songs. Tommy sings a favourite romantic nationalist song about three martyrs for Ireland (94–95). Later his Orange counterpart, Grigson, bursts into "The Orange Lily O." (117–118) Songs like these have been of prime importance in whipping up the passions of contending factions in Irish history. Tommy and Grigson get as drunk on them as they both do on alcohol. Their singing is the culmination of a process of lending themselves Dutch courage through boasting speech. The songs are the quintessence of this form of self-hypnotisation. Their voices rise to a shout—they shout down the world and become for the time being oblivious of the real danger brought down on themselves and others by their reckless singing. The ritual songs will lend them invulnerability and save the necessity for action.

Thus the function of the songs here is the opposite to the way Brecht uses songs. Brecht "alienates" (distances) the action through the songs. They are "alienating-effects." O'Casey alienates or distances us from the songs through the action. The action in general functions as an alienating-effect in relation to the songs. This is determined by the role of these songs in Irish history as indicated above. In line with O'Casey's de-heroicising and myth-debunking strategy it was necessary to let the emotional hot air out of the songs and force us to take a cool look at the kind of attitudes that they represent.

The ways are manifold in which conventions, myths and rituals determine the people's relationship to reality, making them mistake the shadow for the substance. They do not always take the direct form of the word.

Mrs Grigson lavishes all her considerable powers of self-sacrifice, responsibility and devotion on a good-for-nothing object–her husband. When he is away from her at the pub she is capable of seeing him for what he is. If she were a girl again, she says, she'd think twice before she'd get married. But when he is on the scene she forgets the evidence of her senses, for, according to the social convention sanctioned by religion, he is her ordained lord and master. The Holy Scripture says that "the woman shall be subject to her husband" and Mr Grigson is going to make sure that his wife keeps the teaching of the Book "in the letter an' in the spirit." (116–117) Mrs Grigson acquiesces to this ritual sanctioned by the Word and introduced into the people from outside.

In its essence Minnie Powell's relationship to Davoren is quite similar. This constitutes one of the complex systems of inner parallels in the play. In taking Davoren for an I.R.A. gunman and then falling in love with this self-created form Minnie also goes against the actual evidence of her senses. The romantic myth or convention of the freedom fighter and his devoted sweetheart who is ready to lay down her life for him blinds her to this evidence. She has imbibed it from her earliest days in songs and stories about patriot-lovers such as Robert Emmet. It is a "form" which has shaken itself loose from all real content, become an independent entity imposing its own arbitrary and illusory "content" upon reality, making the latter correspond to the illusion. It paralyses Minnie's ability to treat reality on its own terms (she, like the others, fails to suspect Maguire of being a gunman) and to learn from experience. It induces her to squander her capacity for heroism and selfless devotion to another human being and to a cause on an object unworthy of it–Davoren. Minnie in her fascination with the myth, the convention, must bear her share of responsibility for creating the deadly shadow of a gunman which ends by destroying her.

Certain critics have written a great deal of gushing nonsense about little Minnie Powell. Armstrong says that "The archetypal quality of O'Casey's central character [Minnie] raises his play far above the level of topical realism."[1] Hogan maintains that "The theme of the play concerns the difference between true and false bravery. The characters who are truly brave—Maguire, Minnie, Mrs Henderson—are not talkers, but doers."[2] In talking of women characters like Minnie and Juno (*Juno and the Paycock*) David Krause pronounces the women to possess "the only kind of untainted heroism that O'Casey recognizes."[3] This has become something of an "established truth" in conventional O'Casey criticism. Nevertheless, it is not true. As regards Minnie—bravery functioning in the context sketched in above is functioning falsely and is therefore not true concrete bravery. For the same reason she cannot function as a heroic alternative to the pseudo-heroic figures. Minnie is herself conceived by the dramatist as part of his systematic exposure of empty heroism and his puncturing of out-of-date and deadly heroic myths. As things are, Minnie is still only *the shadow of a hero*.

In this way the very qualities of courage and devotion which ought to be helping the people to emancipate themselves are made to function in the opposite direction, against the people, as factors contributing to their own destruction. The women suffer to an important extent from the same basic "disease" as the men. Minnie eggs Davoren on along the line that leads to disaster. In this sense she is his "accomplice."

Minnie sees in Davoren the traditional Irish *poet*-rebel— a word-magician. That is, she sees him basically in the same terms as Mrs Henderson sees Gallogher. In sacrificing herself for a man unworthy of such a sacrifice she is doing the same as Mrs Grigson in relation to her husband. So the relationship on the tragic level is paralleled by similar relationships on the comic-grotesque level. On the one hand this is a method of generalising the statement, showing that this is a social phenomenon characteristic of all walks of life. On the other hand it distances us from the Minnie-Davoren action. It is a kind of alienating-effect, and one widely used by O'Casey. It prevents a total emotional involvement in the tragic aspect of this relationship by indicating that it also has its ridiculous side. Once a phenomenon has been shown to be ridiculous as well as tragic it no longer appears as inevitable, but as an aberration which, because it is grotesque, must and can be done away with. This is one of the strategic uses of the comic element in O'Casey's work as a whole.

Their belief in the power of the sign, the convention, ritual, myth, the word, i.e. in form and formulas, is put to the test in the second half of the play (Act II). Do these things have the power over reality which they attribute to them, the power to shield them against the forces of destruction and to defeat these forces?

They turn out to be worse than useless.

Grigson's thundered Orange song fails to keep the raiders away from the house. Neither the holy statues and pictures in Seumas' room nor their "loyalist" counterparts in the Grigson household protect their inmates against the inroads of the Auxiliaries. Far from being intimidated by them the latter use them to terrorise and mock those who put their trust in such things. Just before the "Auxies" burst in, Grigson lays the Bible–that incarnation of the Word as the power that shapes reality–open on his table. He has marked a text in red ink, which calls upon people to submit to the temporal authority of the king. The "Auxies" are not impressed. They throw the holy gospel on the floor and force Grigson to perform the conventional word-rituals of prayer and hymn-singing for their amusement. Lessons can be learnt from the most unlikely people–even from the Auxiliaries. There is something symbolic here. These people who fondly believe that signs, forms, symbols are possessed by them, at their command, are in fact subjugated with the help of these things, which are really controlled by the enemy.

Grigson escapes unscathed. This is on the comic plane. But not Minnie. Her name bracketed with Davoren's on that piece of paper and put as armour against her breast has no magic potency to stop the bullet piercing her heart.

The irony is that the people, in their hearts, know better. Just as Mrs Grigson recognises in her saner moments that her husband is "too far gone in the horns" ever to reform, so they are all ready to admit, on occasion, that the magical rituals and conventions are mere playthings in the hands of the oppressors. "Nobody now cares a traneen about the orders of the Ten Commandments," says Seumas (118 to 119), while Grigson adds that it's all one to the Brits what you profess to be. Loyalists are made to sing "The Soldiers' Song," and Republicans "God Save the King." There is not only irony in this, there is also hope and a touch of optimism, a hint that, in the Brechtian sense, things could conceivably take a different course if the people could really bring into play what is best in them. But O'Casey, as always, refuses to simplify the stubbornness of the problem. Grigson fails to learn from his experience and as soon as the coast is clear he is his old self, weaving myths of how he tamed the wild "Auxies" with mere words. Seumas too, after the event, banishes the bad men by referring to a magic word-formula: "'I don't know of any clause,' says I, 'in the British Constitution that makes it a crime for a man to speak in his own room,'—with that, he just had a look round, an' off he went." (128–129)

How do the two central characters, Donal Davoren and Seumas Shields, fit into all this? Why does O'Casey choose to expand the portrayal of these two in particular?

Davoren and Seumas are people who have, or have had, intellectual and cultural aspirations, intelligent men possessing insight. If the people are to get the particular kind of guidance and leadership they need, then it should be expected to come from men of this background. They are themselves of the people, sharing many characteristics with the masses from which they emerge. They are, as personalities, battlefields on which the dramatic contradictions defining the popular character fight it out with particular vehemence and impact.

Take Seumas Shields. His ties with the mass of the people are more direct and obvious than Davoren's. O'Casey calls him a "primitive man," (80) but he is—or at least was—more than this. He is a man with a history. This differentiates him from the other characters. We find out something about how he developed from what he was to what he is.

He was once an active patriot, with the cause of Irish freedom at heart, and a man of real culture: "I remember the time when I taught Irish six nights a week, when in the Irish Republican Brotherhood I paid me rifle levy like a man, an' when the Church refused to have anything to do with James Stephens, I tarred a prayer for the repose of his soul on the steps of the Pro-Cathedral." (84) The maudlin self-exoneration of this passage as a whole should not obscure the fact that his claims are almost certainly true. He is at least as well and widely read as the "poet" Davoren. He talks of having been fast in the arms of Morpheus, and when he asks Donal whether he is right in thinking that Morpheus was the son of Somnus and that the poppy was his emblem, the man of letters has to admit that he doesn't know. (80–81)

When Davoren answers his query regarding the time by quoting Shakespeare, Seumas immediately places it—*Richard III*, Act Five, Scene III. It is Seumas, as against Davoren, who raises the demand that "a poet's claim to greatness depends upon his power to put passion in the common people." (107)

Above all he is capable, on occasion, of deep and powerful insights:

Seumas. [on the I.R.A.] . . . an' their creed is, I believe in the gun almighty, maker of heaven an' earth—an' it's all for the 'glory o' God an' the honour o' Ireland.'
Davoren. I remember the time when you yourself believed in nothing but the gun.

Seumas. Ay, when there wasn't a gun in the country; I've a
different opinion now when there's nothin' but guns in
the country. [. . .] You're not goin'–you're not goin' to
beat the British Empire–the British Empire, by shootin'
an occasional Tommy at the corner of an occasional
street. [. . .] It's the civilians that suffer; when there's an
ambush they don't know where to run. Shot in the back
to save the British Empire, an' shot in the breast to save
the soul of Ireland [. . .] I believe in the freedom of Ireland, an' that England has no right to be here, but I draw
the line when I hear the gunmen blowin' about dyin' for
the people, when it's the people that are dyin' for the
gunmen! (110–111)

A great part of the play's statement is summed up here in a
nutshell. Here is also real honesty about himself, and a kind
of grasp of the fact that ritual has taken on a devastating life
of its own.

But the thing about Seumas is that he has degenerated.
Despite his insight, or because of it, he is in full retreat
from life and responsibility. He has become an empty boast-
er, a hero-in-retrospect, a coward, procrastinator and bitter
maligner of those whose souls aspire, like those of the poet
Shelley or little Minnie Powell, to something beyond themselves. He has become a cross between a slothful petulant
child and a cave-man, completely self-centred. He has no
real loyalties, no real relationships with other people. His
commerce with life and with his fellow humans is symbolised, quality-wise, in his actual commerce as a pedlar of rub-
bishy knick-knacks. Like old Luka in Gorky's *Lower Depths*
all this once remarkable self-educated man can do for his
neighbours is try to "keep up their spirits" with perfunctory "comforters" like telling Mrs Grigson not to be down-
hearted, her husband might suddenly turn over a new leaf
one day. He has been so turned in on himself that he can no
longer see himself steadily in relation to the world at large.
The irony is that he himself is the very embodiment of all
the weaknesses and follies which he imputes to Ireland, but

never to Seumas. He has washed his hands of that "hopeless country," and retired to bed. His advice to those that seek it is—"go to bed."

In this way it comes to a contradiction between insight and action, a contradiction which has bedevilled Irish history and which is the direct result of centuries of colonial frustration. Seumas' very insights degenerate into arid unproductive rituals, covering the same ground again and again. They atrophy into mere formalism. Seumas is satisfied with these rituals. Having gone through them he feels he has taken valid action. The possibility of real action, instead of being encouraged by insight, becomes obscured by it, as it were. Thus, having "defeated" the landlord in a childish verbal duel, he puts the quit-notices behind him, or rather behind the holy statue on the mantlepiece, as "settled."

His relationship to cultural tradition has also withered into formalism. As we have seen above he has an almost pedantic knowledge of chapter and verse, of the letter. This is all that remains of this self-taught enthusiast's relationship to the classical heritage. The spirit of the humanist heritage has become totally alien to him. It is of no help to him, or through him to the others who so badly need a real relationship to literature and poetry in their daily lives.

Just as Seumas puts the quit-notices behind the holy figure so he puts omens and the formal ritual of the Catholic Church between himself and the inroads of reality, hoping to be preserved thereby. This mindless ritualism pours in and fills the vacuum left by his falling away from his former social involvement. There had been a time when he had not stood in such awe of the church—witness his slogan for James Stephens on the steps of the cathedral, but now, "Thanks be to God I'm a daily communicant. There's a great comfort in religion; it makes a man strong in time of trouble an' brave in time of danger." (111)

In his case too, the second half of the play puts this to the test. Despite his Hail Marys and his appeals to various saints and holy figures the "Auxies" burst into his lair too, and use his holy figures to mock him. But he is no longer willing to learn either from experience or his own better knowledge. The only lesson he draws from the raid is, "I knew things ud go wrong when I missed Mass this mornin'." (121) Ritual rules. The hopelessness of Seumas' case and the ingrained stubbornness of the problem as such is underscored by the very last line, given to Seumas: "I knew something ud come of the tappin' on the wall!" (130) Power lies in the portent, the sign. On the other hand Seumas fails to recognise the gunman in his friend Maguire, though the signs are there. Form and content fall apart. The people cannot relate the two and so cannot cope with reality.

If Seumas had not retreated into total self-absorption, if he had been able to relate appearance and essence in the case of Maguire, Minnie's death might have been avoided. Not only are the people dying for the gunmen, they are also dying because of everyday failures like Seumas, the *shadow* of what he could have been.

How did this happen to him? In general he has been marred by the material and mental deprivation in which he has been forced to lead his life. But in particular, as O'Casey indicates, the fault lies with a national liberation movement which has failed to make itself into a real mass movement serving the true needs and interests of the people, and has thus failed to mobilise and revolutionise the rank and file of the people. The poverty of the relationship between the liberation army and the masses is indicated in the way the gunman Maguire moves through them fleeting and unrecognised. The process of this separation of the liberation movement from the true needs of the masses, its tendency to degenerate into objectively anti-popular terrorism putting all its faith in the ritual of the gun, is graphically sketched in his speech about their creed being belief in the Gun Almighty, quoted on p. 31. In withdrawing from a movement that had taken this direction, Seumas displays sound human sense. But the trouble is that this is the only element in his environment which could have provided a focal point for his constructive qualities. In not fulfilling this obligation the nationalist organisation delivers Seumas over to the forces of demoralisation and itself becomes one of the strongest of these alienating pressures.

Donal Davoren is, at first sight, at the opposite pole to his room-mate. Seumas is a man sunk to the level of a worm. Davoren is a "man of the spirit," an aspiring poet, a "sufferer," free of religion and superstition. And yet there are obvious similarities. Both are capable of important insights. Davoren's, however, are somewhat different. They are not closed insights gained in the past and going rotten, but open, current insights. He sees through the shams of Seumas: "Your religion is simply the state of being afraid that God will torture your soul in the next world as you are afraid the Black and Tans will torture your body in this." (82) He recognises Minnie's qualities, calling her a pioneer in action as he is a pioneer in thought–the two powers which in combination will take the sorry scheme of things and remould it nearer to the heart's desire. "Lovely little Minnie, and brave as well; brave little Minnie, and lovely as well!" (93)

He grasps what is necessary and sees where his responsibility should lie. In contrast to the others he is able to penetrate beyond appearances to essences. This is a hopeful quality in the context of the play. The misery of the world is real to him. He pities "poor Maguire" while Seumas pities only himself. He is susceptible to the beauty of nature (flowers) and of human beings (Minnie). He longs to destroy the ugliness. He has the will and the ability to teach others and to help them free themselves from ignorance. He introduces Minnie to the beauty of simple wild flowers and tries to explain something of the nature of poetry to her. Clearly he is "the man for the job." But this man, Davoren, fails to live up to his responsibility towards the people.

The same pressures that are driving Seumas down into animality, are driving Donal up into an arid introversion. The paradox is that these two opposites, driven to their extremes, meet on common ground.

The landlord and the tenement-dwellers take Davoren for a gunman on the run. In fact he is on the run–from life. He is on stage all the time, hiding from life. He never leaves the room, even when Minnie is taken away.

He is the man who might have helped the people to gain a real mastery over words. But where Seumas fails to use his acquaintance with the cultural heritage, Donal misuses it. Under the stress of the petty daily miseries he utilises the poetry of the revolutionary Shelley mainly to escape into self-pity and self-dramatisation. It is one of the functions of the early Landlord-Seumas scene to make this process clear. There is an ironic discrepancy of levels between the "low" squabbling of these two and Davoren's "high," formal reaction to it–his repeated intoning of Prometheus' wail "Ah me! alas, pain, pain ever, for ever!" from Shelley's *Prometheus Unbound*. Here it becomes a kind of formal chant or ritual reminiscent of Mr Gallogher and his formal-letter reaction to his unruly neighbours, and in fact Gallogher and his letter is one of several parodies or caricatures which help to distance us from the solemn Davoren. Nevertheless, O'Casey is also suggesting here that the "petty" misery of having to live like this *is* comparable with Prometheus' titanic sufferings on the rock.

Shelley is a highly political poet. But Davoren, who would emulate him, says, "I know nothing about the Republic; I have no connection with the politics of the day, and I don't want to have any connection." (94) The reason why a sensitive man like Davoren should thus react against the nationalist patriotic politics of his day is indicated in Seumas' description of the terrorist tendency of the nationalist movement. It thus fails to provide him with a valid field of activity and prohibits him from being able to establish a creative relationship to the Shelley heritage. Davoren feels the inadequacy of the traditional rebel songs as *the* poetic response to the demands of the modern situation. His disgust at the emotional self-indulgence and evanescent catharsis connected with them drives him to reject *all* attempts to get to grips with "Ireland" in poetry: "Oh, we've had enough of poems, Minnie, about '98, and of Ireland, too." (90) He feels there is no adequate heritage here for him to latch on to as a poet. In fact it tends to frighten him off political poetry.

In these ways the movement as it is fails to provide a man like Davoren with the political and cultural context which would enable him to make a stand against the pressures towards demoralisation which pervade his environment. In fact the movement itself contributes towards this state of affairs.

All this encourages Davoren in a tendency towards a formal, art-for-art's-sake, cult-of-beauty approach to poetry-writing, embodied in his own insipidly conventional effusions the production of which is his only systematic life-activity. He knows that there can be no deliverance through Beauty: "There is an ugliness that can be made beautiful, and there is an ugliness that can only be destroyed, and this is part of that ugliness." (105) Yet he is driven into the classical ivory-tower concept—"The People! Damn the people! They live in the abyss, the poet lives on the mountain-top; to the people there is no mystery of colour: it is simply the scarlet coat of the soldier; the purple vestments of a priest; the green banner of a party; the brown or blue overalls of industry. To them the might of design is a three-roomed house or a capacious bed. To them beauty is for sale in a butcher's shop. To the people the end of life is the life created for them; to the poet the end of life is the life that he creates for himself; life has a stifling grip upon the people's throat—it is the poet's musician. The poet ever strives to save the people; the people ever strive to destroy the poet. The people view life through creeds, through customs, and through necessities; the poet views creeds, customs, and necessities through life." (107)

What an intermingling of insight and confusion this is! He recognises that the mass of the people are crippled and blinded by their belief in the magic power of formal rituals, "creeds," etc. On the other hand he blames them for being insensible to his own somewhat "higher" cult of formalism ("design," etc.) and for seeing beauty only in "low" practical things that they need to make life tolerable. Unfortunately, as the play shows, these Irish plebeians and workers largely lack this clear grasp of the realities. The poet should be helping to foster this realism in the people, which is essential if they are ever to loosen life's "stifling grip" on their throats. But Davoren is not the poet to do it, for he suffers from the same disorder as they do—a deadly fascination with "form," a confusion of shadow and substance, appearance and essence, an inability consistently to relate these aspects of phenomena correctly with one another, Davoren is more sophisticated than the others in that he composes his own word-formulas, but even here he is not qualitatively different from Gallogher: Donal's poems are as conventional in their formulations as Gallogher's letter: "Or when sweet Summer's ardent arms outspread,/Entwined with flowers,/Enfold us, like two lovers newly wed,/Thro' ravish'd hours . . ." (80) Thus Seumas, Gallogher, Grigson, Minnie and the others, in themselves, and in their relationships, emerge as comments on Davoren and Davoren a comment on them. In this sense they are parodies on him, distancing and relativising him, bringing out the ridiculous aspect to him. On the other hand he brings out the grave implications for the intellectual life of the people involved in their absurdities. This system of hidden parallels socialises the phenomenon for us. Similar types, relationships and results are being reproduced continuously and simultaneously at all points in the social life of the masses. There can be no excuse that Davoren is a special case, an eccentric. What is true of the pedlar in this Ireland, is also true of the poet. What is true of the Catholic republican is equally true of the Protestant loyalist, etc.

Left to his own devices as he is, Davoren cannot find the inner strength to be guided by his own best impulses. He cannot resist the illusion of romance and self-importance which enters his grey existence for a moment when Minnie falls in love with what she thinks him to be. He boasts of imaginary gunman-activities before her and reveals himself to be just as much an empty braggart as Grigson or Tommy Owens. The difference is that he is aware of the dangers of replacing reality by shadows–"A gunman on the run! Be careful, be careful, Donal Davoren." But he immediately puts it behind him–"And what danger can there be in being the shadow of a gunman?" (104) Because of this awareness Davoren's responsibility for the tragedy is so much the greater.

When the raid comes we find this man of the mountain-top crouching at floor level in abject terror alongside his very earth-bound room-mate. Ariel and Caliban in one boat.

At the moment of catastrophe, when Minnie is sacrificed for them, Davoren at last is obliged to face up to what they really are: "Ah me, alas! Pain, pain, pain ever, for ever! It's terrible to think that little Minnie is dead, but it's still more terrible to think that Davoren and Shields are alive! Oh, Donal Davoren, shame is your portion now till the silver cord is loosened and the golden bowl be broken. Oh, Davoren, Donal Davoren, poet and poltroon, poltroon and poet!" (130)

This is an important step. His faculty for critical insight into people has developed into the faculty for critical insight into himself. He seems to be moving away from total self-absorption towards regaining a sense of responsibility. A step forward, but one made at the cost of the best life among them.

But in how far has he really changed? There are danger signs in this last speech. As it progresses there is a growing tendency towards self-dramatisation and to that formalised word-ritualism where his genuine emotions are turned into a peg on which to hang "beautiful" phrases. Here, as in Seumas' final remark, O'Casey underlines how deeply ingrained and elusive the problem is and what sustained effort will be necessary finally to root it out. There are no simplified solutions for the sake of a neat ending. This is one of the measures of O'Casey's uncompromising realism.

Many critics contrast Davoren and Maguire, seeing the latter as the real, non-shadow alternative which the play offers. But they have difficulties in fitting him into this role. Herbert Goldstone complains, "Nor is the contrast between McGuire [sic], the real gunman, and Donal, the shadow of a gunman, sustained enough to be effective."[4] Kosok remarks, "Had it been O'Casey's intention to present Shields' views as the 'message' of his play it would have been essential to downgrade Maguire, to show him [. . .] as a cynical and brutal fanatic."[5] Only when one realises that this was indeed O'Casey's intention and that Maguire, for all his undoubted physical bravery, is in no way conceived as a real contrast to Davoren, can this play be fully understood.

In his fleeting appearance among the people the main impression Maguire leaves is that of thoughtlessness and irresponsibility. He is late and his language is "breezy." When Seumas asks if he can't postpone his "business" till the next day, he replies that it "Can't be did, can't be did, Seumas; if I waited till to-morrow all the butterflies might be dead. I'll leave this bag here till this evening. *(He puts the bag in a corner of the room.)* Good-bye . . . ee." (84) He is away before Seumas is aware of it.

This deadly "butterfly" is there only long enough to leave his "time-bomb" which later explodes, so to speak, in the people's faces. He is as responsible for Minnie's death as Davoren is. The menacing shadow of the "real" gunman, as well as that of the fake one, is cast over the whole scene. He bears out the truth of Seumas' assertion that the gunmen are not dying for the people, but vice versa. Minnie is not shot by the British but by the "real" gunmen.

Maguire is also the shadow of a gunman. In this sense he and Davoren are complementary ways of looking at the same thing. They are a comment on each other. Thus the system of parallels, which is the organising principle of the play, is completed. There is a metaphorical aspect to Davoren. Although not a member of the movement himself, he nevertheless emerges as symbolic of certain grave weaknesses within the national movement. Through the image of Davoren O'Casey gives us his view of this movement—a romantic thing with its head too much in the rarified, formal and abstract realm of the poetic clouds, with a dangerous lack of contact and interest in the actual "low" needs of the people (see for instance Davoren's contempt for the people's bread-and-butter problems in his speech about the role of the poet), with more than its fair share of "butterflies" fluttering in airy space and irresponsibly turning the heads of ignorant romantic youth, as Donal turns Minnie's. Thus Donal is simultaneously the shadow of a gunman and the real thing, both the fake and the genuine article, because O'Casey sees the "genuine" article as a shadow of what it should be, as, in an important sense, a fake, and the movement, symbolised by him, as a mere shadow of what a genuine mass revolutionary movement should be.

The play indicates that this type of movement in its weaknesses reflects weaknesses within the masses. It is to a certain extent *produced* by them as they are. At the same time it is a pressure reacting back on them, preying on and encouraging that very weakness, leading them to disaster rather than helping them to overcome it, as a mass movement should. Like Davoren, self-immured in that room, it is both of the people and not of them. Clearly the responsibility to change this lies with the people. Do they have the key?

The position is certainly tragic. It is not the tragedy of potential leaders who go to the wall because they are ahead of their times, but the tragedy of the people whose leaders are not adequate to the demands of the people and the times. Nor is there any sign that the masses can, if things stay exactly as they are, produce adequate leaders in the foreseeable future. Is there no perspective? There is, and it is embodied in the portrait of the people, in their contradictoriness. All the human qualities necessary for liberation are there, and there alone, even if they are only potentially positive qualities at the moment, being often turned into their opposite, i.e. into actual menaces, through functioning in a false context.

The most important of these have been brought out in

the course of this analysis: the qualities of the women, their lack of self-centredness, their capacity for loyalty, responsibility and self-sacrifice, their courage, their inherent interest in poetry. Minnie is the most concentrated expression of this. Yet it is not the women against the men. There are important qualities shared by both sexes. There is a spontaneous solidarity (for all their confusions they do not betray Davoren). Minnie and Maguire are willing to lay down their lives for something beyond themselves (what they believe to be the good of the nation). There is Davoren's struggling ability to learn from experience and his partial breakthrough to self-insight. There are their insights in general, sometimes profound, usually fleeting, penetrating to the true essence of things behind appearances. Above all, perhaps, there is their speech with its unruly vigour and inventiveness. (The qualities of their language will be dealt with in more detail in connection with *Juno and the Paycock*.)

All the elements are there, vibrating between the lines of the critique. This accounts for the backhanded beauty of these characters.

Is O'Casey implying that the masses must be freed "from outside" before their best qualities can be de-alienated and so turned into real qualities? On the contrary, he shows that there can be no liberation without these qualities being brought into play. His genius for the creation of contradictory, that is realistic, character constitutes a kind of strategic alienating-effect in that it creates the growing awareness of a possible alternative inherent in "things as they are." This, perhaps above all, brings O'Casey and Brecht into line with each other. As a result of this working out of *productive* contradiction one is made to realise that the direction taken by events in the play is not by fate ordained, not necessarily the only direction they could take. Enough productive potential has been laid bare to make it clear that, given some–quite conceivable–modifications in the general context, events could be swung into another, better direction. This is most intensely expressed in Davoren. We are not quite sure, up to the last minute, which way he will go. Things seem to hang in the balance within him and it is perfectly imaginable that with some slight alteration in the balance of forces he could take the other, better course.

Notes

1. William A. Armstrong, *Sean O'Casey* (Writers and their Work, No. 198), London, 1967, p. 13
2. Robert Hogan, *The Experiments of Sean O'Casey*, New York, 1960, pp. 30–31
3. David Krause, *Sean O'Casey, the Man and His Work*, New York, 1962, p. 104
4. Herbert Goldstone, *In Search of Community, the Achievement of Sean O'Casey*, Cork and Dublin, 1972, p. 29
5. Kosok, op. cit., pp. 27–28 (translated by JM, as well as all other quotations from Kosok)

II JUNO AND THE PAYCOCK

Written 1923-4; produced 1924 (Abbey Theatre, Dublin);
published 1925

> "We suffer not only from the living,
> but from the dead."
>
> Karl Marx, *Capital*

The time is 1922, during the civil war between "Free-
Staters" and "Republicans"–former comrades-in-arms. The
setting–the Boyle family flat in a slum tenement in Dublin.
The Man of the House is "Captain" Jack Boyle, heavily
built, about sixty years old. The "Captain" is a work-shy
proletarian Falstaff, in constant running battle with his wife,
Juno. He spends his days in the local pub or, when Juno is
at work, in the flat, blarneying with his lumpen-proletarian
butty, Joxer Daly. With Joxer's connivance he has woven
a myth round himself in which he figures as a heroic Irish
patriot or sea-captain–both at some time in the past. A
blustering, strutting, self-centred "paycock." Meanwhile his
wife, Juno, captains the family as best she can between the
rocks of poverty. She is the bread-winner and also the family
servant, an ignorant, god-fearing determined woman. Boyle
fears her sarcasm and her unflagging demands that he get a
job.

They have two grown-up children. Mary, the daughter,
works in a factory. At the moment she is on strike in solidarity with a victimised workmate. She is wooed by young
Jerry Devine, a minor trade-union official with aspirations
to a better paid post. Mary rejects him, mysteriously. The
reason is that she is becoming involved with the well-to-do
Charlie Bentham, who can offer better prospects. The son,
Johnny, hides himself in the back bedroom. Every knock at
the door sends him into semi-hysteria. He has taken part in
the Easter Rising, in which his hip was shattered, and in
the civil war, in which he lost his left arm. He cannot work.

Into this situation comes Bentham with the news that
Boyle has been left a legacy by a rich relation. The family
go on a spending spree with money borrowed on the prom-

ise of this legacy. The ever more lordly Boyle organises a musical party in the flat to which Bentham, Joxer, and a neighbour, Mrs Maisie Madigan, are also invited. The revelries are disrupted, however, by old Mrs Tancred passing down the stairs on the way to her son's funeral. Her son, Robbie, a Republican, has been killed in an ambush. Johnny hysterically denies ever having been the dead boy's friend.

Rumours grow that the legacy is not going to materialise. Creditors close in. Bentham makes himself scarce, leaving Mary pregnant. The enraged Captain repudiates his daughter and announces that there's going to be no legacy, thanks to some inaccuracy in the wording of the will. He retires with Joxer to the pub. Jerry Devine comes and tells Mary that he's willing to have her back, despite everything–until he hears "the worst." Men come and remove the furniture. Other men remove Johnny, who is taken away and shot for betraying Robbie Tancred.

Juno and Mary come home to an empty, denuded flat. Juno bears up under the news of her son's death. She and Mary will go and leave Boyle to his fate. When they have left, Boyle and Joxer return roaring drunk. From floor level the Captain announces that the world is in "a terrible state o' chassis!"

At first sight this looks rather like the conventional "naturalist" family drama of drunkenness and defeat, and it was often enough judged to be such. A closer look however reveals a sophisticated inner structure and artistic unity in this supposedly "photographic" play. The unity of structure brings out a unity of theme. Almost all the characters have, in their relationship to living in the present, something in common. An unwillingness to face reality and grapple with it. Each of them makes an attempt to hide from it, or escape from it, while leaving it socially intact.

First there are the attempts at physically getting out of the slums and the proletariat. For all her proclaimed devotion to the principles of solidarity, Mary makes two such attempts. The first is via the careerist trade-union official,

GOSHEN COLLEGE LIBRARY
GOSHEN, INDIANA

Jerry Devine; the second is via the bourgeois intruder, Bentham, who can outbid Jerry. Both these men corrupt and almost destroy their working-class victim. Mary's native realism is almost obliterated by a half-digested rehash of attitudes imported from Devine and Bentham—"Jerry says this..." or "Charlie says that..." Both her "outside helps" abandon her in her moment of greatest need. This road, then, leads nowhere.

Some critics would like to see Mary's disaster as a proof that O'Casey was distrustful of all "general principles" of living. But it is clearly not Mary's "principle" (class loyalty and solidarity) that is wrong, but that she does not stick to it systematically—a contradiction between theory and practice. This happens because her grasp of principle is too abstract. It is evident in her defence of Johnny when the pragmatic Juno justly attacks his abstract principles— "He stuck to his principles, an', no matther how you may argue, ma, a principle's a principle." (9) Clearly there is also a contradiction between one part of Mary's practice and another. We will meet this again. In this case it arises from a lack of sufficient confidence in herself, for she is not only a proletarian but a young woman, conditioned to be dependent on men.

Of the two men involved here, one is an outsider (Bentham) and therefore not an escape-candidate. As far as facing reality is concerned O'Casey puts his own people to shame in the person of this presumed Englishman. Bentham professes a pseudo-scientific spiritualist "philosophy"—theosophy (scorned by Boyle who has no time for religions), and yet, when Johnny runs out of the bedroom during the party screaming that he has just seen Robbie Tancred's ghost in there, Bentham is the only one with enough courage to go in and report that there's no spirit there. This bourgeois Englishman does not let his absurd philosophy come between him and a sober appraisal of reality. The spirits of the dead, in his case, are kept in their place. This is a contradiction between word and deed of a very different sort, in which the almighty Word is put in its place.

If Bentham's late-bourgeois philosophical principles are corrupt and of no possible use to anyone, it is Jerry's lack of a scientific and principled philosophy which leaves this trade-union official open to corruption. Typical of the play-safe post-Connolly-Larkin leadership of the union, his main aim is to escape by making his career within the union. He succeeds in this personal escape, but at the expense of his fellow workers and his humanity. Jerry does, in his social-democratic way, contribute to a vaguely critical and human-ist view of the world. The poem, which Mary heard him quote at a lecture and quotes back at him when he deserts her, voices the tragic paradox of life in class society which lies at the heart of the play: "An' we felt the power that fashion'd/All the lovely things we saw/[. . .] Was a hand of force an' beauty,/With an eagle's tearin' claw./[. . .] Like a glowin' picture by a/Hand unsteady, brought to ruin;/[. . .] Like the agonising horror/Of a violin out of tune." (67) Thus word and deed, insight and action fall apart and the critic becomes a contributor to the alienated reality he criticises.

Johnny's flight from the mad reality which he has helped to create is also, at one level, physical—into the back bed-room, from which he only rarely emerges. This is symbolic of an escapism in him of a much more insidious kind—into abstract Principle, in his case that of the "Republicans." These principles, once filled with the democratic life given to them by Wolfe Tone, had dwindled down to a sorry ab-straction. As Peader O'Donnell says, "The Republican movement was inspired by 'pure ideals.' In the grip of this philosophy the Republican struggle could present itself as a democratic movement of mass revolt without any danger to the social pattern [. . .] under the shelter of pure ideals the Irish middle-class held its place within a movement it feared."[1] For someone in Johnny's position these principles appeared as a sacred, finished, total reality, needing no thought and demanding preservation, not change. Within their charmed circle one can live a quasi-heroic life without getting involved in the real problems of one's existence.

What destroys Johnny is principle so abstract that it turns into its opposite—total lack of principle: he betrays his friend and comrade Robbie. Death pushes its way between Johnny and life. Death's coming for him at the end is only the logical conclusion of this process. Death will not allow him to live. It is fear of the dead Robbie that drives him into a hole. Ireland is rich in dead heroes. As we have seen in *The Shadow of a Gunman* O'Casey sets out to rid his country of this dead weight of heroes, in the veneration of whom his countrymen so often found a convenient substitute for doing anything on their own account. Here, in Robbie and Johnny, he shows that their lives and deaths are heroic, in many cases, only in the romantic and impotent imaginations of the survivors.

This *diktat* of the dead over the living pervades the whole play. There is one moment where the forces of life and reality seem about to achieve a victory—during the party in Act II. They are just going to put a record on the gramophone—in this context partly a symbol of modern living—when they are interrupted by Mrs Tancred passing down to her son's funeral. At last they get the gramophone going only to be interrupted by Needle Nugent, another neighbour, bursting in and demanding whether none of them have any respect for the Irish people's National Regard for the dead, to which Mrs Boyle answers that "Maybe, Needle Nugent, it's nearly time we had a little less respect for the dead, an' a little more regard for the livin'." (49) The funeral gets under way, not to the music of the gramophone but to the moaning of a hymn. The celebration of death, romantically decked out, wooes them from their celebration of life:

Mrs. Boyle. Here's the hearse, here's the hearse!
Boyle. There's t'oul' mother walkin' behin' the coffin.
Mrs. Madigan. You can hardly see the coffin with the wreaths.
Joxer. Oh, it's a darlin' funeral, a daarlin' funeral! (49)

This death-dominated, death-dealing reality which Johnny

has helped to make, invades his "castle," winkles him out and destroys him. Thus the Johnny-figure is the mediator between the "private" context of the Boyle family and the "public" context of the civil war. They interpenetrate and determine each other, so that the myth about the separateness of private and public life becomes hard to maintain. This civil war has not only nothing to do with the real needs of the people—its negative, destructive nature is partly a reflection, a product of the weaknesses of the people themselves. So long as they remain as they are they will not be able to produce, out of themselves, a true revolution in their own interests. So it is not simply that these people inhibit their own ability to live as a result of their distorted relationship to reality. They simultaneously distort social reality itself, which in its turn breaks in and almost destroys them. They are responsible for reality. Reality (environment) is not portrayed as simply something to be contemplated and understood, as something which determines people, but as human practice, as something determined *by* the people. This dialectical and revolutionary portrayal of the relationship of man to his environment lies at the very heart of O'Casey's specific contribution to realism in the drama.

But to return to the escapists. Mrs Madigan's escape is into her own past, her youth, and that of others. Her contributions to the party are rambling, astonishingly detailed total recalls—"I remember as well as I remember yestherday . . ." (42) She remembers it better than yesterday. Her grasp on present living seems weak. She manages only one verse of a song, for her voice, she says, is too husky now, though she remembers the time . . . Her memories are made up of confused surface detail, so that her own past experience cannot really help her to come to grips with the problems of the present.

Is Joxer Daly an exception? Joxer is indeed a realist in a certain restricted sense. He has sized up the situation and has come to terms with it: "It's betther to be a coward than a corpse!" (20) All the others, in refusing to face up to reality, at least repudiate it. Not Joxer. It is his element. He has reduced his demands and aspirations to the level of this impoverished environment. They mutually correspond and he manipulates the latter to serve his almost animal ends. Joxer's "practice" cannot be aimed at changing this reality but at cultivating it. Thus his "realism" is that of a parasite content to live off and degrade another larger parasite (Boyle), who in turn lives off and degrades the degraded (Juno). Joxer is an extinct planet now become a satellite and evil influence on one which will itself soon be extinct. Boyle produces a Joxer. Joxer reacts back on Boyle "producing" him and dragging him down to the Joxer level, thus "manufacturing" a new and even more pernicious Joxer. Joxer is the end of the road being pursued by Boyle. This end is embodied in the last prostrate scene. Juno instinctively grasps the terrible danger represented by this "lovable clown," and harries him incessantly. Joxer is a plague-spot in the workers' community, the type of man reduced to absolute bodily and spiritual pauperism—a widespread and ever-threatening fate characteristic of an age-long process of colonial degradation.

In order to "live with" alienated reality on its own terms Joxer, too, needs something with which he can insulate himself from the real facts of life. To this end he builds a kind of screen out of a jumble of half-remembered quotations and tags from literature plus a ready flow of proverbs and maxims from popular tradition. This system of prefabricated reactions saves him the trouble of grappling with the specific difficulties of a situation. On the one hand this contains O'Casey's statement that the traditional peasant wisdom can no longer provide an adequate world-view for the people's needs in the new proletarian context. Take three proverbs used by Joxer on one page: "It's betther late than never," "It's a long lane that has no turnin'," "God never shut wan door but He opened another." (12) The fate of the people in this play makes nonsense of these particular bits of popular "wisdom." Another set of principles is necessary.

On the other hand it brings up a question touched upon in *The Shadow of a Gunman*–that of how the cultural heritage is absorbed and used. Joxer has put his nose in a surprising number of books: "Didja ever rade *Elizabeth, or Th' Exile o' Sibayria?* . . . Ah, it's a darlin' story, a daarlin' story!" (21) He has a preference for exotic, escapist stuff. Culturally deprived and without guidance he has been unable to profit from the better things he has read. Now, instead of using literature to help him grapple with experience, he misuses it to escape. This failed relationship of Joxer to the cultural heritage is epitomised in his performance at the Boyle party. He, the legendary man of literature and song ("give us wan of your shut-eyed wans"), is the only one present who cannot sing a single song through to the end. What is this but a facet of that general contradiction between the word and the world?

Mary, culturally speaking, is in a somewhat similar position. She is reading Ibsen, a remarkable enough activity for a girl of her background. But the influence of Ibsen on her daily behaviour seems nil.

Jerry Devine, on the other hand, uses literature in his work, building bits of socialist and rationalist verse into his speeches to add emotional appeal. This is in the typical old social-democratic tradition, but in his case, too, this contact with culture has brought about no humanising of his own basic behaviour patterns. When Mary casts the poem back at him it is she who remembers it; he has no recollection of it. When, at the end, Mary turns this poem against Jerry and uses it to define him, the poem begins, through her, to function as it should–as a way of grappling with life. It would seem that Mary's reading of Ibsen has not been entirely in vain after all. This is part of the real perspective that she carries with her into the future.

This theme of the relationship to cultural tradition will be picked up again in connection with Boyle and Juno.

The most conscious, dextrous, enthusiastic and finally tragic exponent of the art of flight from reality and responsibility is Captain Jack Boyle. He is the central embodiment of the theme.

With the aid of Joxer, Boyle escapes at every opportunity into a fantasy world, an *ersatz* reality where he is an Irish hero-patriot of yore and a gallant sea-dog, a Ulysses, braver of storms: "Them was days, Joxer, them was days. Nothin' was too hot or too heavy for me then. Sailin' from the Gulf o' Mexico to the Antanartic Ocean. I seen things, I seen things, Joxer, that no mortal man should speak about that knows his Catechism. Ofen, an' ofen, when I was fixed to the wheel with a marlin-spike, an' the win's blowin' fierce an' the waves lashin' an' lashin', till you'd think every minute was goin' to be your last, an' it blowed, an' blowed— blew is the right word, Joxer, but blowed is what the sailors use." (23)

Like Joyce, O'Casey too, has his parody-Ulysses! The dream has been something crucial to the Irish character. The Irish people, having for so many centuries suffered national abasement and the foiling of all aspiration at the hands of a foreign conqueror, have tended—as have other peoples in similar circumstances—to sublimate their thwarted action in the form of a vigorous life of the imagination. This has produced great creative achievements, of which O'Casey's own plays are one of the highest expressions. But it has another important side to it, as the Irishman Larry Doyle points out in Shaw's *John Bull's Other Island* (the play that opened O'Casey's eyes to a lot of things):

Oh, the dreaming! dreaming! the torturing, heart-scalding, never satisfying dreaming, dreaming, dreaming, dreaming! No debauchery that ever coarsened and brutalized an Englishman can take the worth and usefulness out of him like that dreaming. An Irishman's imagination never lets him alone, never convinces him, never satisfies him; but it makes him that he can't face reality nor deal with it nor handle it nor conquer it; he can only sneer at them that do, and be 'agreeable to strangers' [. . .] He can't be intelligently political; he dreams of what the Shan

Van Vocht said in ninetyeight. If you want to interest him in Ireland you've got to call the unfortunate island Kathleen ni Houlihan and pretend she's a little old woman. It saves thinking. It saves working. It saves everything except imagination, imagination, imagination.*[2]

This is what lies behind Boyle's tremendous dramatic "presence." It is partly what gives his performance its strangely impressive aplomb and flamboyance. He is working in a long tradition.

In a sense Boyle is an expression of that "Irish malady"– the worship of past, romanticised heroes as a substitute for action in the present–here embodied within one personality. But the image also has other implications.

O'Casey was a great champion of fantasy. The trouble with Boyle's fantasy, however, is that it is infertile. Reality as Boyle has lived it has been too impoverished to feed it. Neither does it draw on the national cultural traditions (the Irish have *not* been a sea-going nation). It is fantasy as pure escape. It lies in the nature of such a fantasy that the isolated self, denied expression in the actual world, must be in the centre. Boyle in his dream is lonely monarch of all he surveys, the apotheosis of self in an empty, undynamic world. His ship is forever sailing, never reaching port. Clearly this absolutising of the self in such an isolated world must lead to the emptying and destruction of the social self in the actual world. There is an irresistible urge towards total self-centredness; the self, torn out of its real context, turns inward. On the one hand Boyle's ability to relate to others in a truly social way is undermined. On the other hand, being confirmed in the free-flying world of fantasy and being thus negated in the real world, absolves one of all social responsibility and even of the necessity of appraising one's own objective position. It subverts the willingness and ability to learn from real experience because one's experience is not accepted as being fully real. The disastrous

---

* I owe this apt quotation to David Krause who uses it in his *Sean O'Casey, the Man and His Work,* pp. 105–106.

result of this for Boyle and those dependent on him under existing circumstances is, at one level, the subject of this play.

The paradox is that the concrete needs of this free-flying Man of the Spirit tend to be reduced to mere bodily, biological appetites. The spirit and the flesh fall apart. Absolutising the imagination calls forth its opposite–absolutising the bodily appetites. In this polarisation it is the appetite which holds the whip hand. "I'll show them I've a little spirit left in me still! (*He goes over to the press, takes out a plate and looks at it*) Sassige! Well, let her keep her sassige," says the great Boyle (19)–and at once falls to and fries it. The chief *raison d'être* of environment and fellow humans is to satisfy these appetites on demand.

So the imagination, which should enrich life and struggle, is turned into its opposite, a force destructive of life. This aggravation of the poverty of life-experience leads in turn to a further destruction of the basis for the development of productive imagination. Split personalities like Boyle impoverish both life and imagination. Once again objective reality is seen as human practice. Boyle's failed relationship to reality and to himself is part of the process distorting reality at large. At the end, lolling drunk in the devastated home, he declares, between hiccups, that as a last resort he can always join a flying column.* So a distorted freedom movement is seen as the logical end-product of a distorted relationship to life in ordinary people like Boyle.

This transformation of great and necessary potentials such as imagination into the people's worst enemies at the very point in history when they are most needed lies at the heart of the tragedy of *Juno and the Paycock*. The time is overripe. The necessary heroes of a new type are not yet there.

But is Juno not a heroine? The mother-cult has played a big part in Irish consciousness from the Virgin Mary to Mother Machree waiting for her sons and daughters to re-

* A mobile strike-force in the Irish Republican Army.

turn from exile, and Juno too, is named after the Mother of Gods (what Gods!). Does O'Casey the myth-breaker make an exception here and add his mite to the myth? Many critics have thought so. Krause says she has "the heroic stature of her namesake."[3] Cowasjee agrees: "Juno, the greatest of O'Casey's heroines, has often been referred to as the greatest mother in drama. In the midst of shirkers, braggarts, the wrong-principled and the good-for-nothings, she alone shows courage and common sense."[4] In the opinion of the Soviet critic Sarukhanyan, however, "O'Casey does not idealise his heroine,"[5] but sees her as a calculated rebuff to the glorified figure of Kathleen ni Houlihan as symbolic of Ireland.

It would be foolish to deny that there is a kind of heroism in Juno. She possesses certain outstanding and essential qualities in contrast to the others: a grasp of realities, practicality, courage, a capacity for selflessness and devotion to others, inexhaustible mother-love, insight into the shortcomings of those around her. She is the master myth-destroyer and puncturer of puffed-up peacockery. Above all she develops her innate ability to learn from experience and her own mistakes.

Is Juno, then, free of the contradictions which define the other characters?

Near the start she launches a bitter attack on her son Johnny's "principles": "Ah, you lost your best principle, me boy, when you lost your arm; them's the only sort o' principles that's any good to a workin' man." (27) This one principle of Juno's, so pithily put, is nevertheless the denial of all attempts of consciousness and action to raise itself above the hand-to-mouth pragmatic level. It is the class-consciousness of the proletariat at its most primitive level. Pure survival is her one end in life—the survival of her family. This principled fear of all principles is that of an ignorant, deprived, warm-hearted mother who has seen her family damaged and endangered by the fanatical adherence to an abstract principle which contains no answer to her daily problems. The environment she lives in fails to supply any adequate social and political force or philosophy which can really help her, so she is obliged to take the whole burden on her own scarcely adequate shoulders. Under the circumstances she cannot extend the range of her concern beyond the perimeter of the family. It is the limit of her power as an individual possessing the level of consciousness which she has.

Thus the working-class community is, for most of the time, alien territory to her, beyond the pale. When the news comes of the murder of her neighbour's son her morbid curiosity is no whit less than that of the others, and she's relieved that her Johnny's had nothing to do with him for some time past. It is a territory fraught with danger to her nest—imagined danger and real. This wider working class with its organisations is continuously producing principles like solidarity, the strike, class pride, etc. She mocks the principle of class solidarity adhered to by Mary. Mary's too superficial grasp of the class struggle is epitomised in her stubborn repetition that "a principle's a principle," but it is her grasp and not the principle which is inadequate. This differentiates her from Johnny. But for Juno both their principles are the same, i.e. for her too, a principle's a principle.

Anything which draws unwelcome attention to the family is bad. She scolds Mary for wearing ribbons while on strike because she believes it will make the employers think they're giving the girls too much money. The way to survive is to keep one's head down. Man's appropriate position is on his knees. Boyle is "constantly singin', no less, when he ought always to be on his knees offerin' up a Novena for a job!" (7) Juno's appreciation of the fact that man does not live by bread alone has been almost obliterated. So we have a certain amount of sympathy with the conspiratorial antics of Boyle and Joxer just as we do for their ancestors Toby Belch and Andrew Aguecheek conspiring against the puritan killjoys in *Twelfth Night*.

In turning in on her family Juno's grasp of reality is narrowed and distorted. Is this not also a kind of flight from reality in the broader sense? A flight downwards to the worm's-eye view of cooking-pots and knees. This contraction which is bound up with the rejection of all general principles distorts Juno's efforts at human behaviour within the family. Her attempts to guarantee its well-being contradict themselves. Having no defined class standpoint Juno is left wide open to petty-bourgeois infections and is ready to embrace any possibility of a local "break-out" for her family.

As with the others, Juno's worst petty-bourgeois traits are brought out by the news of the supposed legacy. When Bentham is about to enter with this news, which Juno already knows, she banishes from sight all the vulgar utensils of work, including the moleskin trousers which she has just badgering Boyle to put on prior to going out and getting a job. One can hardly speak of the courage of one's convictions here. At the first chance she caves in and takes the line of least resistance.

It is Juno who forces the pace, for all her customary caution, in building up a world of empty show—a Jack Boyle world, on the insubstantial foundation of the will. She sees a light at the end of the tunnel, a bolt-hole. In order to make it come about she abandons her most deeply held convictions: she allows the middle-class Bentham, much more of an outsider than the lumpen Joxer, to penetrate, with her connivance, into the closely guarded family fold. For this slip-up in Juno's defences they all have to pay dearly. She and Mary at once go on shopping sprees, filling the flat with a conglomeration of tawdry furnishings. For the sake of a will-o'-the-wisp she actually eggs those around her on along the very same road to ruin against which she has so often warned them. One of her first reactions, for instance, is to say to her husband, "You won't have to trouble about a job for awhile, Jack." (29)

This contradiction between word and deed, insight and action also characterises her everyday treatment of her family. On the one hand she scourges them, especially Boyle, for their fecklessness, self-centredness, and complete dependence upon her and her toil. On the other hand, because she has no other guide to action but her instinctive protectiveness for the inhabitants of her nest, her only answer to invasion by the surrounding "chassis" is to pander to their immediate bodily comforts. In this way she encourages their parasitism at her expense. Her cure-all is the "nice cup o' tay." Johnny tells her, "Tay, tay, tay! You're always thinkin' o' tay. If a man was dyin', you'd thry to make him swally a cup o' tay!" (8) In fact they *are* dying, and this is her only medicine. As Johnny says (without meaning to apply it to himself), "You're to blame yourself for a gradle of it—givin' him his own way in everything." (64) So Juno's great mother-love, functioning in this alienated context, becomes itself a deadly danger to the people she loves.

Juno's lack of any principle or guide to action beyond the immediate creature comfort of her family is one of the elements making for the destruction of the family. There is truth in Herbert Goldstone's statement that "like Mother Courage, Juno simply doesn't realise that she has let the very conditions of life which have victimised her become her ultimate standard of value."[6]

Juno is no "positive hero" shining among the human dross. To an important degree her characterisation is part of the general process of hero-breaking. With the others she shares the squandering and misapplication of potentially productive qualities. Her family-centricity is, up to a point, similar to the egocentricity of the others. Nor is she free of self-dramatisation in the role of hero-martyr in her frequent histrionic confrontations with the Paycock. There is as little justification here as there was in the case of the *Gunman* for maintaining that O'Casey glorifies the women characters as against the men.

Despite these similarities Juno's basic trouble is the opposite to Boyle's—wingless pragmatism. Juno and Jack Boyle. Their relationship to each other lies at the very heart of the play. They are not really a unity but a destructive clash of opposites. It is the falling apart of the "practical" and the "speculative," realism and imagination, materialism and the "things of the spirit," things that should form one whole. Here the polarised elements, isolated and absolutised, turn into dangerous caricatures of themselves.

Here in *Juno* already O'Casey's image of the family "unit" begins to take on hints of a metaphorical-symbolic dimension in which it stands for Irish society as such. Thus the above split calls up associations with that tragic separation of the militant Labour movement and the nationalist movement after the death of Connolly. The trade unions had become entirely pragmatic, concentrating on winning tactical economic concessions, while the nationalists, deprived of their proletarian-revolutionary leaven, swung to the pole of "pure" nationalist sentiment. At the "public" and the "private" levels national life suffers from the same alarming symptoms. Each level puts its stamp on the other.

At the same time this mutual alienation of things that should form a unity also emerges here as the result of woman's subordinate position in the family in exploiting society. Traditional conceptions of their respective roles, embedded in the minds of Juno and Boyle, contribute to the disaster. Up to almost the last moment Juno instinctively thinks of her husband as her decision-maker and runs out to fetch him from the pub when the men come for the furniture.

Thus this self-alienation, this splitting of the human personality under capitalism, is shown as something not confined to the sphere of the psyche but as a practical threat to the unity and advance of the people, as a source not only of their spiritual but also their physical destruction. Its overcoming—the re-establishment of a synthesis of realism and materialism with ideals and imagination—is seen not as a humanist ideal only, but as a mere necessity for survival and progress. Only this reunification can lay the basis for the establishment of a true "principle," an ideal based on the real needs of the people. As things are, each of the "opposites," once it has separated from the other, works on the other, driving it further towards its respective pole. This is the tragic dialectic of Juno and her Paycock.

To sum up. None of the slum-dwellers have (in the main body of the play) an adequate relationship to reality and experience. None of them are heroes. All are engaged in some attempt to escape or hide from reality and their own position and function within it. All these attempts are doomed. On the surface this has a certain similarity to the contemporary tradition of "slum naturalism" in bourgeois literature and drama. These naturalists showed the submerged masses as mere products and passive victims of environment. Therefore all their attempts to free themselves are doomed to failure from the start, the only result of their efforts being that their last state is worse than their first. The latter is certainly true of the people in *Juno* and several critics have labelled O'Casey's "Dublin" plays naturalist. In fact nothing could be further from naturalism than O'Casey's picture of the people. He certainly does not underestimate the formative influence of environment. Of Mary he says in the stage directions, that her speech and manners have been degraded by her environment and are marked by the struggle of opposing forces. There are similar remarks in the stage directions describing Juno, etc. Boyle's distaste for work is shown as conditioned by the degrading circumstances surrounding wage labour—"I don't want the motions of me body to be watched the way an asthronomer ud watch a star." (15) Boyle's attitude to work is also formed by Ireland's history. In a situation where work, the attempt to improve one's position, was used against one, say in the form of a raised rent for the poor tenant farmer who had been foolhardy enough to "impove" his holding, "laziness" became a kind of defence-mechanism.

Nevertheless these people emerge not only as victims but as makers of the alienated environment. They have an active relationship to their environment—albeit a negative one under the given conditions. Their efforts to escape fail, not because all efforts are worse than useless, but because they are the wrong kind of efforts. In engaging in them they are making the situation worse. Their "solutions" are traditional, superannuated self-comforters and attempts at local "break-outs" which leave the total set-up intact. Their hopes of such break-outs are based on rescue through outside agencies rather than through their own efforts. The affair of the legacy is the point of focus for all this.

The legacy device, the discovery that the poor hero or heroine was, after all, the heir to a fortune, was a favourite *deus ex machina* of bourgeois literature and drama, the Happy End of the well-made play. It was an especially popular plot device in the Victorian melodramas which O'Casey so enjoyed. He takes this convention, as he takes others, and remoulds it to his own purpose. In *Juno* the great expectations do not materialise and there is no happy end. But the real irony is that it is not the non-materialisation of the legacy which hastens the disaster, but the naive assumption that it *will* materialise. This, as we have seen with Juno, aggravates all their most negative features. So the legacy-line in the plot is not merely a means of heightening the tension or of forwarding the plot, as some critics have maintained.[7] It is a focal point for organising the statement of the play, bringing out the fact that the characters all have important weaknesses in common, i.e. that these weaknesses are social rather than individual.* The final implication is that the situation would have been even worse (Juno, for instance, might have been corrupted beyond redemption) if the legacy had materialised. Moral: the only thing worse than building false hopes on help "from above" is if these hopes do not prove false and the "help" were to come true.

So one is led to the conclusion that Juno is right when she says, "Sure, if it's not our business, I don't know whose business it is." (47) They must free themselves. They are

---

* O'Casey's attitude to the newly established "Free State" has already been mentioned. He saw it as a petty-bourgeois *nouveau-riche* fool's paradise. If one appreciates the image of the Boyle family metaphorically, as, at one level, a symbol of Irish society as such, then the affair with the legacy can be read as a comment on the Free State. What is true of the slum is true of the State.

continuously moulding reality; it is time they learnt to mould it in their own interests instead of against them. All O'Casey's images infer a) the latent qualities necessary to achieve this, and b) that these qualities themselves are a part of that truly human way of living that one must fight to achieve. It is a measure of the deeply popular nature of O'Casey's realism that he is able to make these potentially world-changing qualities shine through between the lines of his criticism.

They give unfailing stature to the characters from the working people. They are a decisive part of the immanent all-pervading perspective. O'Casey's message is that they must be mobilised *now*. The fact that these potential strengths instead of being a means of liberation are still so often a means of enslavement is an important aspect of the tragedy. What transforms this from a largely abstract perspective into the beginnings of a real, concrete one is that a few characters, here above all Juno, do begin to mobilise them in an effort to move forwards.

The famous contradictoriness or ambivalence of O'Casey's characters is the expression of this inner tension between the two opposite and conflicting possibilities coexisting closely and precariously within these qualities—a tension between the actual and the possible.

The language of these people is the most universal carrier of their "double" nature.[8] This is concentrated in one word in Boyle's justly famous phrase, "a terrible state o' chassis." On the one hand this kind of thing is an expression of the environmentally imposed illiteracy and mental confusion of the characters. On the other it bears witness to their creative, highly individual manipulation of the tool of language. These Irish word-forgers make their own rules and break the old rules. These "unruly" people have a spontaneously creative approach to English. There is nothing sacrosanct about it for them. They are not inhibited by the weight of literary and academic authority, or their use of it dulled by the meticulous and sobering demands of "commerce and industry." It is the absence of this latter influence which makes their speech so "Elizabethan" rather than the mere historical fact that English was imposed upon them in the time of "Good" Queen Bess (before English had become castrated in the "motherland"). They have put their own stamp on the language. Today, in the rhythm and form of almost every phrase, the transforming spirit of the people's old Gaelic tongue has "subverted" the King's English. So the English language, forced upon them as a means of their enslavement, has been partly transformed into a tool to express *themselves*, their particular receiving-end view of the world. In the word "chassis" the all-invading aggressive essence of capitalist anarchy is expressed in the anarchic form of the word itself. But let us take a longer passage from the play so that the characters can speak for themselves. It will also give us the opportunity of going on to a wider discussion of the potentially positive side of the conflicting opposites on which the characterisation is based.

The infuriated Boyle is relating to Joxer how Jerry Devine brought him the terrible news that Father Farrell had a job lined up for him (Boyle).

Boyle. . . . I'm goin' to tell you somethin', Joxer, that I wouldn't tell to anybody else—the clergy always had too much power over the people in this unfortunate country.

Joxer. You could sing that if you had an air to it!

Boyle (becoming enthusiastic). Didn't they prevent the people in '47 from seizin' the corn, an' they starvin'; didn't they down Parnell; didn't they say that hell wasn't hot enough nor eternity long enough to punish the Fenians? We don't forget, we don't forget them things, Joxer. If they've taken everything else from us, Joxer, they've left us our memory.

Joxer (emotionally). For mem'ry's the only friend that grief can call its own, that grief . . . can . . . call . . . its own!

Boyle. Father Farrell's beginnin' to take a great intherest in Captain Boyle; because of what Johnny did for his country, says he to me wan day. It's a curious way to reward Johnny be makin' his poor oul' father work. But that's what the clergy want, Joxer—work, work, work for me an' you; havin' us mulin' from mornin' till night, so that they may be in betther fettle when they come hoppin' round for their dues! Job! Well, let him give his job to wan of his hymn-singin', prayer-spoutin', craw-thumpin' Confraternity men!

The voice of a coal-block vendor is heard chanting in the street.

Voice of Coal Vendor. Blocks . . . coal-blocks! Blocks . . . coal-blocks!

Joxer. God be with the young days when you were steppin' the deck of a manly ship, with the win' blowin' a hurricane through the masts, an' the only sound you'd hear was, 'Port your helm!' an' the only answer, 'Port it is, sir!'

The Captain now launches upon his seafaring fantasy already quoted on page 52, culminating thus:

Boyle. An', as it blowed an' blowed, I ofen looked up at the sky an' assed meself the question—what is the stars, what is the stars?

Voice of Coal Vendor. Any blocks, coal-blocks; blocks, coal-blocks!

Joxer. Ah, that's the question, that's the question—what is the stars?

Boyle. An' then, I'd have another look, an' I'd ass meself—what is the moon?

Joxer. Ah, that's the question—what is the moon, what is the moon?

. . . *the door is opened, and the black face of the* Coal Vendor *appears.*

The Coal Vendor. D'yez want any blocks?

Boyle (with a roar). No, we don't want any blocks! (22–24)

The salient features of Boyle's language here are concreteness combined with the large rhetorical gesture. His images are markedly mimetic, depicting vigorous bodily actions. He is able to give expression to precise and deep critical insights into society. There is a drive to dramatisation and confrontation. Rhythm, originality, imagination and passion fuse into an aggressive energy. These qualities in Boyle's speech are highlighted by being juxtaposed to Joxer's derivative echoes. Joxer's speech is a blunted tool by comparison.

Boyle and most of the others throw their whole personality into this prodigal and prodigious talking. All the force, revolt and inventiveness which should by right find its main field of realisation in deeds, is poured into the *word*. This too, bears witness to the frustration of all endeavour and action in Ireland's bitter history. Functioning in this circumscribed context these potentially revolutionising energies are squandered on trivialities, posturing and internecine bickering—word-fights. But they are there—a repository of aggressive, explosive potentials. There is nothing here of that "dogged inarticulateness" which middle-class authors sometimes like to portray as a characteristic "virtue" of the working class.

The scene quoted is a good example of the more general interaction and interpenetration of conflicting elements in Boyle. He launches a passionate and true attack on the historical role of the Church hierarchy, but he falters in full stride and the mood slips into maudlin self-pity. How precarious is the boundary-line! Jago-Joxer at once pounces on the weakness and fosters it. But then Boyle gets going again, and more strongly, building up to an impressive climax. Pathos—bathos—pathos. Danger for Joxer, especially as harsh reality seems to join Boyle in the sobering shout of the coal vendor. At once Joxer cunningly launches the Captain on the high seas of his favourite fantasy, making him reach for the distant stars rather than stoop to the black, hard, dirty coal blocks of reality.

Dangerous and ridiculous this reaching for the stars is, under the circumstances; empty and absurd his philosophical questions—and yet, juxtaposed to Juno's wingless pragmatism, one cannot suppress a certain admiration. There is here a refusal to accept a life defined by coal blocks. It is childish and irresponsible, but a kind of rebellion. Hence, when the alienating-effect of the coal vendor with his question intervenes to bring Boyle down to earth with a bump, our reaction to his savage rejection is not entirely negative.

Characteristically, Boyle is first introduced singing a prayer to the spirit: "Sweet Spirit, hear me prayer! Hear . . . oh . . . hear . . . me prayer . . . hear, oh, hear . . . Oh, he . . . ar . . . oh, he . . . ar . . . me . . . pray . . . er!" (10)

Joxer (outside) comments that it is a daarlin' song, while Juno (inside) is willing to take a solemn "affeydavey" that he's praying for anything but a job.

It is this insistence that in spite of and to spite soul-destroying conditions, man has a right to a soul, to imagination, poetry and song, this reaching, however grotesquely, for the stars, the unswerving pursuit of this need, whatever the cost—and it's a disastrous cost for him—that gives Boyle his backhanded impressiveness. He will have dignity, even if it is a ridiculous dignity. At one level O'Casey is showing his countrymen, through Boyle, that the "stage-Irishman," that detested caricature of the Irish in the traditional English theatre, is nearer to the actual state of affairs than the romanticised heroics of Irish patriotic literature. A bitter, paradoxical piece of O'Casey irony. On another level however the stage-Irishman convention melts before our eyes, an outer shell, falling away and revealing something living, something in which potential greatness is being tragically wasted. In conventional productions aimed at an English audience the Boyle figure is used to curry laughs at the expense of this supposed stage-Irishman *par excellence*. Serious productions must avoid this pitfall, and the laughter called forth by Boyle's antics must be of a much more complex and productive kind.

In Boyle's attitude and effort there is something concealed which, when liberated from its self-alienation, is as essential to the struggle for liberation as is Juno's realism. Unite these two opposites, not in the botched and destructive "harmony" of this Christian marriage, but in a true synthesis, and both will become fertile again. On this basis new and better heroes can arise, heroes who can master life.

In connection with all this it is time to take another look at the legacy business. We shall see that it is no mere mechanical convention used to forward the plot or something filched from melodrama to heighten the suspense. Its effect on the action is contradictory. Certain positive potentials are discovered or fostered under the conditions arising from the promise of the legacy. Alongside its negative influence it provides them with the basis for a kind of "flowering"– limited and fleeting and deeply compromised as it is. The "prosperity," false though it is in every real sense, functions for a time as if it were real. Juno, for instance, who has never had a breathing-space, now seems to feel solid ground under her feet for the first time and can push out her horns, extend her concern a little. In this way one catches a fleeting glimpse of what might and could be under conditions of genuine security and well-being. In its way it is a proof of their capacity to live and not merely exist.

There is nothing miserly in their behaviour on the basis of the expected money. They use the credit given in anticipation of it not as a capitalist would, to invest and make more money, but in a human way, to procure the good things of life, however tasteless they may be in form. They use it to satisfy real needs which neither the Free State nor the Republicans are satisfying for them. Joxer gets liberal hand-outs. Mrs Madigan is entitled to as much whiskey as she can drink so long as it's there.

Their behaviour and relations become, in a sense, "socialised" under the new conditions. In true Irish style they throw a party whose culmination is a musical "session" where each is expected to perform his or her party piece. Thus Boyle's ideal of social life, "a quiet jar, an' a song or two" (34), is to a certain extent realised.

As has been indicated, Boyle's worst characteristics are aggravated by the "great expectations," but some of his better ones also seem to gather strength for a time. Fleetingly he wins an element of genuine poise and even–at one point–true dignity. His taking command of the proceedings is at once ridiculous and rather efficient. A hint of potentially real captain-talents is suggested. There is a new note in his rising tendency to ridicule their fairy godfather and potential son-in-law, Bentham, to his face. The latter's highfalutin "Prawna" (life-spirit) is too mystical for that man-of-the-spirit, Jack Boyle–"Prawna; yis, the Prawna. *(Blowing gently through his lips)* That's the Prawna!" (37) His penchant for realistic social insight and generalisation seems to gain in steadiness, especially his critique of that favourite anathema of his–religion. Religion, he says, has had its day and is passing like everything else. The Dubliners of today are better acquainted with Charlie Chaplin than with Saints Peter and Paul. His pagan hedonism comes more strongly to the fore. It is something much more necessary to the people in their historic task than the traditional religious belly-crawling of Juno. Then there is that remarkable poem of his, the recital of which is the high point of the "session":

Shawn an' I were friends, sir, to me he was all in all.
His work was very heavy and his wages were very small.
None betther on th' beach as Docker, I'll go bail,
'Tis now I'm feelin' lonely, for to-day he lies in jail.
He was not what some call pious–seldom at church or
    prayer;
For the greatest scoundrels I know, sir, goes every Sun-
    day there.
Fond of his pint–well, rather, but hated the Boss by
    creed
But never refused a copper to comfort a pal in need. (48)

This is simple and dignified and devoid of bourgeois literary convention. It strongly reflects the class pride and consciousness born during the 1913 strike. It is set in a popular and working-class ballad tradition which Boyle must have been acquainted with. His cultural potential seems to have received a boost through the anticipation of a little well-being. It is new enough to surprise Juno–"God bless us, is he startin' to write poetry!" (48) At this point Boyle, who has revealed little or no contact with literary tradition, is suddenly able to create this poem out of nothing, it would appear, except his experience coupled with his imagination. This original creativeness puts his contribution to the session in a different category to those of the others who are content to reproduce the artistic creations of others.

Juno too, is stimulated–perhaps more than Boyle. She shows tendencies towards an inner synthesis of her own qualities with those found in Boyle. There are growing signs of interest and participation in the world beyond her nest, the beginnings of her socialisation. For the first time she ventures a comment on the state of her society–"when we got the makin' of our own laws I thought we'd never stop to look behind us, but instead of that we never stopped to look before us!" (36)

In contrast to the impression she has made hitherto, Juno now reveals a genuine feeling for things artistic. Standing together, she and her daughter sing "simply" the Verdi duet "Home to our Mountains." The fact that this song is from another country and people is in itself a sign of her modest "expansion." It is as if the participation in this cultural activity stimulates the broadening of her human concern. Not long after she has sung her song she hears Mrs Tancred passing down the stairs with the other mourners to her murdered son's funeral. She stops Boyle putting a record on the gramophone. She'd forgotten they were taking the body to the church that night; now she tells Mary to open the door and give them a bit of light on the landing. She wants her light to shine out for others.

The sing-song, then, is a moment of synthesis, a high point in the expression of the positive potential of these people, their capacity for living. Only Joxer fails to come up to the mark.

But death and death-dealing reality break in on the festivities more and more massively in connection with the mourning procession for Tancred. The high moment is lost in morbid fascination with the trappings of death. Boyle's behaviour at this point is ominous. He washes his hands of all responsibility for what is happening to people: "That's the Government's business, an' let them do what we're payin' them for doin'." (47) This is the money ethic victorious. The socialising effect of the anticipated legacy has not been as strong in his case as its corrupting influence. This is really the final parting of the ways between Boyle and Juno and foreshadows his rejection of his pregnant daughter because the scandal will damage his image.

Boyle fails the test because his grasp of reality and therefore his sense of responsibility are initially too undermined to provide any basis. Juno on the other hand has been able to profit from the experience of this bit of "good living." For her it has brought out the contrast between what might be and the way things have been. The fiasco of its quick collapse under the blows of circumstances heightens her awareness that one must not accept these circumstances but fight them. But the realist O'Casey does not simplify her progress or the difficulties which will continue to face her. Indeed, Juno finds the strength for the final break only when the tragedy has been completed with the death of her son.

Juno derives the strength to take the decisive step from her experience and what she has learnt from it. This she is able to do because all along she has had to face up to reality, and her experience has therefore been real to her. When Mrs Madigan comes to tell her that Johnny has been shot her comment is, "I've gone through so much lately that I feel able for anything." (70) This great quality is indicated on a lower key in Mary and Mrs Madigan.

Juno abandons Boyle—"he'll be hopeless till the end of his days," (71) and goes off with Mary. This is an epoch-breaking step for Juno: *she splits the family,* the former be-all-and-end-all of her life, for the sake of deeper and wider human considerations. Together with her daughter she intends to found a new type of family unit, an unorthodox one without a male "head of the house," one which will recognise its debt and its responsibility to the working-class community as a whole.

Her last famous speech is almost word for word a repeat of Mrs Tancred's lament for her son, spoken in Juno's presence: "It's well I remember all that she said—an' it's my turn to say it now: What was the pain I suffered, Johnny, bringin' you into the world to carry you to your cradle, to the pains I'll suffer carryin' you out o' the world to bring you to your grave! Mother o' God, Mother o' God, have pity on us all! Blessed Virgin, where were you when me darlin' son was riddled with bullets? Sacred Heart o' Jesus, take away our hearts o' stone, and give us hearts o' flesh! Take away this murdherin' hate, an' give us Thine own eternal love!" (71–72)

This "quotation" from Mrs Tancred is of a different nature from Davoren's repetition of his favourite Shelley lines at the end of *The Shadow of a Gunman*. Davoren partly misuses Shelley to express that fatal narcissism which even at the bitter end he has not finally overcome. Juno's quotation on the other hand (which, curiously enough, contains an unmistakable echo of the second stanza of Shelley's *Adonais*) expresses her new level of socialisation. Quotation is the fitting form for the content of the speech, which is a realisation of the need for understanding and solidarity with those working people like Mrs Tancred in the same plight as herself. It is the perfect way of expressing Juno's total identification with this "outsider" ("it's my turn to say it now"). In her moment of deepest emotional disturbance the words of a "stranger" are suddenly the very words she needs and finds to express her most personal and heartfelt thoughts. The quotation form is an act of solidarity. It is the second link in a chain reaction, a process of growing socialisation; in her speech, Mrs Tancred had already made the first link-up by breaking through to an understanding of Mrs Manning who had lost her son in an ambush led by Robbie Tancred. It is a way of generalising Juno's experience. The form and direction of this speech also suggests that Juno can, in the coming time, develop that imaginative capacity which had hitherto been alienated from her in the pernicious form of Boyle.

But is this last speech not also evidence that Juno has not freed herself from one of the most inhibiting elements in her environment—religion? Having renounced the family god Boyle, is she not passing the buck on to the Holy Virgin and her son? It has even been suggested that this is a religious play, advocating, through Juno, that the only hope lies in a revival of the true religious spirit.[9] If one ignores or falsifies the potential dynamic embedded in the characterisation as a whole such an interpretation may be made to look superficially plausible, especially if Juno is put on a pedestal. In fact the speech is quite in keeping with the contradictory logic of her character. Her whole emotional upbringing has been bound up with the church and so it is natural for her to express herself in its terms at a moment of deep emotional turmoil. But the religiosity of the speech is really mainly in the form. Indeed, it contains a basic questioning of the relevance of religion to life ("Blessed Virgin, where were you . . .?"), a question forced on Juno and the audience by the whole development of the action which has insisted on man's own responsibility for his plight and his liberation. Juno learns from life but her conscious world-view is not yet as far advanced as her actual doing: there is deep unconscious irony in her plea for God to replace their hearts of stone with hearts of flesh, for this heart transplant is exactly what she has already achieved by her own efforts. She has shown that there is no need for God. Juno—that name so indicative of godlike sovereignty—now ceases to be a mockery of her who bears it.

O'Casey chose to close the play with Boyle and Joxer, incapably drunk, alone on the scene. And he gives Boyle the last word on the state of the world—"chassis." Why?

First, the scene shows the end of the road for Boyle. All his potentials have come to this. He subsides to the floor on a level with Joxer. The "man of higher things" is himself the very embodiment and epitome of the "chassis." As soon as Juno abandons her hold on him he sinks as quickly as she rises. At the same time the scene is an alienating-effect in true O'Casey style. It provides a kind of "comic relief" while in essence being anything but comic. With its calculated bathos it reminds us of Seumas' last line in the *Gunman*. It is a technique we shall meet again. It lowers the emotional pressure built up to a catharsis-like situation in Juno's great preceding scene, bringing us down to a more normal temperature. This enables us to appreciate that Juno and her action are still an exception and that the Irish scene remains largely defined by the Boyles and Joxers and the helpless anarchy for which they stand. They remain "in occupation." Juno's way is going to be no easy one.

The release-in-laughter of the final scene also allows us to sit back and take a cool look at the implications of the action as a whole, freeing us from the intense fascination with Juno's great moment alone. In making us laugh under these circumstances it forces us to ask ourselves *why* we laugh at this and why we have laughed at these characters. It raises the question–is laughter alone the adequate response? Thus the comic side of this tragedy and the laughter it evokes emerge, not as something coexistent with the tragic, but a key, a way in to a more profound understanding of the tragedy.

Lastly it places Boyle's persuasive summing up of the world in a critical perspective, encouraging us to test it and question it.

Notes

1. Quoted by James Plunkett in *The Gems She Wore*, London, 1972, p. 193
2. G. B. Shaw, *John Bull's Other Island*, Act I
3. Krause, op. cit., p. 104
4. Cowasjee, op. cit., p. 26
5. Alla Sarukhanyan, *Tvorchestvo Seana O'Casey*, Moscow, 1965, p. 38 (translation, JM)
6. Goldstone, op. cit., pp. 39–40
7. See for instance Krause, op. cit., p. 125, and Goldstone, op. cit., p. 42
8. For a detailed and discerning study of O'Casey's use of

speech levels see Thomas Metscher, *Sean O'Caseys drama-tischer Stil*, Braunschweig, 1968

9. See for instance Gabriel Fallon, "The Man in the Plays," in *The World of Sean O'Casey*, ed. S. McCann, London, 1966, p. 207

III THE PLOUGH AND THE STARS

Written 1925; published 1926; produced 1926 (Abbey Theatre, Dublin)

> "So they have decided against bringing the rough energy and virile splendour of the workers to the definite aid of the National Movement. Well, to hell with them then!"
>
> Sean O'Casey, *Drums under the Windows*

The events take place between November 1915 and Easter 1916. Setting–the Dublin slums. The action opens in the little flat of Nora Clitheroe and her bricklayer husband, Jack. Nora has two lodgers–her uncle, Peter Flynn, a labourer and nationalist of childish mentality, and the Young Covey, a fitter, anti-nationalist and doctrinaire socialist. The latter so provokes the older man with verbal jibes that Peter attempts to attack him with an ancient cavalry sword, part of the outlandish regalia which he is donning for the great Republican rally to be held that evening. Nora comes home and puts the two "children" firmly in their place.

When the others have gone Nora tries to persuade her husband Jack to stay in and spend the evening alone with her. Jack is a member of the Citizen Army, the workers' militia, which has now joined forces with the nationalist Irish Volunteers. He has been less active lately, some say because he wasn't made a captain. Enter Captain Brennan of the C. A. Jack is called "Commandant" in the order he brings with him from General Connolly. Jack knows nothing of this promotion. It turns out that Nora has burnt the letter to Jack containing the news. Furious, Jack goes off to the parade with Brennan. But Nora is not left in peace for long. First Mollser, the consumptive daughter of a gossipy neighbour, Mrs Gogan, creeps in. She too, has been left to fend for herself while her mother goes off to the rally. Next Bessie Burgess barges in, a loud-mouthed loyalist fellow slum-dweller, whose son has gone as a volunteer with the British army to France. She insults Nora and pours vicious invective on the Irish stay-at-homes.

Act II is set in a pub. Outside, the great Republican rally is under way. A speaker standing on a platform outside the pub window sways the gathering with mystical rhetoric. His words can be heard within from time to time. Rosie, a young prostitute, sits customerless in the emptied pub. Presently others—the Covey, Mrs Gogan, Bessie Burgess, and Fluther Good, a pugnacious carpenter and trade-unionist—drop in to relieve their thirst. They quarrel and it almost comes to blows, first between Mrs Gogan and Mrs Burgess, then between Fluther and the Covey. Peter is left holding the Gogan baby. Brennan, Clitheroe and Lieutenant Langon (the latter of the Irish Volunteers) rush in. While they drink to imprisonment and death for the sake of Ireland, Fluther and Rosie slip off to her place.

By Act III the Rising is in full swing. The scene is the street outside the tenement. Fluther leads home the hysterical Nora who had run off in the night to find and bring back her Jack. Bessie jeers and sings "Rule Britannia" from her upstairs window. Peter and the Covey play pitch and toss to a background of gunfire. Presently these two, followed by Bessie and Mrs Gogan, run off to the town centre to loot shops and pubs, despite being shot at by the Volunteers. Mollser and the baby are again forgotten. Brennan, Clitheroe and the badly wounded Lieutenant Langon enter. Nora rushes out and tries to reclaim her Jack, who is finally persuaded to brush her aside. Fluther appears, fighting drunk, having looted a pub. He rants outside, while Nora, giving premature birth, screams within the house.

Act IV. Back inside the slum, up in Bessie's attic flat, a few days later, Fluther, the Covey and Peter play cards near a coffin containing the dead Mollser with Nora's still-born child in her arms. Firing and shouts for ambulances outside. Brennan, now dressed in civilian clothes, brings news that Jack has fallen in battle. Nora should be proud. But Nora is now insane. Brennan refuses to leave although his presence endangers the others. Two British tommies come in and round up all the men in the house. Bessie, trying to drag the raving Nora away from the window, is shot from outside. The tommies are left in sole occupation. They brew tea and join with soldiers outside in singing "Keep the Home Fires Burning." Dublin blazes around them.

There is clearly a new departure here in the scope of the setting and the radius of action. In the two foregoing plays the action was compressed within one tenement room. A claustrophobic, ingrown atmosphere was thus created which became part of the plays' statement. Here the action bursts these bounds, widening out, first to take in the pub, and next the street. Then it shrinks back again to end as it started in a tenement room, this time a garret up under the roof. But even here there is no refuge. The people are driven out into the void and alien forces are in occupation. This expansion and contraction is characteristic of the play as a whole.

There is also a new development in the way the action is structured. The preceding plays were still making brilliant use of certain traditional "intrigue" (plot) elements—the legacy, the sudden change of fortune, reversals, discoveries, etc. The action revolved round one or two central figures, culminating near the end in catharsis-crises which produce a kind of "purifying" of the main character and open up the possibility of radical change in him or her, as a social personality. Now O'Casey abandons these Aristotelian rules, or transforms them, to branch out into a type of structure with growing similarities to the Brechtian or "epic" plot.

Now each scene gains a kind of independence, becoming a fully rounded dramatic episode in its own right. Aristotle says of this: "The episodic are the worst of all plots and actions; and by an episodic plot I mean one in which the episodes have no probable or inevitable connection."[1] In the traditional Aristotelian plot the parts are nothing in themselves but rungs on the one ladder that leads with fatal inevitability to the climax or catastrophe. Diverting episodes were frowned upon as blurring the focus and disrupting the unity of action whose duty it is to unfold the central, main-line personal plot. This type of structure had certainly helped to bring discipline into the drama as a way of modelling reality, and, in the hands of a master, could, and perhaps still can, be a productive approach. The disadvantage—and this became more and more obvious in the plays of its latter-day middle-class exponents—lies in its inherent tendency to narrow the drama's ability to embrace society in its manifoldness and the totality of its interrelations.

O'Casey had already begun to depart from it in his previous plays. Now he goes completely over to a form of action-structure containing several embryonic individual-story elements, none of which is exclusively developed at the expense of the others. Several critics disapproved of this new departure of O'Casey's from the established norms.[2] In fact it gives the playwright a much freer hand to express social totality and complexity. Each episode or scene can now exploit to the full the whole breadth of social implication inherent in it. Organic unity is achieved nevertheless because all the relatively independent "bits" are moulded towards a common point of reference—the underlying social theme or subject of the play. Each makes its special contribution to this grand theme. But, besides this, O'Casey uses specific techniques to establish his artistic unity. Above all perhaps there is his system of inner contrasts and parallels. This was one of the things he "picked up" from his master, Shakespeare. In *The Plough and the Stars* this technique reaches a new level of sophistication. The apparent looseness of the "epic" structure is a fallacy. In fact this system of contrasts and parallels knits the whole and its parts so tightly together that there is far less "superfluous" material in an O'Casey play, despite appearances, than in the conventional "well-made play."

What has been said up to now implies a broad panorama of figures rather than concentration on a particular hero or central character. Which is the case. This too, works as a distancing-effect. It stops us from becoming too massively involved with certain individuals and their personal fates and encourages critical insight into the social causal nexus as a whole. As Sarukhanyan says, "Nora's fate is only one episode in these tumultuous days [. . .] The main thing in the play is the tragedy of the people as a whole."[3]

The Plough and the Stars continues O'Casey's general campaign in the "Dublin" plays to de-heroicise and de-mythologise the Irish working people's view of themselves. At a pivotal point in their history, the Easter Rising–a moment surrounded in their minds with a romantic aura–he shows them to be anything but a people of saints, scholars, virtuous women and brave patriots. They are disunited, quarrelsome, childishly petty, ignorant, self-centred, self-deluding, self-dramatising, word-worshippers, negligent of their own true state and real needs, squanderers of their splendid energies. All these familiar characteristics are however woven together into a much broader, more universal and turbulent pattern. No single element of their disturbed relationship to themselves and reality becomes the main focal point here. In fact, in the final analysis, this tragically distorted everyday relationship to reality is no longer the main theme in this play because it was not yet the foremost problem in the objective historical situation with which the play deals, i.e. the Rising of 1916.

The basic contradiction which the play sets out to lay bare is established in the pub scene (Act II). It is the contradiction, the gulf, between the movement for national liberation in its present form (represented in this scene by the Voice beyond the window) and the state and real needs of the people. The relationship between the national movement and the masses now becomes the chief and specific object of study.

The Voice conjures up a mystical and idealised vision of the Irish people which is negated by their actual behaviour in the pub. The abstractness of this approach is symbolised in the fact that the Voice is disembodied. The people of Ireland need war, it cries, a blood-sacrifice to purify them–"Heroism has come back to the earth. War is a terrible thing, but war is not an evil thing. People in Ireland dread war because they do not know it. Ireland has not known the exhilaration of war for over a hundred years. When war comes to Ireland she must welcome it as she would welcome the Angel of God!" (169)

In fact it is obviously not war but an end to poverty and ignorance that they need. They need an end to the conditions that force Rosie Redmond to lie in wait for men in the pub so as to be able to pay her rent, the conditions that bring people like Bessie and Mrs Gogan, Fluther and the Covey, to the point where they attempt to attack each other physically. These people have known nothing else but war for the last hundred years and more. Peace is what they have not known—war against want and exploitation. What they need is the exhilaration of true peace, an end to *senseless* war, so that what should be joined together in harmony may be joined. But the earthy plough of the people's life and the starry plough of the ideal are sundered. Noses are too close to the grindstone; heads are too high in the stars. The fusion of the two which the great banner signifies is not realised in fact. It is the theme of Juno and her paycock played out on a higher social and political plane.

How could such a state of affairs have arisen? The play has something to say about this.

Certain characteristics of the working people—their weaknesses—are reflected in the weaknesses of the liberation movement and its members.

Poor Peter Flynn is totally absorbed in appearances—regalia, finery, cutting a figure. His longing for colour in a drab life is understandable if ridiculous. Even in Nora Clitheroe there is a shadow of it behind her basically healthy wish to express her respect for herself through dressing well and refusing to be defeated by her environment. Mrs Gogan's vicious remarks about Nora getting "notions of upperosity" (137) are, like much that comes out of the same mouth, not without shafts of insight which help us to grasp the contradictory nature of all we see. Mrs Gogan, despite her derogatory remarks, is herself fascinated by dress and formal paraphernalia. She tries on Nora's new hat, handles Peter's sword and frilly shirt (part of his Foresters uniform). When she remarks that "The Foresthers' is a gorgeous dhress! I don't think I've seen nicer, mind you, in a pantomime," (167) she is hovering between real admiration and fun-poking. Thus Jack Clitheroe's preoccupation with his officer's uniform and insignia of rank, his urge to cultivate an image, are commented on through a system of parallels. It is a method of generalising, showing the soil out of which Jack's weakness arises. At the still higher level of the organised movement as such the same thing is embodied in the great parade. There is a subtle parallel between this and the looters in Act III, decking themselves out in plundered finery in the midst of battle.

Mrs Gogan is fascinated with death and dying, understandable up to a point considering her circumstances (a dead husband and a dying daughter). She frightens Fluther by telling him a story about a seemingly strong woman who was carried off suddenly by a little cough. She depresses her own daughter by saying she thinks she's been coughing more lately. She dreams of Jack staggering in spattered all over with his own life-blood. Is it such a long way from this to Clitheroe's, Brennan's and Langon's toast to wounds and dying, or to the Voice's mystification of dying as blood-sacrifice?

The characters in *The Plough and the Stars* are among the most passionate of O'Casey's proverbial word-wielders. In their great rhetorical set battles they forget the realities of life, neglect the things that really need their anger. The better to deal with Bessie Burgess Mrs Gogan lays her baby down on the pub floor and promptly forgets it. It is there even in the Covey. His reaction to all situations is to intone high-sounding abstract generalities from Jenersky's *Thesis on the Origin, Development, an' Consolidation of the Evolutionary Idea of the Proletariat*. This avoids the necessity of grappling with the specific demands of real situations. At this level the Covey is similar to his anathema, the Voice, whose empty rhetoric he derides.

In these ways O'Casey shows how the immature sides of

the masses insinuate themselves into the national liberation movement. The love-scene between Jack and Nora Clitheroe in Act I is of decisive importance in this connection.

Nora, initially, is the person with most insight into what life should be like and where the dangers lie. She is all for life. She realises that the nationalist adventurers are divorced from the real needs of the people and that people are more important than idealist abstractions. She grasps that happiness is something concrete and has to do with human harmony and fulfilment. Under the circumstances her instincts are right in trying to keep Jack at home and away from the nationalists.

But their marriage shows the impoverishment of the man-wife relationship in their society. Jack has the traditional attitude. Nora tells him, "Oh, yes, your little, little red-lipped Nora's a sweet little girl when th' fit seizes you; but your little, little red-lipped Nora has to clean your boots every mornin', all the same." (154) He has an insufficient grasp of her as a human being, a real life-partner. He sees her as a part of his image, like his uniform. They are basically at a loose end with one another. This impoverished relationship cannot hold or fulfil him or her. He must look for his fulfilment elsewhere.

Nora is aware of the danger. She seeks to hold him. Her weapons are those he expects and understands. She descends to playing the prescribed role of sex-object; she knows no other way. There is truth in Mrs Gogan's "catty" remark that "She dhresses herself to keep him with her, but it's no use—afther a month or two, th' wondher of a woman wears off." (138) She persuades Jack to sing their special love-song from the early days of their courting. She is trying to lead him back to the unsullied spring of their relationship so that they can try again and perhaps find a better path. She succeeds in reawakening some of the old emotion in him, but the moment of harmony is very frail. It is too purely nostalgic, without the makings of anything new in it. One can understand her having a better lock put on the door and wishing she was out of the crowded slums when the knock of Captain Brennan of the nationalist movement breaks into the budding idyll. After the discovery that she has suppressed the letter with the news of Jack's promotion she tries the "little red-lipped Nora" approach on him in her desperation. His retort is—"None o' this nonsense, now." (158) Her only magic fails her. She has been unable to bring to their relationship the quality which might have saved it. This is dictated partly by Jack's limitations, but also by her own. In her efforts to keep him she actually drives him into the arms of her "rival." Once again a basically healthy urge is turned against itself. In this way the love-scene and its consequences illustrate the process by which the weaknesses of the people are channelled into the national movement.

Nora's tragedy arises from her position as a woman in capitalist society. She appears to have no existence, no justification of her own outside and beyond her husband. All her demands, hopes and aspirations are exclusively focussed on this one object. When he goes off to fight she says, "They have dhriven away th' little happiness life had to spare for me." (186) Just before this she tells Mrs Gogan that she sometimes thinks she's going mad. And indeed, the well-spring and logic of her growing *mania* lie here. She sees the be-all-and-end-all of her existence—her husband—going out willingly to be "butchered as a sacrifice to th' dead." (184) The desperation of her position drives Nora to exaggerated reactions. She resorts to petty subterfuges which belie and belittle her real stature. Negative tendencies already within her are encouraged—her preoccupation with appearances, her petty-bourgeois self-centredness, her lack of a sense of social responsibility and her developed sense of property, of possessiveness. There is still clear justification in her early demand that they should forget everything but their two selves for the evening. (156) But later this begins to take on a hysterical note—"What do I care for th' others? I can think only of me own self." (184) She "cursed the rebel ruffians an' Volunteers that had dhragged me ravin' mad into th' sthreets to seek me husband!" (185)

The progress of her insanity is the malignant growth of this exclusive preoccupation (forced upon her) with her husband. When she tries to drag Jack away from the dying Langon she is still right on an abstract level but her humanity and sense of moral judgement are already seriously impaired. The end of this process is reached in Nora's "mad-scenes" in the last act. These aren't simply something taken over from Shakespeare or the melodrama in order to lend pathos to the climax of the play. They are the culmination of a process. Again O'Casey takes a convention which seems to be played out and breathes new life into it.

Her hallucinations all revolve round a struggle between herself and certain mysterious forces for the possession of her husband. Her mania has taken over complete command. Once again she ignores the need of someone dying of wounds, this time poor Bessie Burgess of whose motives in acting as she does there can be no doubt—she gets the fatal wound trying to save Nora. But all the once active and humane personality Nora can do now is to stand helpless and cry for her Jack to come and comfort her. Being deprived of her *raison d'être*, her husband, has lamed her personality, killed her as a human being *before* Bessie sacrifices her life "saving" her at the window. The historical and social conditions under which she lives reduce her to only one facet of the full personality she might have been. She is then deprived of this one plane on which she can function and so broken, disqualified from life. In this sense she harks forward to Harry Heegan in *The Silver Tassie*.

In the story of Jack Clitheroe's family life we see how the poverty and immaturity of the people's everyday living encourages them to "escape" into a movement of the kind depicted, thus helping to mould that movement. They appear as being themselves partly responsible for the movement which fails them. But this also implies that the responsibility and the *ability to transform it* also lie in their hands. As things are, only their weaknesses are taken up into the movement.

Yet the main emphasis is not on the people's responsibility for the kind of movement they get, but on the movement's failure of responsibility towards the people, its inadequacy to them. Despite the masses-movement connections that have been indicated, the national struggle as O'Casey depicts it is not shown as a truly popular movement of the masses. It has shaken itself loose, become an "independent" alien entity, objectively opposed to their interests. This movement reflects the people one-sidedly and is therefore inadequate to them. The actual social personality of the masses is portrayed as being so rich and contradictory that it can contain the weaknesses without being finally defined by them. The movement, in embodying only a certain facet of the masses, lays itself open to corruption and alienation through bourgeois forces. Writing of the early twenties O'Casey says that "The cause of the Easter Rising had been betrayed by the commonplace bourgeois class."[4] Here he shows how this betrayal was already beginning to make itself felt in the Easter Rising itself. The men who "lead Jack astray" are of middle-class background. Brennan, though a member of the workers' Citizen Army, is a chicken butcher (!) and Langon of the Volunteers is a civil servant. At one point Captain Brennan savagely demands of Clitheroe why he had fired over the heads of the looters instead of firing to kill. Jack protests that, bad as they may be, they are all Irish men and women. Brennan's answer to Jack and the people's distress is, "If these slum lice gather at our heels again, plug one o' them . . ." (194)

This nationalist movement, as O'Casey depicts it, far from helping the people to overcome their weaknesses, actually aggravates and consolidates them, while failing to mobilise and utilise their strengths.

We have already traced the process by which it brings out the worst in Nora and in Jack. The pub-scene in Act II provides a symbol or metaphor for this process. For there is not only a contrast between the meeting and the words of the Voice on the one hand, and the goings-on in the pub on the other; there is also a hidden parallel. This movement is like a pub. It intoxicates the masses. Having just experienced the traditional nationalist emotional catharsis outside at the meeting, the characters are still under its spell when they storm into the pub. They order and drink "with the fullness of emotional passion." (163) Fluther forgets his pledge. Clitheroe, Brennan and Langon *enter hurriedly. Captain Brennan carries the banner of The Plough and the Stars, and Lieut. Langon a green, white, and orange Tricolour. They are in a state of emotional excitement. Their faces are flushed and their eyes sparkle; they speak rapidly, as if unaware of the meaning of what they said. They have been mesmerized by the fervency of the speeches.* Clitheroe (*almost pantingly*). Three glasses o' port!" (177–178)

In their "intoxicated" state they toast, not life, but imprisonment, wounds and death (i.e. assumed defeat!) for Ireland. In this way they give voice to the tragic fallacy and divorcement which the play sets out to expose.

The effectuality and "holiness" of this typical catharsis situation (nationalist rhetoric with its mystical aura) are put into question by the *contrast* and *parallel* between the meeting and the pub. Thus a similar thing happens as with the songs in *The Shadow of a Gunman*: the public, or reader, is distanced from a traditionally accepted, emotion-steeped, anti-rational catharsis situation, and made to examine it coolly and critically. The main action (here the scene in the pub) relativises and de-mystifies the *inserted* element (the speech of the nationalist orator). This again is the equivalent of the Brechtian alienating-effect except that the relationship between inserted element and action is reversed (see p. 26 above). Brecht sets out to prevent emotional intoxication taking place in the theatre; O'Casey, via the theatre, aims to discourage it at certain quite crucial points in the actual daily life of the Irish masses. This difference of emphasis is partly determined by the relatively different national and historic problems with which the two writers had to grapple.

Fluther Good is forever taking the pledge and then breaking it. A comic convention. But, as so often with

O'Casey, we are led into the heart of the tragedy through a comic detail. Fluther has certain sterling qualities. He would use them "only he's too dhrunk," (199) as Bessie says, when she has to go herself to fetch a doctor for Nora. A genuine liberation movement would have given him the backbone necessary to stick to his pledge and overcome his drinking.* But he is left to himself. Worse—Fluther's "drunkenness," which is a wider thing than just his addiction to alcohol, is actually fostered by the movement as it is.

The Covey challenges Fluther—"what's the mechanism of exchange?" (174) Driven into a corner, Fluther roars, "How th' hell do I know what it is? There's nothin' about that in th' rules of our Thrades Union!" (174–175) Fluther has taken active part in the battles of the Labour movement, but his horizon is that of classical empirical trade-unionism. Fluther needs theory, the idea, to realise his potential—a clear view of the stars of the title. But practice and theory are divorced.

On the one hand the idea has been monopolised and turned into a confusing emotional appeal by the bourgeois nationalists. Fluther is too down to earth to be more than momentarily caught up and moved by this. On the other hand he and his like are not caught or fired at all by the idea (theory) as represented and expounded by the Covey. If the nationalist "idea" has commandeered all the emotion, the Covey's mechanical, doctrinaire "socialist" sloganising has no emotional appeal whatsoever. Although he is right in the abstract he can find no way in to these people. It is a sign of their humanity that they *can* be moved, even if it is by the rhetorical demagogy of the nationalists. The fact that the Covey is not moved by it, even for an instant,

---

* This in fact happens in *The Harvest Festival*, an early attempt of O'Casey's rejected by the Abbey Theatre. A worker named Bill, a great drinker, gives up the drink completely when he becomes involved in the organised class struggle during the Larkin-led class war in Dublin. The same thing happens with Brannigan in *The Star Turns Red*.

is somewhat ominous. He stands for a sectarian socialism divorced from the masses, as divorced in its way as the petty-bourgeois nationalists are in theirs. The sundering of the plough of real life and its needs and the stars of the ideal is repeated within him, and both halves of this thing that should be whole, having fallen apart, atrophy. The Covey is not physically a coward, but he is frightened of life. The advances of the prostitute Rosie Redmond, that is of life-in-the-flesh with all its degradation and sensual joy, terrifies him. He turns in disgust from what should be his main preoccupation. The insulted Rosie calls him a louse and no man, and this is part of the truth. Like the national-ists he shoves a flow of rhetoric (phrasemongering) be-tween himself and real life. He is incapable of positive hu-man relations, keeping human beings at arm's length.

This he also does with a barrage of insults. Here he dis-plays a concreteness and energy which is lacking in the ap-proach of the nationalist movement. For all the abstract aridity of his "revolutionary" dictums this man becomes one of the most inventive, forceful and ferocious verbal "soul-movers" in all O'Casey when he gets down to the petty business of provoking the simple Peter Flynn—"Isn't that th' malignant oul' varmint! Lookin' like th' illegiti-mate son of an illegitimate child of a corporal in th' Mexican army!" (152) There is nothing quite like this in English-speaking drama between the Covey and the curses in *King Lear*. He can find no way in to Fluther or Rosie with his theory, but he can *move* Peter to a white heat of emotional reaction by vocal variations on the one word "cuckoo!" An energy and ability squandered. Given a national move-ment which truly latches on to the real needs of life, the Covey might have found in it a mobilising centre from which to overcome this crippling compartmentalisation with-in him.

In these ways the national movement as it is cultivates what is worst in the people and fails to mobilise what is best.

*

The underlying shift of emphasis in this play is towards the great revolutionising potentials possessed by the masses. It was inherent in the preceding plays. Some of it has already emerged in what has been said about this one.

Their energy, discontent and creativeness find their most general and spontaneous expression in their speech. Almost all of them possess the verbal vigour we have noted in the Covey. There is an aggressiveness here that surpasses anything in the earlier plays. The rhetoric of the Voice is but a flat and disembowelled shadow of it.

But they have more to offer than their language. The qualities initially possessed by Nora have already been discussed. A potential leader of the *right* kind goes a-begging in her. She is a commanding figure among the "children" until she herself is reduced to a whimpering child. There was a hopeful breadth of humanity in her. Mollser senses this and goes to her for comfort when left alone. There is, within her, *an alternative Nora.* Given somewhat different conditions Nora's story could well have been told differently. Her fate is not preordained.

But not all are crushed or distorted. Bessie Burgess's qualities are made of sterner stuff, and she takes over something of Nora's organising role before she is senselessly and almost accidentally wiped out. "Ideologically" Bessie is a rabid Protestant loyalist which tends to split and isolate her from her Catholic neighbours. This ideology, superimposed on her by church and state is as alien to her true needs and inclinations as is that of the nationalists or the Covey's phrase-chanting. Her "theory" is not the true stars either. In one sense Bessie's view of the imperialist war in France, where her son is fighting, comes ominously close to the Voice's demagogy about blood-sacrifice. There's a storm of anger in her heart, she says, thinking of the poor tommies in France, her own son among them—young men "with th' sunny lust o' life beamin' in them, layin' down their white bodies, shredded into torn an' bloody pieces, on th' althar that God Himself has built for th' sacrifice of heroes!" (168)

But note the conflict behind her words. The difference

between Bessie and those under the spell of nationalist demagogy is that she is instinctively in inner and outer rebellion against the anti-human implications of these ideologies, including her own. Bessie is, at bottom, an honest, direct, brave and compassionate person. It is savagely ironical that death should "pick her out," for death and dying exercise no fascination over her. It outrages her humanity and she fights against it at all points. She is the only one who thinks of the consumptive Mollser (symbolic in many ways of the people's true state and needs) and gives her help in the midst of the chaos. In the struggle of conflicting forces within Bessie practical humanism triumphs. Her environment has failed to provide her with a focal point to mobilise her rebellion, but it does not succeed in crippling this ordinary proletarian woman as it does the more petty-bourgeois Nora.

But O'Casey's fullest embodiment of the sterling stuff inherent in the masses and waiting for a catalyst, is not a woman in this case, but the carpenter Fluther Good. In his Autobiography O'Casey talks of "the arrogant courage, and [. . .] jovial determination, which, under different conditions, might have made a great man of Fluther."[5]

When Fluther is introduced in the first act he is the only person, besides Nora, who gets anything useful done–he mends the door-lock. The healthy grip on the concrete things of life implied here, triumphs in the pub-scene. For a fleeting moment the impressionable Fluther is swept away by the Voice's demagogy, but he quickly regains solid ground. At the end of the scene, when the "intoxicated" Clitheroe, Brennan and Langon toast wounds and the destruction of life "for Ireland," Fluther turns a deaf ear to the bugle-ball to sacrifice, and goes off instead with Rosie Redmond, that example of lusty living in the hereand-now. She sings a different toast at the end of the act, a pledge to the production of human beings and to their real needs:

I once had a lover, a tailor, but he could do nothin' for me,

> An' then I fell in with a sailor as strong an' as wild as
> th' sea.
> We cuddled an' kissed with devotion, till th' night from
> th' mornin' had fled;
> An' there, to our joy, a bright bouncin' boy
> Was dancin' a jig in th' bed! (179)

In this case the song distances us from the action, creating a critical attitude to an otherwise dangerous catharsis situation (the dazed fervour of the three soldiers).

This scene illustrates not only that the nationalist movement is divorced from the real state and needs of the people, but that the two are mutually exclusive. The essential nature of the people is diametrically opposed to the essential nature of the movement under its present middle-class leadership.

This opposition works itself out in the second half of the play. The people of the slums are not left totally unmoved by the situation created when the Rising actually occurs. They come out of their cellars and garrets on to the street. A kind of movement, a possibility, has stirred the stagnation of their existence. But the Rising remains something essentially apart from them. For reasons already indicated it cannot "capture" the masses, where the material for a real rising resides. This cannot be Bessie's and Fluther's movement. It cannot provide them with a basis on which to overcome their confusions and divisions and pool their abilities.

The geography of the action symbolises this divorcement. The actual battle takes place somewhere off stage, away from the tenements. The people take part only as fleeting observers, bringing back more or less garbled reports to their own "country." Far from entering in and helping their "heroes" their only activity is looting. In fact they get in the way of "their" soldiers and are fired upon by them. The lack of any conception of something beyond their immediate material advantage, their lack of some inkling of "the stars," is certainly indicated in this.

But if they do not involve themselves in the Rising, the

latter soon involves itself with them. Its result, as far as they are concerned, is to drive them back in on themselves, off the open scene and into the slum rooms from which they had begun to emerge. All it manages to give them is not the spiritual exaltation and purification promised by the Voice, but demoralisation and the puncturing of empty bellies. The kind of rising portrayed here by O'Casey is a tragedy for the people.

But there is more to it than this. Left to their own devices these people begin to exploit the situation in their own way. They go out and bring something back which is very different from the wounds and death brought home by the insurgents and those pursuing them. They seize the unexpected opportunity created by the chaos to get themselves some of the necessities and the good things of life, those good things of which they have always been deprived and which the Rising itself is failing to deliver—"An' th' Volunteers is firin' on them. I seen two men an' a lassie pushin' a piano down th' sthreet, an' th' sweat rollin' off them thryin' to get it up on th' pavement; an' an oul' wan that must ha' been seventy lookin' as if she'd dhrop every minute with th' dint o' heart beatin', thryin' to pull a big double bed out of a broken shop-window!" (Bessie, 187 to 188) Bessie herself arrives back with a new hat, a fox fur, three umbrellas and a box of biscuits.

There is some reaching for the stars in this after all! In the course of the looting there are real signs that, under certain circumstances, divisions and enmities can be laid aside in favour of unity for concrete ends (Fluther joins forces with the Covey, Bessie with her "enemy" Mrs Gogan). Their best potentials begin fleetingly to find a focal point in bettering their material condition in this way. And other qualities are revealed which were scarcely suspected. Courage and realism are here combined with aspiration and a spirit of enterprise. So we see that the people are willing to make the most strenuous efforts and to go through fire and slaughter provided it is for a tangible betterment of their lives.

There is a certain similarity between this "strange flowering" of the people in the looting episodes and the "flowering" of the Boyles in their expectation of the legacy in *Juno*. And the implications are even more marked here: if they can achieve this much fleetingly, in a false context, what might they not achieve in a true one?

Are we not reading too much into this? O'Casey, in his Autobiography, has this to say about his attitude to the looting in 1916:

> Sean watched their wonderful activity, and couldn't desecrate their disorder with dishonour. All these are they who go to Mass every Sunday and holy day of obligation; whose noses are ground down by the clergy on the grindstone of eternal destiny; who go in mortal fear of the threat of a priest, he thought; but now he was glad to see they hadn't lost their taste for things material. In spite of the clergy's fifing and drumming about venial and mortal sin, they were stretching out their hands for food, for raiment, for colour, and for life.[6]

Already in the looting there is the beginning of a tendency to close ranks, the first suggestion of a community with a specific aim. This is underlined in their brusque repulsion of a frightened middle-class lady who comes whining for help, having gone astray in the midst of the fighting. They have not gone astray. They are finding their feet, in a sense, beginning to see themselves as a special social entity with a frontier dividing it from that which is outside and alien to it. The middle-class woman is "beyond the pale."

This tendency to congeal becomes, for a time, more marked in the struggle for survival that follows. The major part of Acts III and IV is marked by a growth of civilised relationships. The petty enmities between the Covey, Fluther, Bessie, Mrs Gogan, etc. tend to be replaced by a new mutual respect and understanding. Their best qualities, those of courage, resourcefulness and solidarity cease, temporarily and up to a point, to be purely individual characteristics and begin to take on the nature of a mass social phenomenon—a kind of collective. Poor Nora, who has been forced to the opposite pole, driven completely into herself, is, unlike the middle-class lady, taken in and shielded. So is Brennan, the ex-rebel on the run, although he shows no signs of a growing appreciation of social obligation beyond himself. On the other hand, while opening its ranks to these "broken" members, the community closes them sharply against the attempts of the "outsider," Corporal Stoddart of the Wiltshires, to involve himself, in a friendly way, in their affairs. Their attitude to this working-class and vaguely socialist British soldier clearly indicates a limitation as well as a strength. This is typical of O'Casey's art: inner contradiction stimulating and challenging our active, critical faculties even in seemingly peripheral details.

This "community" begins to throw up its own more genuine heroes and leaders in people like Fluther. It is epitomised in the way he abruptly tells the demoralised traditional hero-leader, Brennan, "Thry to keep your hands from shakin', man," (207) when playing cards in Bessie's garret and they hear British soldiers moving about the house. Fluther takes over complete command, trying to calm all concerned by means of the game. When he says, "You lead, Peter," he makes it clear who is actually leading. Single-handed he confronts the British soldiers, telling them not to talk rubbish about a fair fight.

In the later scenes of *The Plough and the Stars* the second or alternative possibility, hitherto suggested mainly in individual figures, is diffused through the composite portrait of the working-class community as a whole and so appears as a mass phenomenon inherent in the working class.

The necessary stuff is there at this historical turning-point. With certain modifications things could have been made to take a different, better, truly revolutionary course. There is nothing preordained about the path they take. A leadership at the head of an organised movement based on the masses and with a practical revolutionary programme, could have found and forged a working class ready and willing to do the job. The advances and experience of the great proletarian battles of 1913 were still there. The people were not yet defeated. Revolution was on the agenda.

But the historic opportunity is worse than wasted. This is the tragedy of *The Plough and the Stars*. Those who have got the leadership in their hands lag behind the masses and the times. The working people are left to their own devices and so their rallying can only be partial and fleeting. It comes too late. It is too purely defensive, and it is contradicted and undermined by the weaknesses already indicated. The demoralising pressures begin to work on them from without and within. Forced back into their holes and into social inactivity in the aftermath of the Rising, they become the mere objects or playthings of events and the cracks between them again begin to widen.

This is suggested in their petty bickering over the card-game while Dublin burns. Peter Flynn re-imports dissention, relapsing back, in the face of the enemy (British imperialism represented by the tommies), to his puerile feuding. When devastation in the shape of the fatal bullet catches Bessie unprepared she too falls back (partly) into her habitual viciousness: "(*To* Nora) I've got this through ... through you ... through you, you bitch, you!" (215)

The people are tired out by the terrible ordeal which they have to bear alone and unequipped. Their grip tends to slacken. O'Casey several times emphasises Bessie's tendency to fall asleep in the last scene. This and her continuous battle against it are symbolic of the pressures and the struggle to remain wakeful and active at the necessary level. It is significant that Bessie begins to reiterate her old bigoted King and Country credo after "sinking into sleep [and] waking up to a sleepy vehemence," (210)—that is, while struggling with a state of exhausted mental twilight. The others too, remain true to their "creeds"; the Covey to his Jenersky quotations, Fluther to his lightly worn Catholicism, even Mrs Gogan to her preoccupation with death.

Their self-mobilisation and their self-produced leaders

such as Fluther and Bessie cannot get beyond the immediate daily horizon to a longer perspective because they have been starved of a practical and dynamic ideology. When the Covey advises Fluther to reserve some of his looted whiskey for later Fluther's answer is, "Keep a sup for tomorrow? How th' hell does a fella know there'll be any tomorrow?" (202) It is there too, in Bessie's song of comfort for Nora: "Keep Thou my feet; I do not ask to see/Th' distant scene—one step enough for me." (207) A new type of world-view is called for by implication, one which will provide the basis for reuniting the plough with the stars.

Not all the gains are lost again. Fluther has grown permanently in stature. Even Mrs Gogan has gained a new concern for life. At the end she fills the gap left first by Nora and then by Bessie. The people have reserves in depth. Nevertheless, demoralisation is on the counter-offensive. That the working people as a whole are forced down below their initial positions as shown in this play is documented by O'Casey's portrait of them in his two preceding plays. These describe the state of the people *after* they have been defeated and the opportunity of 1916 squandered. Their later ingrown, cave-man existence is traced to this. O'Casey says: "Meanwhile, I remembered that I had written a play about the Black and Tan period; about the period of the Civil War; but no play yet around the period of the actual Easter Rising, which was the beginning of all that happened afterward. So I set about illumining and ravaging my mind for a new play about the Easter Rising..."[7] There is a logic, then, in the order of creation of the three plays. The first two led the author back to the source. A trilogy indeed.

The first Abbey performances of *The Plough and the Stars* in 1926 were disrupted by protesting nationalists who declared that the play was an insult to the hero-martyrs of 1916.

O'Casey had his own views on the Easter Rising and these did not coincide with those of the nationalists or even, at all points, with those held by many socialists. Some of his views he elaborates in this play, but not all of them. In his Autobiographies he gives a rounder, more "balanced" view of those who took active part and of the historical significance of the Rising. In the play he chose, in the interests of preparing his people for a new and better revolution, to place certain critical emphases. His aim is to highlight certain grave inadequacies which were objectively present. He is not interested in giving a "complete" picture, but in distancing his fellow Irishmen (and others) from something which had become so encrusted with sentimental and romantic legend as to be no longer a subject of rational and realistic analysis. The whole play is an O'Casey "alienating-effect," encouraging people to take a cool, realistic look at a decisive turning-point in their recent history. A certain amount of distortion was necessary to achieve this realist purpose.

On this basis he was able to work up an artistic model which is a) of enduring relevance to the specific conditions of the mass revolutionary struggle in Ireland and elsewhere, and b) a profoundly realistic investigation of the splintering and self-alienation of man under capitalism.

Notes

1. Aristotle, "The Poetics," in *Aristotle on Poetry and Style*, translated by G. M. A. Grube, The Library of Liberal Arts, Indianapolis/New York, 1958, p. 20
2. See for instance A. E. Malone, "O'Casey's Photographic Realism" in Ayling, *Modern Judgements*, op. cit., p. 75: "... it is not so good as Juno. It is little better than a series of disconnected scenes [...] the theme gets lost in the multiplicity of incidents."
3. Sarukhanyan, op. cit., p. 43 (translation, JM)
4. *Inishfallen, Fare Thee Well*, op. cit. p. 138
5. Ibid., p. 147
6. *Drums Under the Windows*, in *Autobiographies I*, London, 1963, p. 654
7. "*The Plough and the Stars* in Retrospect," in *Blasts and Benedictions*, op. cit., p. 97

The two full-length plays, *The Silver Tassie* and *Within the Gates*, plus the one-acters, *A Pound on Demand* and *The End of the Beginning*, constitute what can be called the second period in O'Casey's dramatic career.

The narrowness and bigotry of life in the "Irish Free State" drove O'Casey to do what almost all great Irish artists had done before him—emigrate. He settled in England in 1926. The nationalist riots at the Abbey against *The Plough and the Stars* were the last straw, but not in themselves the reason.

O'Casey's analysis of the causes of the failure of the Irish revolution was complete. Ireland, up to 1922 a storm-centre of the contradictions of the capitalist world, was fast becoming a social, political and cultural backwater. At the very moment when the Irish bourgeoisie saw themselves as at last overcoming the country's age-long status as a mere province they were in fact launching it well and truly into provincialism.

The state of social crisis, which had had a focal point in Ireland, had now taken a grip of the capitalist world as a whole. O'Casey, with his unerring feel for the main issue and the point where his art could step in most effectively, felt the time had come to spread his wings, both personally and artistically. What had happened and was happening to the Irish people had now to be generalised upon and related to the context of capitalist exploitation and oppression on a world scale. The themes of the "Dublin" plays had to be raised to a new level, and new themes interwoven with them. This meant expanding his subject-matter beyond purely Irish events, and, at this stage (in *Within the Gates*) it meant taking this subject-matter from entirely non-Irish material.

It also involved developing new dramatic methods and techniques. The first priority was no longer to impress his public that what they were watching (or reading) was a mirror, reflecting reality "pure." Now it was a matter of lugging the whole capitalist world as a complex system of exploitation and struggle on to the stage, of creating model microcosms of a whole society. The way he chose to achieve this was to move further away from the traditional "illusionist" realism, which presented the world in the "everyday forms of the world," to a more symbolic, imaginative and "theatrical" realism of heightened effects. Thus artistic logic and necessity induced O'Casey to move in a direction which had always interested him and been congenial to his genius.

What was the main underlying danger facing the working people in this period? In one sense of course it was fascism and war. In the last resort, however, these were but aggravated manifestations of the basic, deep-rooted disease. International capitalism was in a short phase of relative "peace." But the British General Strike of 1926, the fascist take-overs, and the international economic crisis of the late twenties and early thirties showed that the system was becoming more and more deeply embroiled in its general crisis, bringing with it a vastly stepped-up pressure towards mass demoralisation and bodily and spiritual sabotage as part of the preparation of the masses for a new world war. This was clear for all to see in the fascist states. More difficult to recognise were its workings through the "everyday," "peaceful" processes of life in the bourgeois democracies—above all through the medium of economic crisis.

In *The Silver Tassie* (1928) and *Within the Gates* (1933) O'Casey sets out to expose the anti-human essence of this "innocent" everyday capitalism and to show the deadly danger inherent in its daily subversion of the spiritual and bodily health of the people. This is just as true of the *Tassie* as of *Within the Gates*, despite the fact that the former is set during the First World War and partly on the battle-front. In order to survive and to mobilise the strength for the necessary counter-offensive, the "human spark," the vision of poetic humanity had to be kept alive, fanned into a flame. Concern with the bread-and-butter problem of immediate bodily survival was essential, but not enough.

This O'Casey does without crying his socialist programme from the housetops. He wanted to reach a public and did not wish to neutralise the effectiveness of his art from the start by a too direct confrontation with deeply ingrained political prejudices. Nevertheless, the directors of the Abbey Theatre thought *The Silver Tassie* a presumptuous enough piece of work from someone whom they considered their very own pet slum-protégé. They rejected the play, telling the prickly proletarian, who had clearly moved beyond their ken, that the cobbler should stick to his last (to slum plays in this case). This was not an act of murder but of suicide. The Abbey Theatre, having robbed itself of its one dramatic genius, steadily declined into nonentity. O'Casey was now without a theatre and his contact with actual theatre work was confined to very occasional rehearsal visits from now on. The disadvantages of this need no comment. The advantage was that he was now free to develop his revolutionary artistic ideas and methods without hindrance. This meant that the commercial theatre became more and more reluctant to touch an O'Casey play. With time he perfected his own inimitable combination of the highly individualised dimension with the symbolic and fantastic in his image-building. In this way he created a basis from which he was later able to return to the raw material of his original inspiration—contemporary Irish life, and, for all its current provincialism, make revolutionary world drama out of it.

IV THE SILVER TASSIE

Written 1927–8; published 1928; produced 1929 (Apollo Theatre, London)

> "And there will always be a strain towards war, international and civil, while the lust of profits is allowed to mar the mind of man."
>
> Sean O'Casey, *Rose and Crown*

Act I. A slum flat in an Irish city, presumably Dublin. Time—during the First World War. Harry Heegan, a young manual worker, is a volunteer with the British army in France. Harry is the star of the local football team. Home on leave at the moment he is playing for them in the cup final. Several people await his triumphal return from the field: Sylvester Heegan, Harry's father Simon, Sylvester's crony (both elderly ex-dockers), Mrs Heegan, Harry's ageing mother, and young Susie Monican, an apparently puritanical young lady. Simon and Sylvester recall Harry's feats on the sports field and in knocking down policemen. The evangelising Susie tries to win them from the sinful worship of the flesh to the life of higher things. Old Mrs Heegan is anxious lest Harry miss the troopship. Young Mrs Foran from upstairs likewise can't wait to see the back of her husband Teddy, also a soldier on leave. Teddy terrorises his wife and, as a parting gesture, he smashes her wedding bowl.

Enter the victory procession, bearing Harry, the scorer of the winning goal, and the silver cup. Jessie Taite, his girl friend acts priestess to his god. At parting he pledges love, youth, and strength in wine from the cup, then sings Burns' love-ballad, "The Silver Tassie." The others hustle him, his somewhat dull mate Barney Bagnal, and Teddy off to the boat.

Act II. Set directly behind the front line in France. A moonscape scene of desolation. A unit of the army has just returned from a twelve-hour stint of ammunition transport. They are congealed into a grey, anonymous mass. The only recognisable person is Barney, who has been spread-eagled on a gunwheel for stealing a chicken. They are "resting" in a ruined monastery, part of which has been made into a Red Cross station. Opposite Barney stands a war-damaged Christ-figure on a cross. The scene as a whole is dominated by a huge howitzer gun. The cowering swaddies put their misery, perplexity and resentment into a series of dreamy chants in the form of Gregorian plain-song. The singing is led by a death's-head-like soldier, called the Croucher, squatting above them on a ramp. Synchronised with his intoning comes the sound of a Latin chant from an inner part of the monastery, hymning the mercy of God. The soldiers are designated only by numbers. Their semi-stupification is broken into by three outsiders–their Corporal, a rich civilian on a sight-seeing tour, and a "Staff-Wallah" who reads out fatuous, inhuman orders. Chanting stretcher-bearers bring the wounded to the Red Cross station. The enemy attacks. Under the direction of the Staff-Wallah the soldiers gather round the howitzer and address a hymn of praise to it and to God.

Act III. A hospital ward. Simon Norton, Sylvester and Harry Heegan are patients. The staff address them by their bed-numbers. Sylvester and Simon have nothing recognisably wrong with them. Harry is in a wheel chair, lamed from the waist down. Susie Monican is now a smart, officious nurse. Surgeon Maxwell is more interested in cuddling with her than in tending his patients. Harry is embittered. Jessie now only has eyes for her new champion, Barney, who was awarded the Victoria Cross for saving Harry's life.

Act IV. Dance at the Avondale Football Club. Jessie and Barney try to shake off Harry who dogs them in his wheel chair wherever they go. Susie and Maxwell dance happily together. In the boisterous fun of the balloon dance the revellers dismiss the war-damaged Harry from their minds. The latter surprises Barney and Jessie in a love-scene. He showers them with bitter invective and Barney is barely stopped from strangling him. Harry batters the silver tassie into a shapeless mess and goes off with the blinded Teddy Foran, his only "comrade" now. The others get on with the dance.

If there is one thing about *The Silver Tassie* on which all the critics are agreed it is that the play is an anti-war play. Some interpret it as condemning war as such, with O'Casey making no attempt to place responsibility or blame.[1] Manfred Pauli is more specific: it is "an attempt to depict imperialist war in a new way."[2] But, he writes, "in this parable-depiction, too, only the outward manifestations of war are attacked; its roots and essential nature are not revealed [. . .] So in the last resort he was only able to penetrate to the pacifist half-truth that wars are dreadful."[3] The view is widespread that O'Casey's position in *The Silver Tassie* is pacifist.[4]

What kind of an anti-war play is this? As an anti-war play is it adequate to its subject? Is it enough to define it as an anti-war play? Is it really pacifist?

In trying to answer these questions one must begin by looking at the symbolic war-model constructed in the second act. The crucial fact is that it represents war as seen from the perspective of the common soldier. (Many of the songs used are actually soldiers' folk-lore from the First World War.) This was O'Casey's intention in this act, rather than to lay bare the economic sources and the mechanics of capitalist war (which he understood well enough). His model is designed to bring to life the impact that imperialist war *makes on the psyche* of the rank-and-file participants—what it does to the personality and to human relations. He does this because it is essential to an understanding of his main theme and intention.

What are the effects of war as shown in the second act? These only emerge fully when this act is considered in relation to what comes before and after it. The dominating impression relayed is of an uncontrollable and incomprehensible Juggernaut which has burst unaccountably into their lives. It destroys and maims their bodies and with it their individuality and dignity. The very things that give their laborious lives some significance and worth—youth and strength, and the pride and joy in these things, are melted down in the fire of war to this one grey, anonymous lump of misery. If war ever partook of the romance embodied in "The Silver Tassie" song, it is now, in its "modern" form, the denial and reversal of all that. War, which once gave the Champion the chance of earning his lady's favour, now rifles him of this same chance, sunders him and his lady, making him impotent, and so incapable of claiming her The old song, "None but the brave deserve the fair" has been turned into a mockery.

By means of this contrast war emerges, not as an eternal category, but as something with a history, something that changes, and therefore as something that can be stopped.

The song "The Silver Tassie" is related to the play's action in a more complex way than are the songs in the *Gunman*. As in the earlier play, the action (portrayed reality) distances us from a well loved piece of the popular cultural heritage (the song), relativising it so that we learn to appreciate such songs with awakened critical faculties rather than lose ourselves in a dangerous flood of emotional identification. But unlike the songs in the *Gunman*, "The Silver Tassie" song is truly beautiful. In its contrast relationship to the action it serves to bring out the sordidness of the reality portrayed. The action is a comment on the song, but, in this case as in Brecht, the song is also a comment on the action.

This war turns people who were once independent individuals into a mere series of numbers. Harry, with his forceful, colourful character, is totally submerged. There is no sign of him at all in Act II. Some critics have criticised this, but it is precisely the point that O'Casey is making. He begins to use absences from the scene to make certain points—a part of the general urge in this play to utilise the possibilities of the stage universally.

In this maelstrom Harry's strength of personality is as chaff in the wind. Nor is this reduction confined to the actual war zone. It spreads like a contagion into "normal" life—see the regimentation of the hospital inmates in Act III. Not only the broken Harry is conceived of as a mere number (28), as a kind of relic in a museum, but that lively pair, Simon and Sylvester, have also become numbers for the powers that control them. The how and the why of their hospitalisation is left vague. Both live in easy-going retirement so it is unlikely that they are there under their own auspices (malingering). They have somehow got into the clutches of the para-military authority, who are out to make good, clean, regimented citizens of these two irrepressible clowns. (There is a running battle between them and Nurse Susie about their having to take too frequent baths.) All that may be necessary to bring them into line is a little interference in their most intimate sphere, in the form of a minor surgical operation.

This process of depersonalisation has its epicentre in Act II, in the war zone. The "choral" level of characterisation used in this act is dictated by the nature of the statement being made about human relations under these circumstances: that individual personality is obliterated. Here we have an image which is profoundly realistic because it is not highly "individualised."

The action in Act II is carried forward largely through the songs. To a high degree they *are* the action—in a more organic way than is the case in most operas. They are the means by which the soldiers can still achieve some freedom in coming to grips with what is destroying them. They use the cultural heritage, particularly their own subversive tradition of ballad-making to express their true position. As the chief mode of existence of the action the down-to-earth singing of the Cockney soldiers functions as an alienating-effect over against another type of singing which does *not* express the realities of the situation—the Latin Christian litany. Significantly we do not see the singers of the latter. Like the Voice in *The Plough and the Stars* they are disembodied. In this juxtaposition the litany is divested of its time-honoured emotional aura, "made strange" so that it emerges as an outlandish incantation, the voice of a church with less than nothing to offer. The fact that some of the soldiers' songs are identical to church music in their *musical form* (plain-song) and partly parody passages from the Bible, defines the distancing-effect:

Croucher. And the hand of the Lord was upon me, and carried me out in the spirit of the Lord, and set me down in the midst of a valley.

And I looked and saw a great multitude that stood upon their feet, an exceeding great army.

And he said unto me, Son of man, can this exceeding great army become a valley of dry bones?

(The music ceases, and a voice, in the part of the monastery left standing, intones: Kyr ... ie ... e ... eleison. Kyr ... ie ... e ... eleison, *followed by the answer*: Christe ... eleison.

Croucher (resuming). And I answered, O Lord God, thou knowest. And he said, prophesy, and say unto the wind, come from the four winds a breath and breathe upon these living that they may die.

(As he pauses the voice in the monastery is heard again: Gloria in excelsis Deo et in terra pax hominibus bonae voluntatis.

Croucher (resuming). And I prophesied, and the breath came out of them, and the sinews came away from them, and behold a shaking, and their bones fell asunder, bone from his bone, and they died, and the exceeding great army became a valley of dry bones.

(The voice from the monastery is heard, clearly for the first half of the sentence, then dying away towards the end: Accendat in nobis Dominus ignem sui amoris, et flammam aeternae caritatis.

A group of soldiers come in from fatigue ...

1st Soldier. Cold and wet and tir'd.

2nd Soldier. Wet and tir'd and cold.

3rd Soldier. Tir'd and cold and wet.

4th Soldier (very like Teddy). Twelve blasted hours of ammunition transport fatigue! (48–49)

This kind of war not only erases all individuality. It also brings with it a huge aggravation of the pressure to alienate and splinter the human personality and relations. That which should be whole and harmonious falls apart and is divided against itself.

The Harry Heegan we meet in the first act seems to possess something of the "Renaissance-man" quality of totality which O'Casey regarded as essential–the urge to live fully in the present, in the glory of the moment, the synthesis of the bodily and cultural-intellectual appetites – the integrated, poetic personality. At parting he succeeds in fusing the drinking of wine, the kissing of Jessie, and the triumphant singing of the great ballad, which casts an aura of high poetry over the moment. This self-sufficiency and apparent wholeness of Harry is annihilated by the war. He and the blinded Teddy are turned into bits, which, when added mechanically together, can never make up a whole again:

Harry. I can see, but I cannot dance.
Teddy. I can dance, but I cannot see.
[. . .]
Harry. There's something wrong with life when men can walk.
Teddy. There's something wrong with life when men can see.
Harry. I never felt the hand that made me helpless.
Teddy. I never saw the hand that made me blind.
Harry. Life came and took away the half of life.
Teddy. Life took from me the half he left with you. (98–99)

War disqualifies them from life, unmans them (Harry is made impotent), sends them into exile. Those most richly endowed are those who are most totally cast down. Their strength is turned into their weakness. The memory of one's one-time glory becomes the source of even deeper embitterment. All things are turned into their opposites.

Thus the analysis of the dangerous disintegration of the human personality and relations implicit in the "Dublin" plays now comes out into the open to be polemically treated in *The Silver Tassie*, where the characters are physically bits of men.

They never recognised the thing that hit them, just as the policeman in Sylvester's reminiscence never saw Harry's fist. *They cannot pin down who or what is really to blame, so they are driven to blame life.* They become sworn enemies of life. O'Casey called this play a tragi-comedy. Part of the tragedy lies here. Thus their ignorance, their lack of ideological tools, goes hand in hand with war itself. The ability for social insight and analysis could have prevented them from being exiled from life. It would have enabled them to focus on the real enemy and so would have provided a channel for their social re-integration. The lack of it turns them sour. The play is, by implication, about the results of this inability on the part of the untutored masses to recognise where the blame lies, rather than an investigation of the socio-economic and political mechanism of imperialist war. At the same time, however, this opaqueness to the unschooled and manipulated consciousness, the feeling of being helpless prey in the hands of arbitrary forces, is a specific characteristic of "modern" imperialist global war. The tragedy emerges clearly as the product of this kind of war. The situation shown in *The Silver Tassie* could not arise in the case of a revolutionary people's war.

The meanings that have been established up to now have a good deal in common with that considerable body of radical anti-war literature which appeared towards the end of the twenties. In fact the play was written one year before the definitive group of works of this type appeared in 1929.[5]

At the point reached now, however, the specific and unique concern of this play begins to take shape.

The victims hold life to blame, that is, they hold war to be produced by life, an integral part of things. Enough has already been said to make clear that war and its works (the maimed in body and soul) are portrayed as diametrically opposed to life, as a species of anti-life. In the latter "world" the normal becomes the abnormal and the abnormal the moral norm (see the Harry-Teddy dialogue above). Thus the forces of Death-in-Life and Joy-in-Life stand in conflict–

a struggle which would underlie O'Casey's work from now on.

Is this anti-life nevertheless compatible with life as such—an unfortunate but unavoidable part of the whole? The two worlds are out of touch with each other. (The theme of being "worlds apart" and incapable of establishing contact is symbolised in the slapstick episode near the end where Simon and Sylvester wrestle unsuccessfully with the job of answering the telephone.) The two worlds have no "feel" for one another. Harry says that he remembers the different feels of iron, wood and flesh but now "to my fingers they're giving the same answers—a feeling of numb distance between me and the touches of them all." (75) He is an outcast from the essential sensuousness of living which is the hallmark of normal life in the others. This is immediately underlined by the entry of Dr Maxwell, singing a sensuous sex-song in appreciation of his new girl friend Jessie's palpable charms. (75) Maxwell, because he is sensually intact, is plugged in to the current of life. Harry is plugged out. It is quite natural, then, that thoughts of the sensual pleasures of creating new life should continuously divert the surgeon's attention from the world of dying and the affront of sensual numbness represented by his maimed patients. His song is like that of Rosie Redmond in *The Plough and the Stars*. Both are songs of life asserting itself against the dangerous cult of dying and the dead.

On the other hand the attempts of the "normal" world to establish contact with the maimed are equally hopeless. The various scattered bids by the healthy to comfort Harry and Co. are all wide of the mark and aggravate the antagonism. This is epitomised in Harry's hypersensitivity to the repeated platitude "while there's life there's hope." (e.g. p. 77) The attempts at comfort and understanding are bound to be shallow and perfunctory because there can be no appreciation of the "feel" of that other, anti-world. It has its own type of anti-sensuality. This *unfeelingness* for the sensations of the anti-world reaches its most intense expression in the final punch-line of the play, Mrs Foran's well-meaning but totally "insensitive" remark, "It's a terrible pity Harry was too weak to stay an' sing his song, for there's nothing I love more than the ukulele's tinkle, tinkle in the night-time." (106) Ironically the remark is inspired by her own (somewhat shallow) response to sensation – musical sound. Symbolically, the streamers thrown into the anteroom by those in the dance hall envelop only the healthy, binding them together with bands of colour. Harry, it is true, picks up some streamers and loops them round himself, his wheel chair and Teddy (104), but this only underlines the existence of two incompatible groupings. In the light of all this, Harry's and Teddy's final pledge of comradeship and solidarity–"what's in front we'll face like men, dear comrade of the blood-fight and the battle-front!" (105)–does not indicate a hopeful perspective of community but an ominous ganging-up of the life-exiles against life.

The rhythms of the world and its anti-world are different, incompatible. It is one of the main functions of the last act to bring this out. It consists of a jarring juxtaposition and conflict of the rhythmic (the dance) and the anti-rhythmic– the stumbling movements of blind Teddy, and the sudden tank-like, violent jerks of Harry's wheel chair: "He then wheels his chair back and comes on to the centre of the window-frame with a rush, bursting the catch and speeding into the room, coming to a halt, angry and savage, before Barney and Jessie." (102) At one point he whirls round in his chair to the beat of the music, in a mockery, that is, of the rhythm and melody of life. These two rhythms can never interlock. They are incompatible with each other. Thus the anti-world of war's products appears not as an organic part of life, but an alien thing, a piece of irritating grit within its tissues.

But these progenies of war are not simply an anti-world; they are actively and malignantly anti-life, a kind of "fifth column" within life. Harry's programme is, "I'll make my chair a Juggernaut, and wheel it over the neck and spine of every daffodil that looks at me . . ." (84) In his persecution of Jessie and Barney he puts this into practice, and by way of climax he crushes the silver tassie, symbol of youth and beauty. There is a strong hint of Shakespeare's crippled Richard Gloster in all this. The hint is underlined by the "Shakespearian" tendency of the language in the passage quoted and at similar points. Anti-life is a kind of inverted life, with the same insistent demand as true life that everything be shaped according to its measure. It is this inverted life-urge, as strong in its way as the powerful urge of true life, which makes the cripples so venomous and dedicated.

In all this one feels the growing suggestion of a metaphorical or symbolic dimension to the figures and their relationships. Thus the "symbolic" plane which comes to dominate in Act II, is in fact latent to the play as a whole. There can be no adequate understanding of the intention of the play if one grasps the figures, etc. only on the purely individual and non-metaphorical plane.

It is in the light of the above analysis that one must judge the apparent heartlessness and neglect with which Maxwell, Jessie, Barney, Susie and the others behave towards the war victims. Broadly speaking their behaviour is approved of by the author. They are life rejecting a foreign body. As people in the midst of living, with all its sensual joys, they simply cannot keep their minds on these affronts to the senses for very long at a time. Some critics have interpreted their behaviour as part of O'Casey's critique of the break-down of human relations.[6] This, I think, misses the point, which is summed up in Susie's last speech: "Teddy Foran and Harry Heegan have gone to live their own way in another world. Neither I nor you can lift them out of it [. . .] As long as wars are waged, we shall be vexed by woe; strong legs shall be made useless and bright eyes made dark. But we, who have come through the fire unharmed, must go on living. *(Pulling Jessie from the chair)* Come along, and take your part in life! *(To Barney)* Come along, Barney, and take your partner into the dance!" (106)

These people are refusing to make the fateful mistake

made by so many in the "Dublin" trilogy–to cultivate dead heroes to the detriment of life. To treat these be-medalled "heroes" as real heroes is to concede the "glory" of imperialist war in retrospect and so help prepare misguided cannon-fodder for the next one.

In fact the "healthy" people in the play are remarkably considerate to the crippled. The accusation against the latter that they have allowed themselves to be turned into the enemies of life is still only implied–though strongly so, through O'Casey's obvious approval of their being exempt from honour. O'Casey, as always, holds his working people responsible for their own actions, because he knows them to be the only shapers of history, one way or the other. Harry and Teddy were not conscripted. As Irishmen they volunteered. Therefore, in a certain sense, their wounds are self-inflicted. Thus they can never be fully tragic figures in themselves, but the objects of satire more than pity. This is why the play is a tragi-comedy. In his next play, people like this who allow themselves to be beaten by circumstances, are openly and directly shown up as a danger to the community.

We have now worked out one important facet of O'Casey's image of the working people: the healthy urge of the community, its instinctive "yes" to life and "no" to death, its resilience and recuperative powers. In this sense the play expresses O'Casey's strategic social optimism more definitely than do the "Dublin" plays. This optimism is well embodied in the control which life exercises over these products of war (admittedly after the event of war). The representatives of Death-in-Life are put up with only so long as they behave themselves. If they overstep the mark they are refused more wine, half throttled, threatened with being sent home from the party.

If war is not an organic part of life there can be no wellsprings of war inherent in life as such. War can therefore be rooted out. There is little point in trying to cure the after-effects of war. There is no way of rejoining the war-damaged parts with life. It must be prevention, not cure. This is possible, and life has potentially the health, the strength and the will to do it.

This is one of the particular statements being made about war in this play. It suggests that O'Casey does more than penetrate to "the pacifist half-truth that wars are dreadful." There is certainly nothing pacifist about the attitude of the people towards the war-damaged and, by implication, towards war.

The so-called non-realistic techniques used in Act II are perfectly designed to bring out this basic statement about the foreignness of war to life. To portray war in its immediate, everyday terms would not have done this. Through the generalised type of image it is divested of its massive "presence," its "part-of-life" aura. We are made to see it with new eyes. The everyday is revealed as astonishing, not true to life. Brecht would have approved. It is given a dream-like quality. The actors behave as in a dream-nightmare. There is no noise of battle, only flashes, and we are told that every feature of the scene is distorted somewhat from its original appearance. (48)

A favourite bone of contention among the critics is the question of whether the second act of *The Silver Tassie* is influenced by expressionism or not. One thing is certain. O'Casey's world-view had nothing in common with the irrationalism and extreme subjectivism of the expressionist trend of thought. Certain critics, while pointing this out, nevertheless insist that O'Casey was influenced in his techniques here by plays like Toller's *Masse Mensch* and *Hinkemann*.[7] It would be equally possible (and unfruitful) to speculate on surrealism or the methods of the old morality plays as possible models. Hans Nordell records that O'Casey "told the writer that when he was writing 'The Silver Tassie' he 'didn't know the difference between expressionism and impressionism.' He was surprised when critics described the second act as expressionistic: he intended it to be a kind of ritual."[8]

In order to make his extremely strategic statement about the relationship between war and life O'Casey had to make his picture of war work on a high level of generalisation. Nevertheless there are sufficient indications that this is not just any war, but a war against the people, a war manipulated by the people's oppressors. The scene is somewhere in France and the whole set-up is unmistakably that of the imperialist war of 1914–1918. Added to this are the savagely satirical portraits of the Staff-Wallah and the Visitor. These types are alien to everything human as embodied in the soldiers. Again there is an incompatibility of rhythm. Against the strongly rhythmic chanting of the soldiers is placed the jumpy, mechanical, telegram-talk of these two: (Visitor) "Seriously, Corporal, seriously please. Sacred, sacred: property of the citizen of a friendly State, sacred. On Active Service, serious to steal a fowl, a cock. (*To Barney*) The uniform, the cause, boy, the corps. Infra dignitatem, boy, infra dignitatem." To which Barney answers, "Wee, wee." (52–53) For Barney, the Visitor–that "man-of-property" for whom he is suffering–is at least as foreign as the French. It cannot be his war and Barney's, for it is being fought around that most sacred thing, private property. That is why the Visitor and the Authorities take such a "serious view" of Barney's insignificant theft: Barney, tied to the gunwheel, is like the Christ hanging opposite him, an image of the common people being crucified to preserve the sacredness of private property. Once again O'Casey strikes at the heart of the matter through an apparently almost superfluous comic detail.

In the light of the above one is driven to ask how, and why, the West-German critic Heinz Kosok could come to the conclusion that "in *The Silver Tassie* it is not important [. . .] what war it is. The ties with reality are reduced essentially to those elements characteristic of *every war*."[9]

There is a second aspect to O'Casey's specific concern in this play that still remains to be discussed. The long, turbulent first act stands in a contrast relationship to the second, war-front act, as we have seen. But at the same time–and this is less obvious–there are also inner parallels between them, or rather, lines leading organically from Act I to Act II.

Imperialist war transforms whole men into bits of men. But how whole *are* the personalities and human relationships in Act I? In the introductory scene of broad comedy there is already an absolute polarisation of the physical and the "spiritual." Sylvester and Simon are totally absorbed in the vicarious enjoyment of Harry's physical exploits, especially in the blow-by-blow description of how he knocked down the policeman. Opposed to them is Susie's soul-saving evangelising with its denial of "the flesh." There is danger in this absolute dichotomy. There is a core of insight within the religio-mystical form of Susie's challenge: "When the two of yous stand quiverin' together on the dhread day of the Last Judgement, how will the two of yous feel if yous have nothin' to say but 'he broke a chain across his bisseps?'" (23)

Susie dimly feels the necessity of something to life beyond the spontaneous physical moment–a moral dimension. But her sense-denying vista of the spiritual life is ill designed to open up wider spiritual horizons to these men of the muscular moment. Thus the "spiritual," languishing in the wilderness turns sour, while the "purely" physical, deprived of the things of the mind, dominates the scene. There is a path leading from this basic "peace-time" situation to the tragedy in Flanders.

The nature of their lives as exploited manual workers and workers' wives forces them into this one-sided emphasis on the "bodily." They are accustomed to earning their living and defending their rights by their physical strength. They are used to a situation in which the mere material struggle for survival comes first and last. Their "spiritual needs" are looked after by the clergy.

In old Mrs Heegan this process has gone so far that the fact of a regular income in the form of maintenance money makes her, a mother, welcome war and hustle her own son off to the trenches. In this queer way war seems to give her a little freedom from insecurity. The same is true of young

Mrs Foran. She can't wait for her husband to be off. His absence will free her from the physical slavery and injury of male-dominated marriage–"I'll be single again, yes, single again;/An' I goes where I like, an' I does what I likes,/ An' I likes what I likes now I'm single again!" (27)

In this way she is driven to welcome war. Jessie, Harry's girl friend, whose glorification of sensuous physical living matches Harry's, works in munitions, producing the means to destroy the body. This has enabled her to amass a nest-egg of "two hundred an' nineteen pounds, sixteen shillings, an' no pence," in the Post Office Savings Bank, on which she hopes to start off married life with Harry. Thus the material and mental deprivations of "peace" drive the people into the welcoming arms of war.

Out of the soil of this environment grows young Harry Heegan, the epitome of the physical as the absolute. Certainly, Harry personifies that celebration of the full physical life of which O'Casey was so passionate a champion. But the point he is making here is that, as things are under the present set-up, unreflecting celebration of physical being is not enough. It is a kind of suicidal innocence. The conditions of his life and work and the cult of the individual Champion superimposed on the people through all the media of manipulation have forced him into this one-sided gladiator mould.

There is a specific national tradition also involved here. This is the myth of the "foightin' Oirishman," a particular variation on the stage-Irish "hero," the brawny "Paddy" whose best argument is his fist. O'Casey is out to shoot this brand of false and fatal heroics down. There is, however, no attempt to underline this "Irish connection" here. It is allowed to establish itself spontaneously, for the author avoids anything which might hinder generalisation.

Harry's one aim in life is to go on winning honour for physical prowess in the field. This has made him ripe for war and the slaughter. O'Casey tells us that he has gone to the front as unthinkingly as he would go to the polling-station. (38) And he goes as unthinkingly and naturally from the playing-field to the battle-field. The battle of Waterloo is said to have been won on the playing-fields of Eton. Harry was put on the way to losing his battle for life on the victorious pitch of the Avondale Football Club. "Normal" life produces these single-track people, whom war uses and destroys. They are deprived, by war, of the one means allowed to them to fulfil themselves–their healthy bodies, and left without the wherewithal to take part in life. Harry is crippled *before* he goes to war. His later physical crippling is both the result of this and also the outward manifestation of the fact that he has been a one-sided, mutilated personality all along. So once again, the splitting and self-alienation of the human personality, and the need to overcome this, are posed as a practical matter of life and death.

Under the scintillating surface the "whole" Harry Heegan of the first scenes evinces a frightening one-sidedness and poverty of social relations. He and his father live alongside and past each other without ever making real contact. The nearest he comes to his mother is to turn back as an afterthought, when leaving for the front, and give her a hurried kiss. His "friend," Barney, he suffers as a mere hanger-on to reflect his own glory. His girl, Jessie Taite, he treats similarly as part of his champion's entourage, a priestess to his god, a status symbol, his private property. Jessie's charms are "Napoo' Barney, to everyone but me!" (42) There is no breadth or depth of human sympathy hinted at in their relations. They are purely public. This poverty of relationship marks all the characters in the first act. The result is a narrow egotism, an atrophy of personal identity. In this way the annihilation of identity in the war zone appears as the final stage of a process already begun in civilian life.

The apotheosis of the physical produces its own dangerous antagonist–the absolute negation of the body and apotheosis of the "spirit." This process is manifest within Susie Monican, initially in love with Harry. The only fulfilment that Susie recognises as a woman in this society is to be accepted as a physical body, a "love-object." Harry denies this to her and is incapable of offering her any other plane of relationship with him. Thus Susie is driven towards the opposite pole. She represses her healthy bodily urges and embraces a fanatical, life-denying, religious "chastity." Established religion lies in wait, as it were, and provides her with a ready-made form for her alienation, a form which she and the others have had inculcated into them since childhood. Unnatural repression of the body leads to militant denial and hatred of the body. It is therefore quite natural that Susie should be polishing the weapons designed to wound the body (Harry's rifle and bayonet) while letting loose her harangue against "carnality." She is aligned with God in the battle against the physical life. War, then, for her, must be the highest expression of this crusade—"the men that go with the guns are going with God." (41) So one is made to see that the soldiers' prayer to the gun as God ("We believe in God and we believe in thee." 64), which takes place at the moment of crisis at the front, has roots going back into their everyday lives. This reminds one of Seumas Shields' remark on the religion of the I.R.A., as being I believe in the gun almighty, creator of heaven and earth, and is, indeed, a raising of this theme to a more general plane.

Susie becomes a volunteer nurse. One can construe this as a humanist urge coming from her contradictory, healthy self. On the other hand her martinet behaviour in the hospital smacks of an almost sadistic pleasure in her mastery over the powerless bodies of men. She condemns Sylvester's body to the scourge and purification of the bath more often than is demanded by normal cleanliness. Clothed, through war, in a little brief authority, she reduces these vile bodies to clean, tamed, *dis*embodied numerals—26, 27, 28. By this paradoxical path Susie is able to exorcise her "complex" concerning physicality and to regain her true nature. Act IV shows her physically uninhibited, while at the same time her summing-up speech shows that she has now combined this with her penchant for reflecting on life. It is logical that Susie should make this speech.

We have shown how Susie in her crusade puts her trust in God and brute force. Violence and God are fused in her evangelising for the "spirit." She seeks verbally to bludgeon her opponents into submission as violently as Harry downed the copper.

Susie. Bitterness and wrath in exhortation is the only hope of rousing the pair of yous into a sense of coming and everlasting penalties.
Sylvester. Well, give it a miss, give it a miss to me now. Don't try to claw me into the kingdom of heaven. (29)

But Susie is not alone in putting all her trust in the god of brute force. Violence is worshipped throughout. It lurks at the core of the apotheosis of the physical. It has been the one way left open to them for retaliation and fulfilment. In Harry it is disguised by being *poeticised*. Sylvester decorates his narration of Harry's brawl with the policeman: "An' the hedges by the road-side standin' stiff in the silent cold of the air, the frost beads on the branches glistenin' like toss'd-down diamonds from the breasts of the stars, the quietness of the night stimulated to a fuller stillness by the mockin' breathin' of Harry, an' the heavy, ragin' pantin' of the Bobby . . ." (24) The reason for the fight he omits to give, it was of minor importance.

Harry's shooting of the winning goal is celebrated with great ritual. Harry himself, however, unwittingly reveals that it was an achievement of brute force rather than artistry. The full-back, he says, rushed at him like an enraged bull. Slipping past the latter he half-stuns the goalie with the force of his shot, then carries "him, the ball and all with a rush into the centre of the net!" (41)

As Harry builds up towards the climax of the ceremonial parting, the theme of *taking by force* inspires him to flights of poetic fervour. Referring to a bottle of wine, he proclaims, "Out with one of them wine-virgins we got in 'The Mill in the Field', Barney, and we'll rape her in a last hot moment before we set out to kiss the guns!" (41) This has the ring of a Shakespearian swashbuckler. But the times have changed. Harry's Renaissance rhetoric is misplaced cultural heritage. Of course, his ability to express himself with such creative energy is, as always, a sign of tremendous potential, but in the concrete situation here it is the Shakespearian heritage being used to obscure the realities rather than to clarify them. This alienation of poetic tradition is seen at its clearest in the singing of "The Silver Tassie."

Teddy Foran is nakedly that which in Harry is draped with a poetic aura. Teddy's only equipment for dealing with the frustrations of his environment is brute force. This was true of him *before* he went to the front. His wife's joy at having seen the back of him point to a long history. And Teddy's trust in violence seems to bring him results. When he bursts into the Heegan flat to reclaim his "property" (i.e. his wife) by force, his "enemies" bow down before him, hiding under the bed, etc. It is the frustrations, not so much of the war, but of "normal," "peaceful" life that make Teddy crush *his* silver tassie, the wedding bowl. Up to a point Teddy is Harry with the shine worn off—what Harry would have become in the end, even without the war.

For people who are forced and persuaded to look upon brute force as their main means of self-fulfilment, the transition to violence on a mass scale (war) is easily made.

The lack of balance and harmony in these figures and their relations, the falling apart into incompatible extremes, is systematically symbolised in images of clashing heat and cold. In these there is a frantic shuttling between the two extremes, without true warmth ever being achieved. Simon and Sylvester cower over the fire in the grate, but all around them is "cold as a stepmother's breath." (31) Mrs Heegan, pushing her way towards the "fosterin' fire," says, "The chill's residin' in my bones, an' feelin's left me just the strength to shiver." (32) At the other end of the scale are Susie's "scorchin' Gospel," the "scent of burnin'" of Mrs Foran's neglected steak, for which she berates the others—"I can hear the love for your neighbours almost fizzlin' in your hearts." (all 31) Scorching heat without comforting warmth. The sharp chill at the centre of Susie's hot-gospelling is epitomised in her polishing the cold steel of the bayonet as she speaks. The dichotomy is there, too, beneath the surface of the poetisation in Sylvester's description of Harry's hot battle in the frosty night. All this anticipates the pervading coldness of the trenches, lit up by the non-warming fire of the artillery. Significantly, the lecture these soldiers are ordered to attend is on the Habits of those living between Frigid Zone and Arctic Circle. Sylvester, that man of feeling, is, in Act II, martyred between coldness during the medical examination and the anticipation of being perhaps boiled alive in the steaming bath. The lamed and impotent Harry carries this opposition into the last act: "*Jessie.* I'm so hot. *Harry.* I'm so cold." (88) Finally there is his hectic shuttling between choosing red wine, which he associates with the heat of spilt blood, and white wine, which is associated with death and coldness.

It is an irony of history that it is war which first forces these masses into a kind of unity of point of view and action (Act II). Common misery compels them to begin to ask, "Wy'r we 're?" (50) Under the surface there is a remarkable resilience and, in contrast to those represented by the stilted Staff-Wallah and the Visitor, an unbroken humanity, a longing for peaceful life and work, a being *out of their element*, a growing hatred for their oppressors, wit, imagination, poetry and rhythm:

2nd *Soldier (chanting very earnestly and quietly):*
    Would God I smok'd an' walk'd an' watch'd th'
    Dance of a golden Brimstone butterfly,
    To the saucy pipe of a greenfinch resting
    In a drowsy, brambled lane in Cumberland.
1st *Soldier:*
    Would God I smok'd and lifted cargoes
    From the laden shoulders of London's river-way;
    Then holiday'd, roaring out courage and movement
    To the muscled machines of Tottenham Hotspur. (56)

Note the combination of common and individual desires in this. Rich individuality somehow survives and becomes the basis for their rising resentment against the (individual) brass hat, "the red-tabb'd squit," the "lousy map-scanner," etc. Here is a beginning, a possibility. But their spontaneous consciousness, conditioned by the pressures seen at work in Act I, can go no farther. They are aware of the economic argument: "An' all the time the battered Conchie squeals,/'It's one or two men looking after business.'" But the ingrained hero-coward myth leads them to reject it – "An' saves his blasted skin!" (50–51) War, which has brought this degree of collective insight, robs them of the morale and energy to do anything about it. When the crisis comes they fall back on the two things on which they have been conditioned to rely – brute force and religion.

Corporal. Let us honour that in which we do put our trust.
Soldiers (in chorus). That it may not fail us in our time of
   need.
   [They kneel to the gun.] "We believe in God and we believe in thee." (64)

This community gains no qualitatively new depth of insight from the experience of the war. The comic episode of the duel between Simon and Sylvester and the telephone in the last act, in which they fail to make contact with the distant caller, emphasises that the problem of social communication is still acute. The nearest approach to a deeper understanding is made by Susie in her last speech, but this is immediately relativised in typical O'Casey manner by Mrs Foran's fatuous curtain line about the tinkle of the ukulele in the night. In these last scenes there is a strong sense, not only of the ability of life to assert itself over what is monstrous and abnormal, but also of frivolity (balloons and paper streamers), of a lack of hindsight and forethought. In the spontaneous, purely bodily affirmation of the dance there is a suggestion of the same one-sidedness which contributed to the catastrophe.

*

To call *The Silver Tassie* an anti-war play is clearly inadequate. It is this in a special sense, and it is much more than this. As Horst Höhne says, "What O'Casey shows is not so much the impact of war, but that war is the culmination of everything brutal, wrong, and idiotic as shown in the other three acts." [10] But there is more to it, even than this, as we have shown.

The play lays bare a certain aspect of the dialectics of war and peace under capitalism. This is the measure of its realist achievement. War is not immanent to life as such, but it is prepared for and produced by a certain kind of life–by exploiting class society. O'Casey shows how ordinary, everyday, "peaceful" capitalism produces the necessary preconditions for war. This "peace" is a hotbed of war. In a sense there is war all the time, so that the "hot" war appears as stepped-up normality. In fact the war-scene in the play is, in one sense, a metaphor highlighting the quintessence of this "peace." War completes what "peace" begins. War and ordinary capitalism are inseparable:

THE TOP PEOPLE TELL YOU–PEACE AND WAR
Are made of different stuff.
But their peace and their war
Are as the wind to the storm.

War springs from their peace
As the son does from the mother.
He bears
Her brutal features.

Their war kills
What their peace
Has left over. [11]

This was how Brecht, in his own way, expressed the same truth eleven years later. In order to put an end to war one must put an end to the whole condition of society as it is. As O'Casey says, "Till Socialism strangles these [. . .] evils, there will be war, and men, women and children will be mangled senselessly, with malice and with calculated brutality. Ay, and even in peace, without Socialism they will be mangled just as effectively by poverty and disease." [12]

There is no heavy underlining of the causal connection between capitalist exploitative relations and the road to war. Nor does he show the connection to be necessarily direct. All is indicated with his particular lightness of touch, so that he avoids any sense of a fatalistic dominance of environment over people. His people themselves must bear responsibility for allowing things to go this way, and also for taking action to transform the situation.

It has been made clear how *The Silver Tassie* grows out of the "Dublin" plays. Themes from these, such as false heroism, the relationship between the nature of war and that of everyday, private life, the practical peril of the self-alienation of the human personality and social relations, etc., are fused here with new elements, new techniques and emphases, and raised on to a new plane of world significance. His message to the working people is that the "Great" war was not a war to end war but had emanated from the same kind of "peaceful," demoralising set-up as still existed in 1928. "The womb that brought this forth, can still give birth." (Brecht)

By the end of *The Silver Tassie* the implied question of a practical revolutionary alternative has become unavoidable.

Notes

1. See Kurt Wittig, *Sean O'Casey als Dramatiker: Ein Beitrag zum Nachkriegsdrama Irlands*, Leipzig 1937, pp. 42, 46, etc.; and Kosok, op. cit., *passim*
2. Pauli, op. cit., p. 117 (translated by JM, as well as all other quotations from Pauli)
3. Ibid., p. 125
4. For instance Maureen Malone, op. cit., p. 421; also Otto Brandstädter (ed.), *Sean O'Casey, Rote Rosen für mich,*

Aufbau-Verlag, Berlin und Weimar, 1976, p. 803: "... an essentially pacifist condemnation of war" (translation, JM)

5. See Erich Maria Remarque, *All Quiet on the Western Front*; Ernest Hemingway, *A Farewell to Arms*; Richard Aldington, *Death of a Hero*; Robert Graves, *Goodbye to All That* (all published 1929)

6. For instance Krause, op. cit., p. 156: "... in the last two acts we see the real consequences of the war as the wounded soldiers also lose the struggle on the home front. Absolute war corrupts absolutely – those who ignore it at home as well as those who were crippled by it in the trenches."

7. For instance Pauli, op. cit., p. 123; and Kosok, op. cit., pp. 118–119

8. Hans Roderick Nordell, *The Dramatic Practice and Theory of Sean O'Casey*, dissertation, Trinity College, Dublin, n. d., pp. 57–58

9. Kosok, op. cit., p. 112

10. Horst Höhne, "Political analysis, theatrical form and popular language in Charles Wood, Henry Livings and John McGrath," in *Political Developments on the British Stage in the Sixties and Seventies*, documents of a symposium, Wilhelm-Pieck-Universität, Rostock, 1977, p. 11

11. Bertolt Brecht, from *Deutsche Kriegsfibel*, 1939, (translation, JM)

12. Letter to *Irish Freedom*, January, 1941, in *Letters*, op. cit., p. 875

V WITHIN THE GATES

Written 1932–3; published 1933; produced 1934 (Royalty Theatre, London)

> "Capitalism is the regimentation of life towards death."
>
> Sean O'Casey

Within the Gates grows out of *The Silver Tassie* in response to the needs of the working people in the crisis of the early thirties. At the same time it anticipates the later plays. In it O'Casey takes an important step towards his large-scale working models or microcosms of a whole society, in which he seeks to define its moral essence.

The scene is a park, very like Hyde Park, in the centre of London. Period—the early thirties. There are four Scenes which follow the rhythm of the day and the year: a Spring Morning, a Summer Noon, an Autumn Evening, and a Winter's Night. Various characters such as the Atheist, the Man with the Stick, a Man wearing a Bowler Hat, a Guardsman, Nursemaids, etc., gather there, near the war memorial, to take the air, read the papers and argue about philosophy. It is also the haunt of the army of the Down-and-Out, with their muffled drum and dirge of hopelessness. Spiritually near to the Down-and-Out are two decrepit hell-fire Evangelists and two ignorant Cockney Chair Attendants.

The pivotal figure is the Young Woman (Jannice), out of work, and now a half-hearted prostitute frequenting the Park. The Young Woman is physically and mentally on the verge of collapse. The Atheist, her stepfather, who has often helped her in the past, now washes his hands of her. In desperation she appeals for aid to the Bishop, who is out observing low life. But he will have nothing to do with her at first.

The Old Woman, Jannice's broken-down mother, comes to lay a wreath on the war memorial. She is lonely and embittered, having lost her brand-new husband, an Irish dragoon, in the First World War. She and her daughter detest each other. She thinks she recognises in the Bishop the divinity student who once seduced her and left her pregnant with Jannice. The Bishop recognises her and realises that the Young Woman is his daughter. He denies the Old Woman, but secretly resolves to help Jannice. His proposed help is to hand her back into the tutelage of the nuns, under whose regime she spent her childhood. Jannice's instinctive dignity and urge to life make her reject this solution.

Meanwhile, she has made friends with the Dreamer, a poverty-stricken poet and visionary. He wooes her, inspiring her to fight against spiritual capitulation and for a full life. She goes with the Dreamer for a time, seeking peace, but the blandishments of the Salvation Army also exert a passing attraction on her.

Jannice's heart begins to give out. She asks for the Bishop. The Dreamer is her man for life, but she still needs the Bishop for death and for what she fears she may have to answer for after death. The Dreamer fetches him and he appears backed by the encroaching Down-and-Out. He refuses Jannice his blessing and says she must go with the Down-and-Out who have now swallowed up the Old Woman, the Attendants and the Evangelists. Singing his battle-song of life the Dreamer forces the Down-and-Out back from Jannice, clearing a space for her to dance in. She dances till she falls. Dying, she persuades the Bishop to guide her hand in the sign of the cross. The Bishop claims her for the church, but it is the Dreamer who speaks her funeral oration.

Clearly this is, in its method of construction, indeed in its approach to the drama, the systematic development of a tendency already emerging in *The Silver Tassie*. No longer is the action unfolded mainly through highly particularised, richly contradictory individuals; rather the characters are subordinated to the demands of the over-all allegoric-parable concept, and are more strictly limited to their particular function within this symbolic pattern. This was the first play that O'Casey wrote without the Abbey Theatre in view and represents a conscious and militant break with the

"Abbey style" which had made him famous. It is a return at a more complex level to the parable-play style of his early one-acter, *Kathleen Listens In* (1923). O'Casey himself says, *"Within the Gates* tries to bring back to the drama the music and song and dance of the Elizabethan play and the austere ritual of the Greek drama, caught up and blended with the life around us."[1] Drama as imaginative celebration of struggle rather than as slavish imitation of trivialities.

In how far is this programme realised?

In its conflict-structure the play has more in common with the late medieval morality plays than with Shakespeare and the Greeks.[2] In these plays personified representatives of the forces of Good and Evil competed for the soul of a socially indeterminate individual (see *Everyman*). In *Within the Gates* the two opposing forces can be designated as Death-in-Life and Joy-in-Life. They compete for the body and soul of Jannice, the young working-class woman, living through the crisis of capitalism. Thus the classical struggle no longer takes place up in the air but under quite specific historical and social conditions.

This struggle has its subjective and objective aspects which interpenetrate.

Within Jannice the struggle is between superimposed, life-denying, death-oriented religious inhibitions and her natural urge towards full sensuous and "spiritual" living. Outwardly, the same tug-o'-war goes on, with her as the prize, between individuals who represent the same opposing principles.

The play shows how the conditions of everyday capitalism (here in the aggravated form of economic depression) play into the hands of the forces of Death-in-Life, and further, how these same forces are part and parcel of the general social pressure towards the atrophy of body and mind.

O'Casey uses the Park setting to highlight the general atmosphere of depression: on the one hand, the burgeoning life and beauty of the world of nature; on the other hand, a human society denying people the right to live naturally. London parks at the best of times are the focal point for the lonely, the semi-derelicts, the outcasts. In O'Casey's Park there is an underlying atmosphere of rootlessness, homelessness, enforced idleness and aimlessness. People come there in their distress, seeking some kind of peace and the chance companionship. Man, under present circumstances, is, on the whole, a foreign body in the loveliness of the Garden that might be Eden.

Most of those who haunt it are in the grip of the all-pervading pressure towards demoralisation. The end of the descent is to be absorbed into the ranks of the Down-and-Out—spiritual death. The army of extinct humanity is already legion, and it is spreading, infesting the Garden. The image of the Down-and-Out awakens strong associations with the concrete situation of capitalist economic depression, the state of grey hopelessness to which masses of people were reduced by long-term unemployment and cultural destitution. But the Down-and-Out are *not* the unemployed as such.

Dreamer. No; I've got a song shaping in my mind, and I must think it out: Song of the Down-and-Out.
Atheist (indifferently). Oh, hymn for the unemployed?
Dreamer. No, no; not the unemployed. They remain men in their misfortune. I keen for those who whine through to-day and dread to-morrow. (133–134)

The Down-and-Out are a poetic symbol for those who have lost the spirit to resist and so their human identity. They represent the fate threatening everyone, in work or out, in a society which denies the human personality the chance of full and harmonious development.

The mere sound of the Down-and-Out's drum-beat is enough to fill almost all who hear it with chill apprehension. At the same time however they do represent a certain seductive alternative to those who are harried and enervated by insecurity and the break-down of human relations— *a kind of peace and community,* that of the living dead.

Some are ripe to be absorbed: the two miserable Evangelists, broken by years of poverty and religious mind-battering. Some are well on along the same road: the younger and the elder Chair Attendants, disabled by ignorance and an idiot patriotism (each has a stiff leg–shades of Harry Heegan). Their descent into sleepy passivity is hastened by their losing their material source of livelihood, their jobs.

Thus the pressure to spiritual demoralisation and capitulation is shown as the product of capitalist society in general and the Depression in particular. Within this context the world war and its effects also make their contribution. This is seen in the Old Woman. She was once a gay young lass, but has been turned into an embittered old hag by losing her new young husband in the war. Ignorant of the real causes, she blames life. Whenever she appears one feels the dominance of death over life. She has become a priestess ministering to death and the dead. She enters with a wreath held high above her head as a priest elevates the host. Peace is what she too desires most: "Oh, Jesus, is there no rest to be found anywhere!" (168) For her, peace and community are only to be found in death, where she can sleep at last with her murdered man. Death is life for her, and life, death. "There can be no rest nor work nor play where there is no life, and the golden infancy of England's life is tarnishing now in the bellies of the worms." (213) She is a pre-prepared candidate for Death-in-Life and is duly absorbed.

Jannice's own position is highly precarious. Two main factors lower her resistance to spiritual capitulation. The first is her inner wall of superstitions and religious guilt complexes, erected by the nuns, which makes her unable consistently to face towards life. The second is the vulgar fact of her losing her job and being unable to find another without compromising her human dignity. Material distress underlies her mental distress–material distress with its roots in the Depression. Again and again O'Casey draws attention to this.

At the core of Jannice's mental anguish lie loneliness and

lack of security: "Most important thing, too, is peace; most important. Peace most pure and peace most perfect, due to the children of the Prince of Peace. *(Recklessly)* But what have I to do with peace! When I come to the temple of peace, the veil of the temple turns to steel!" (185)

What is the nature of this true peace which the people long for, and which should be their birthright? This question lies at the centre of *Within the Gates*, as it does again, in a more concrete context, in the next play, *The Star Turns Red*.

To whom should Jannice turn in her spiritual crisis but to those who are supposed to be her spiritual ministers and pastors, the representatives of organised Christianity? They are there, ready and waiting. The central figure here is the Bishop, leader of an established church and, symbolically and in fact, Jannice's father. What is the peace and community that he has to offer?

In his person he embodies the basic situation and policy of his church. He is past his prime, but he is at pains "to show to all he meets that he is an up-to-the-present-minute clergyman, and that those who wear the stole are, on the whole, a lusty, natural, broad-minded, cheery crowd." (127) He is intent on "getting close to the common people. Get them to talk with us; laugh and joke with us; and then we can expect them to pray with us." (133) In actual fact he is unable to make contact with the frequenters of the Park, most of whom have an ingrained distrust of him and resent his interference. In Jannice, however, he finds an interested subject. She soon discovers that he and his church are unable and unwilling to provide any real help. His peace is mortification of the body and capitulation of the soul. He fears the independent, harmonious personality. Only after she has been broken by years of penitential servitude to the "good sisters" could he think of helping her to achieve the basis for material existence. That is, he makes material security dependent on spiritual capitulation. This is the most human offer he is capable of making. He is the best the church can offer. Subjectively a sincere and even compassionate man, as a dignitary of the church he must function as he does. His sister is in this sense his grey eminence and emanation, the spirit of the church, which shadows him at every step. This church says, "Blessed are the poor in spirit," and this is his ideal. Thus the solution he offers is to join the Down-and-Out:

Bishop (*pointing towards where the Down-and-Out have gone*). There go God's own aristocracy, the poor in spirit! Their slogan, Welcome be the Will of God; their life of meek obedience and resignation in that state of poverty unto which it has pleased God to call them, a testimony that God's in His heaven, all's well with the world. (*To the Attendants*) Join them, my sons. (*To Young Woman*) Join them, my daughter, in the spirit of penitence and prayer! (196)

Despite all his efforts he can find no new words: "I am here to help you, showing how kind and gentle God can be to–er–a straying lamb, seeking in devious ways to find a way back to the waiting flock." (189) The old played-out images, drained of all sensual-emotional appeal–despite his new-found advocacy of song and dance.

Jannice is also attracted to the Salvation Army, whose representative is at first sight much more promising than the Bishop, being both young and handsome. He promises "peace that is perfect, and peace everlasting." (174) Jannice says she'll go a little way with him to hear more about this peace that seems so far off. The Army is in professed rebellion against the ritual-bound state church which is failing the people in their need. The Dreamer warns her that his voice is not that of peace but of fear. But Jannice feels there might be here that consummation of religion and the sensual life, which she so longs for. She tries him: "Oh, come out of the gloom for a moment, dear! Come into the sun, and kiss me with the kisses of thy mouth!" (173) She offers him a bridge in using the sensuous imagery of his own Bible. But the Salvation Army man cannot cross it. His offer to her is full of nails, crosses, and crowns of thorns.

sensuality taking its revenge; loosed from its connection with the human, it degenerates into mere animality: the Body and soul are sundered. Denial of sensuality leads to Salvation Army man furtively feels Jannice's leg while he is preaching to her.* She realises that, in essence, the Army has the same gloom-ridden view of life as the church. But the Army people play their trump card–*they sing to her:*

> But none of the ransomed ever knew
> How deep were the waters crossed,
> Nor how dark was the night that the Lord pass'd through,
> Ere He found His sheep that was lost.
> Out in the desert He heard its cry–
> Sick and helpless and ready to die;
> Sick and helpless and ready to die. (199)

The ominous power of this song lies in its use of the same time-worn lamb-flock imagery as the Bishop's, but in a new, emotionally effective way. Jannice is "visibly affected." No rational argument, but only the emotional-cum-sensual force of the Dreamer's *counter-song* is strong enough to stop Jannice from becoming a shorn lamb in the "peaceful" community of the mutton-providers.

The last group of religious propagandists are the two Evangelists. These broken-down religious maniacs present no direct threat to someone like Jannice, but they are the same thing working at a lower level. They are a typical O'Casey means of commenting on his more "serious" figures. They are in a sense caricatures of the more sophisticated "men-of-god," laying bare the latters' grotesque and anti-human essence. At the same time they are examples of their victims, the *products* of their efforts, the concrete link between them and the Down-and-Out.

---

* The general social nature of this phenomenon is brought out in the fact that the only uses that can be found for Jannice's sensuality are a) as a *commodity,* and b) as a means of satisfying the mere animal impulses of strangers. Her "friend," the Gardener, uses her in this way too. He has no interest in the *human* partnership of *marriage* with her.

Thus the people's traditional "spiritual guides," far from providing an answer and an alternative, are themselves the chief spokesmen, advocates and creators of the Down-and-Out and all they stand for. The material insecurity aggravated by the Depression makes people exceptionally susceptible to their false visions of peace and community. This the "men-of-god" exploit for their own anti-human ends. They are, in this sense, the serpents in the Garden, tempting Eve. It is they who are in fact the devil's agents, seeking to make a desert out of Eden. They aim to inscribe on the iron gates of this circumscribed garden (such gates are painted on the curtain drawn between the scenes) Dante's motto from the gate of hell–"Abandon hope all ye who enter here!"

Herd-passivity, the abandonment of the will to resist, is the aim and end of this society and its protagonists. Like the war-zone scene in *The Silver Tassie*, the Depression here becomes a metaphor epitomising the essence of life under "normal" (undepressed) conditions in this society. "Peaceful" everyday capitalism emerges as as great a danger to humanity as war itself. It is really *the denial of peace.* War waged against the people with other means. According to the logic of O'Casey's art this aspect of the play's theme calls forth its "opposite"–that longing and quest for true peace, which is one of the main unifying factors in the play, thematically speaking. The spokesmen of Death-in-Life try to "sell" complete capitulation to the-way-things-are as the path to true peace.

This "peaceful" war against the people is also the product of the actual war, and is the preparation for, and possibly the prelude to, a new one, in that it conditions the masses to go like sheep to the slaughter. The Chair Attendants are already clad in khaki, the colour of war and mud. The Down-and-Out call up associations with an exhausted army shuffling to or from the front; grey, anonymous, hopeless, to the sound of the drum. Parallels to the troops in Act II of the *Tassie* are unavoidable but are valid only up to a point. O'Casey never repeats himself artistically. The

Croucher-like figure of the soldier on the war memorial lurks in the shrubbery of the Garden. At first he seems to shrink, but in the last dark winter-scene he looms larger, gleaming like "burnished aluminium" in the night. What has been could be again, despite, and because of, the "war to end war." The conclusions to be drawn from all this, regarding changing the world, are unavoidable. *Within the Gates*, in this way, further explores and develops certain basic statements made about society in *The Silver Tassie*.[3]

Who takes up the fight for true peace and against the forces warring on the body and soul of humanity?

The healthy impulses of the people in general and the youth in particular move spontaneously in a counter-direction. The singing crowds at the start of Scenes I and II sketch in the mass background to the drama in the foreground. The Chorus of Young Men and Maidens are in harmony with the rhythm and energy of nature: "Our mother the Earth is a maiden again, young, fair, and a maiden again./Our mother the Earth is a maiden again, she's young, fair, and a maiden again./Her thoughts are a dance as she seeks out her Bridegroom, the sun . . ." (118)

They challenge those caught up in the cash nexus to "Bellow good-bye to the buggerin' lot 'n come out/To bow down the head 'n bend down the knee to the bee, the bird, 'n the blossom,/Bann'ring the breast of the earth with a wonderful beauty!" (149)

A challenge to get into tune with nature as a whole. Note the series of explosive "b" sounds underlining the energy involved.

It is characteristic of these forces that they express themselves and wage their struggle largely through song and the rhythm of the dance. It is rhythm versus rhythmlessness, anti-rhythm. This was becoming a new dramatic principle in O'Casey's work. Its presence is already marked in *The Silver Tassie*. The essence of healthy natural life is musical.

The two moribund Chair Attendants each have a stiff leg and actively resent song and dance. The Bishop realises theoretically the importance of these things for winning the people, but he and what he stands for are also too stiff to put them into practice. It may be objected that three representatives of the defeated also sing and move in rhythm: the Salvation Army, the Old Woman, and, above all, the Down-and-Out. It has been pointed out that the first of these *misuse* poetry and music for tactical gains (do what the Bishop would like to do). It is alienated rhythm; the tune is enervating, without energy. The latter is also true of the music of the Old Woman and the Down-and-Out. But their songs are sincere and therefore moving, expressing the essence of their spiritual state. O'Casey was artistically right in having them express themselves in song. This brings out their tragedy. It underlines that these people were once different from what they are now, that their defeat has been a process, that they are the shadows of what once were valuable men and women. The completeness of their defeat is embodied in that they give voice to it in song. Song has become here the vehicle of what is opposite to its nature, of anti-life. The Down-and-Out chant:

> We challenge life no more, no more, with our dead faith
> and our dead hope;
> We carry furl'd the fainting flags of a dead hope and a
> dead faith.
> Day sings no song, neither is there room for rest beside
> night in her sleeping:
> We've but a sigh for a song, and a deep sigh for a drum-
> beat! (230)

The dead march of the Down-and-Out is the echo of the poetry and rhythm that once was inherent in a whole mass of people. The Dreamer composes it for them, and this is fitting. It is his elegy for wasted humanity. In this way O'Casey engenders in us a pity and anger at the waste, though, as we shall see, the pity is drastically relativised.

The high points of Jannice's fight-back against the inhibiting pressures take the form of song and dance. Her whole sensual, emotional and intellectual make-up becomes involved, and this is the only adequate weapon. Building on a material basis in the form of two one-pound notes given by Jannice to the Chair Attendants, this weapon can even resurrect these two near-zombies for a fleeting moment or two. Jannice sings and dances to the tune of "Little Brown Jug": "Life is born and has its day,/Sings a song, then slinks away;/[...] Sling out woe, hug joy instead,/For we will be a long time dead!" (195) The Attendants "imitate her in a reckless manner," and join in vigorously until inhibited by the drone of the approaching Down-and-Out. But Jannice's unresolved inner contradiction infects her rebellion itself, giving her song of life a note of suicidal desperation in face of the unknown after death. Her grasp of life here is not strong enough to save the situation.

It has been her new acquaintance, the Dreamer, who has fostered this attempted insurrection in her. But her earlier development, after she got free of the nuns, was under the tutorship of the Atheist, who became her *step*father. The Atheist, for all his rational argument, was never completely successful in liberating her psychologically.

This Atheist seems at first sight to be the logical antagonist of the life-denying forces within the pattern of the play. Their main weapon is God; his—the denial of God. He fails because he is the *pro*tagonist of nothing positive to take the place of what he seeks to tear down—a pure negator. As Kosok says, "If he is finally unable to offer [Jannice] any way out of her plight then it is because he fails to feed her imagination—set in motion by the hell-fire visions of the nuns—with visions of a more joyous nature."[4] The nuns knew the importance of appealing to the emotions and the imagination and exploited this. The Atheist's pure rationalism is too arid to drive the nuns out and occupy these positions. He ignores the poetry *which alone can win the people.* He has drummed Paine's *Age of Reason* into Jannice, but when the Dreamer asks if he ever taught her a song he answers, "Song? Oh, I had no time for song!" (124) Objectively, the Atheist's world-view ends up by being as "soulless" as the philosophy of those he would oppose. He has allowed his scope to be determined by the limitations of his enemies. He cannot inspire, he cannot tempt, as the Salvation Army and others can. His peace is the peace of a human vacuum. In fact he refuses to help Jannice any further because she refuses to knuckle under and live according to his purely intellectual nunnery-regime—"it was all no good—she refused to think as I did." (124) There is just as little true equality and community here as with the "men-of-god."

The Atheist is something of an authority among a group of Hyde-Park-type debators. Here large questions concerning God, time, eternity, the nature of pain, etc., are interminably fought over by people totally unequipped to solve them. Emotions are squandered and tempers raised over issues which are irrelevant to the true needs of the situation. These scenes are classical O'Casey broad comedy. The rationalists are often on the point of convincing their God-fearing adversaries, but never quite manage it—because the centre of their argument is vacant. Man, who should be the reference point of any valid discussion, is left out entirely. The habitués who get caught up in the charmed circle of these abstract cosmic speculations become sealed off from life and its problems. Structurally this is brought home by their participation in the action being confined to episodes, and also by the grotesque humour used to portray them in contrast to the main characters. Getting involved in these debates is like getting hooked on a drug which makes one neglect the joys of physical living.

The Guardsman and the other listeners react instinctively against a cosmos in which "man couldn't be seen, even under a microscope." (Man with Umbrella, 209)

Man wearing Cap. . . . D'ye mean that under your hypothenuse, en hour of the clock would stretch aht into ten years of time?

Man with Umbrella. Exactly that in spice-time; en 'undred years if you like.

Man wearing Cap. Wot? Then in your spice-time, a man doin' eight hours would be workin' for eight 'undred years!

Guardsman (to Man with Umbrella). You're barmy, man!
Wot abaht th' bloke doin' penal servitude fer life? When
is 'e agoin' to get aht? You're barmy, man! (210)

Wearied by their mental gymnastics, the debators sit down
to refuel their minds with the products of the press. Avidly
they devour the salacious and sensationalist "human-interest"
stories, the only fare which the mass media provide. So
they rattle down to the opposite pole from their high
philosophical speculations. Intellectual inquiry and the sen-
sual-human aspect of living are cloven apart, both becoming,
in isolation, corrupt and dangerous. Sensuality turns to animality. The readers peer furtively over their newspapers at the
Young Woman's legs, for which she accurately designates
them a bunch of high-minded toads.

Despite the Atheist's shortcomings he is "Ned," the
Dreamer's best friend and supporter. Though he only ne-
gates he does fight, according to his lights, for the liberation
of the human mind. It is this militancy and lack of humility
which endears him to the Dreamer, whose battle-cry is,
"No one has a right to life who doesn't fight to make it
greater." (121)

Only the Dreamer is the adequate combination of antagonist and protagonist. He, the poet and singer, emerges as
the true alternative to the traditionally accepted "spiritual
guides" who are betraying the people. In him there is something strongly reminiscent of Shelley's definition of poets as
"the unacknowledged legislators of the world." He fights,
not against God, but against the concrete forces threatening
life from within, and above all he fights for a programme—
the affirmation of man's right to the full and harmonious
development of all his faculties, the whole man. In doing so
he offers the one true solution to Jannice's desperate search
for true peace—"only joy can give you peace." (178)

His chief weapon in this fight is song. He does what so
many people in the previous plays, to their cost, failed to
do—he brings poetry and music into fruitful relationship with
life. Art as battle-songs for life. The Dreamer produces his

songs not purely for personal use but in order to give society, in all its contradictoriness, a voice. He provides the Chorus of Young People with their poetic challenge, Jannice with the love-song which becomes the focal point of her defiance, the Down-and-Out with their chant of defeat—and his own counter-song to this. At the critical moment, when they threaten to close in on Jannice and him, he shoulders them back, singing, "Way for the strong and the swift and the fearless:/Life that is stirr'd with the fear of its life, let it die;/Let it sink down, let it die, and pass from our vision for ever." (230)

The function of songs in this play is a development from their role in the war-zone act of *The Silver Tassie*. There, however, they expressed a static *situation* rather than a process. Here the songs become the main vehicle for carrying out the dramatic conflict.

In the Dreamer's songs philosophy, poetry and music become one, a synthesis of the intellectual and the sensual and emotional. Further, in and through them, word and deed, insight and action immediately flow into each other. Philosophy, poetry and action become one seamless unity. Thus while he sings his celebration of sensuous love to Jannice he accompanies it with more palpable advances. Only this whole and integrated personality is equipped to combat the forces of spiritual subversion and cut a path out of the impasse. This vision of the full life must be embraced if humanity is to survive capitalist "depression" (in the narrow and wider sense) and come out fighting. It is suicidal to allow one's demands on life to be reduced. That was the main point to be made under the circumstances. To a critic who reviewed the play, saying that if anything was certain in those troubled times, it was that there was no longer any place for dreamers, O'Casey answered that "what the world wants more than anything else at the present moment is a Dreamer."[5]

At this point one of the basic differences between O'Casey and Brecht begins clearly to emerge. Although Brecht was certainly not against emotions in his epic theatre he gave them nothing like the primary importance bestowed on them by O'Casey. O'Casey was acutely aware of the tremendous emotionality of the working people (whom he always saw as his prospective audience). Because he came of the working people himself he knew their essential capacity for emotional cognition of the things that matter, and their responsiveness to emotional appeal. For him "emotion burns within the veins of life."[6] He was also aware of their emotional generosity, and knew that if we do not fight to win and define the emotional responses of the masses the enemy will certainly step in and misuse them. The theatre for O'Casey was certainly a place in which our ability for cool, critical reasoning should be developed, but at the same time it was a place where our emotions should be feasted and revolutionised and the life of the senses celebrated.

The Dreamer is ruthless with the representatives of Death-in-Life. He has only one query of the Chair Attendants—when are they going to do the world a favour and die? Kosok sees this pitilessness as a human inadequacy built into his hero by O'Casey,[7] but the playwright himself reckoned it a signal virtue of the Dreamer, who is "ruthless to get near the things that matter," a symbol of "rebellion against stupidity; and the rising intelligence in man that will no longer stand, nor venerate, nor shelter those whom poverty of spirit has emptied of all that is worth while in life."[8] What is this but a more conscious and sharply defined version of the spontaneous rejection of Harry Heegan and the other cripples in *The Silver Tassie*?

In this way the theme of the fight against death's domination over life is expanded out of the "Dublin" plays.

Incredible as it may seem, there are several critics who maintain that *Within the Gates*, while criticising institutionalised Christianity is "O'Casey's most Christian play."[9] Goldstone believes that "the play both in a strict religious sense and in a much broader context dramatises the need for salvation."[10] This school of criticism uses Jannice's final "reconciliation" with the Bishop to make its point.

Krause says, "In her death she has resolved the conflicting faiths of the Dreamer and the Bishop [. . .] The Dreamer and the Bishop may worship God in different ways, but Jannice has earned the grace of both their creeds, which for her have become manifestations of the one God." [11] This is false. Nothing has been resolved, and that is the point. This attempt at appeasement runs directly counter to O'Casey's whole undertaking.

Jannice's last appeal to the Bishop is the culmination of her unresolved conflict. Her death from *heart* trouble symbolises this and the deep-seated nature of her dilemma. The ending is typical O'Casey in its contradictoriness. It fits in with his general policy of relativising his emotional climaxes through last-minute restatements of the traditional inhibiting attitudes. This brings out the fact that the contradictions of life never come to a neat finish, with all the ends tied up as in the well-made play, but are part of a never-ending process of struggle. Victory is possible, and we are shown steps on the way, but local victories must be seen as such and not blind us to the depth and ingrained nature of the problem. Such endings encourage us to take action on our own account to solve problems which have been demonstrated as soluble, but not solved *for us*.

What is it that stops Jannice from being finally and completely won back to life?

The Dreamer's hold on her is real and growing, but it is never completed or fully secure. The inhibitions imposed on her subvert her efforts at a very deep level. The true peace of the Dreamer can only be attained *by taking risks* and her whole environment has imbued her with a fear of doing this: "I feel uneasy, feeling so much joy [. . .] I feel afraid of myself." (178)

The Dreamer himself is objectively restricted. Their meetings are by necessity always fleeting. The comings and goings of the Dreamer are largely dependent on his material resources. He, too, lives on the brink of physical destitution, and in money matters he is an absolute realist. When the Bishop gives him three pounds to give to Jannice he prudently pockets one of them himself. When the few financial windfalls which his writing provides are used up he and Jannice can no longer live their life of joy together. His wooing her to Joy-in-Life is therefore severely restricted by the material situation of the Depression. (And by capitalism's inability to provide a poet with a livelihood.) O'Casey leaves little room for the traditional romantic myth that love conquers all. This is the perfectly mundane background to the play's "inconclusive" ending.

Indeed, far from implying a reconciliation of the creed of the full life with the God of the Christian religion, *Within the Gates* is a full-scale attack on certain basic precepts of this religion. It would be less than honest to close one's eyes to this fact in an effort to highlight O'Casey's undoubted emphasis on the common ground shared by Communism and the real humanist achievements of Christianity. The play is by implication an examination of the relevance of certain basic precepts of the Sermon on the Mount to the conditions of capitalism in crisis. The Dreamer's programme is an assault on the theses:

> Blessed are the poor in spirit: for theirs is the kingdom of heaven.
> Blessed are the meek: for they shall inherit the earth.
> Resist not evil: but whosoever shall smite thee on thy right cheek, turn to him the other also.
> Love your enemies, bless them that curse you, do good to them that hate you.[12]

The Bishop, as we have seen, actively propagates this teaching. The catastrophic results are illustrated in the play as a whole and in the Down-and-Out and Evangelists in particular. The latter sum up in a kind of confession which paraphrases Christ's words: "Stricken, we struck not back; we blessed them that cursed us; and prayed for them that took no note of our misery and want." (227) So much for O'Casey's pacifism!

Throughout its history suffering has always held a place of honour at the core of the Christian religion. As the

Evangelists say, in words reminiscent of William Blake: "We have honoured pain; bound up joy with sighing." (226–227) [13] Like its predecessor, *The Silver Tassie*, *Within the Gates* is above all an onslaught on this cult of suffering and martyrdom which comes in so handy for the powers that be in times of crisis. The whole action of the play alienates us from these "time-honoured" precepts. It is quite understandable that the good citizens of Boston U.S.A. banned the play from their stage in 1934.

But it also champions certain of Christ's rules laid down in the Sermon on the Mount. It does so by showing how they are systematically ignored by those who ought to be their chief exponents. The Bishop's behaviour shows up badly in the light of "Judge not, that ye be not judged" or "Why beholdest thou the mote that is in thy brother's eye, but considerest not the beam that is in thine own eye?" [14]

Within the Gates has serious artistic weaknesses. There is a thinness of texture, a somewhat abstract, too constructed quality about the constellation of figures, conflict and action. These are conceived too one-sidedly as metaphors or symbols of certain too generalised moral life-principles. Individual specificity is dangerously reduced. The balance which characterises his later work is not fully achieved here. It is, after all, too much of a modern morality play to fulfil his programmatic demand for a drama that incorporates the richness of Shakespeare and the Greeks.

The reasons for this partial failure are probably complex and not easy to locate precisely. O'Casey himself once said, "it is only through an Irish scene that my imagination can weave a way." [15] Twice O'Casey left this basis–in *Within the Gates* and later in *Oak Leaves and Lavender*; neither play is artistically fully convincing. Nevertheless, the weaknesses in *Within the Gates* cannot, it seems to me, be attributed to this fact alone. The play might have been given the "body" it lacks if O'Casey had been able to tie up his conflict on the general-moral plane with the actual social battles being waged at that time in Britain, for instance with the struggle of the unemployed workers' movement. The strength of the "Dublin" plays and, partly, *The Silver Tassie*, rests on this organic connection with decisive historical events. In *Within the Gates* this connection is not fully achieved with the result that the conflict is carried out almost exclusively on a rhetorical plane, almost as if words and music, song and dance could really drive back the forces of alienation by themselves. Because of this, central figures like Jannice, and especially the Dreamer, cannot be socially placed with any precision and so the proper balance between the specific (individual) and the symbolic (general) is lacking. As has been pointed out O'Casey does indicate the specific social and historical basis for the aggravated spiritual state-of-crisis which he portrays. One feels the Depression massively if somewhat indistinctly. For this very reason the Dreamer as protagonist-antagonist, as hero, fails to convince us that he has the practical weapons to make any real impression on this "scheme of things entire." This means that, although O'Casey as always unerringly puts his finger "on the nerve," he is unable here to give body to the actual social forces which might transform the situation. Thus the play lacks a concrete perspective in the last resort. At best it can encourage in the public a sort of basic attitude towards life–that of the necessity of fighting back.

The reasons for O'Casey's partial failure here probably lie to a certain extent in the stage he was at in his own artistic development. Beyond that, however, they are also to be found, I would suggest, in the actual conditions of the class struggle, and in O'Casey's relationship to this struggle at that time. The class struggle was at this point (1932–33) largely confined to the defensive campaigns of the national unemployed movement. Meanwhile O'Casey was more isolated from the actual struggle than at any other period in his life. His ties with the organised Labour movement were minimal, though his enthusiasm for and contacts with the Soviet Union continued to grow. At the same time he was being actively cultivated by "admirers" in upper-class English circles, people like Lady Londonderry, Lord and Lady

Astor (of the notorious "Cliveden Set") and James Ramsay MacDonald. His relations with his publisher, the young "left-wing" Conservative politician Harold Macmillan, tended to develop into something approaching friendship. Many working-class writers, British and Irish, have been corrupted by such associations. O'Casey never was, but there are statements in his letters of this period which might be construed as showing a kind of wavering in some of his positions. Writing in the *New Statesman and Nation* in 1935 he says, for instance: "And is justice to be vindicated by Black Shirts kicking the bellies out of the Red Shirts, or by Red Shirts kicking the bellies out of the Black Shirts? Oh, what has the artist got to do with the honest and careful reconciliation of these things? He is above the kings and princes of this world, and he is above the Labour Leaders and Proletariat, too. And under the patronage that draws a hiss from Toller many of the greatest and finest works of art were born [...] No, the artist is answerable only to himself and his work is for those finer minds among men who hold varying views upon all other things."[16]

This as it stands approaches the elitist views of a Yeats. Or in another place: "The good taste of the majority! Good taste never has and never will spring from the majority. Man in the mass is vulgar ..."[17] The lack of concrete social "placing" and direction in *Within the Gates* may not be unconnected with this. Despite this, however, his basic standpoint remains unshaken. He compares the anarchy of the capitalist world with the orderly human life being created in the Soviet Union, and says of the former, "If the present things that we know which are called the system of civilisation, continue to be sanctified by custom, God's will and the guns, for a long enough period of what is called time, then the soul of man will turn into a huge arse."[18] The strong sides of *Within the Gates* bear witness to O'Casey's determined efforts to hinder this.

From about 1935 on, the objective situation began to change radically. In the fight for life against fascism and war (epitomised in the part played by the International

Brigades in Spain) the masses began to take the historical initiative on a world scale. The struggle of the champions of Joy-in-Life against those of living death became clearly defined in terms of real, positive, militant action. It began to throw up its own inspired flesh-and-blood heroes. Sean O'Casey, being what he was, was drawn into this and out of his partial isolation. Here he found the social and political context for action which was necessary to him. Real life was about to fill with the bright colours of actuality the black-and-white draft sketched in *Within the Gates.*

Notes

1. Sean O'Casey, "From Within the Gates," in *Blasts and Benedictions*, op. cit., p. 114
2. O'Casey's scattered remarks on the morality plays are somewhat contradictory.
3. See also: Jack Lindsay, "Sean O'Casey as a Socialist Artist," in *Modern Judgements*, op. cit., p. 199
4. Kosok, op. cit., p. 148
5. Letter to the *Evening Standard*, Dec. 9, 1933, in *Letters*, op. cit., p. 480
6. Sean O'Casey, "Art is the Song of Life," in *Blasts and Benedictions*, op. cit., p. 80
7. Kosok, op. cit., p. 148
8. Sean O'Casey, "From Within the Gates," op. cit., p. 115
9. Cowasjee, op. cit., p. 65
10. Goldstone, op. cit., p. 95
11. Krause, op. cit., p. 199
12. *Bible* (Authorised Version), the Gospel According to Matthew, 5: 3, 5, 39, 44
13. Cp. Blake, *The Garden of Love*
    "And Priests in black gowns were walking their rounds,
    And binding with briars my joys and desires."
14. *Bible*, op. cit., the Gospel According to Mark, 7: 1, 3
15. Sean O'Casey, "O'Casey's Credo," in *The New York Times*, Nov. 9, 1958
16. Review by O'Casey of *Love on the Dole* in the *New Statesman and Nation*, Feb. 9, 1935, in *Letters*, op. cit., pp. 538 to 539

17. Letter to Richard C. Boys, March 31, 1935, ibid., p. 552
18. Letter to Jack Corney, Sept. 18, 1931, ibid., p. 435

PART THREE PREPARE TO TAKE POWER

In 1938 the O'Casey family moved from London to Devon. Far from indicating a withdrawal this period saw a new intensification of Sean O'Casey's involvement in the vital class struggles of the time. Indicative of this was his active work on the General Council of the socialist Unity Theatre and the Advisory Board of the *Daily Worker*. The Spanish war moved him deeply. "I am praying to God that the Spanish Communists may win. I wish I could be with them,"[1] he wrote to Harold Macmillan.

His way of being with them and the other fighters against fascism was to write his "revolution" plays—*The Star Turns Red, Purple Dust* and *Red Roses for Me*. The fact that directly revolutionary events and heroes move to the forefront of his work at this point is not in itself proof that O'Casey's socialist-realist drama reached its "highest" level here, only to somehow fall away from this in the postwar plays. Rather the revolutionary emphasis in the plays is in response to a shift of emphasis in reality itself. Again it is O'Casey tuning in to the strategic needs of the era.

The period of the late thirties and the Second World War, with the fight against fascist imperialism and the example of the success of the Soviet people in peaceful and crisis-free construction brought new problems and possibilities to the peoples of the world. When writing the "Abbey" plays O'Casey had been responding to the needs of a period following on a defeated revolution (in Ireland); now the needs were those of a pre-revolutionary era, a time full of revolutionary possibilities. He wrote: "If this war spreads, it will end in revolution . . ."[2]

Capitalist civilisation "deserves fire and brimstone from heaven; and it is getting it. We are all at the bier of Finnegan's Wake."[3]

"When this great world convulsion ends, life will be more active and more promising than the life that you and I knew."[4]

First priority was no longer the exposure of the people's crippling weaknesses or the destruction of old and inadequate heroes, myths and illusions. The job now was to replace them with a vista of practical, attainable ideals, with images of heroes and leaders of a new type, drawn from life, and to emphasise the world-changing capabilities of rank-and-file working people. In the plays of this period, including the less successful *Oak Leaves and Lavender* (not dealt with here), O'Casey poses, and suggests answers to questions like—Where is the true people's heritage to be found? Which sort of people are capable of defending, using and renewing the humanist cultural heritage in the fight against the fascist threat? At this historical point of decision to whom does the future belong, who must take power? In the plays of the twenties he was saying that the times were overripe for change but that the working people (up to a point) and above all the leadership were not equipped for the job (in Ireland). Now he is saying that it is the played-out bourgeoisie who are no longer adequate to the times. The working people can and must take over the world, for "the workers alone have the words of eternal life."[5]

Behind the relaxed self-assurance with which he depicts the workers and pours scorn and ridicule on the exploiters and their minions stands his conviction that despite the setback in Spain and the retreats of 1941 the armies of socialism will be an unbreakable bulwark against fascism and reaction.

In the plays dealt with here O'Casey returns for his raw material to Ireland and to the alternative, revolutionary possibility in her history. In order to project this material and build his models of revolution on it he develops an ever more sophisticated combination of individual everyday detail and allegorical-metaphorical implication. These plays are a kind of revolutionary-romantic and realist anticipation of what could and should happen. Allegory, now incorporating the fantastic as well as the symbolic, was necessary to sketch—from the materials at his disposal, which indicated the direction but did not go that far in themselves–the shape of things to come.

Notes

1. Letter to Harold Macmillan, Nov. 13, 1936, *Letters*, op. cit., p. 642
2. Letter to George P. Brett, March 21, 1940, ibid., p. 852
3. Letter to Gabriel Fallon, March 29, 1941, ibid., p. 882
4. Letter to Rev. Canon Arthur Henry Fletcher, Dec. 1, 1941, ibid., p. 912
5. Letter to George Bernard Shaw, Nov. 24, 1937, ibid., p. 685

VI THE STAR TURNS RED

Written 1938; published 1940 (February); produced March 12, 1940 (Unity Theatre, London)

> "Christ is risen! shouted the Nazis over to the Reds, knowing that this was a Russian exclamation common on Christmas or Easter Day – they couldn't remember which.
> – He is risen, indeed! shouted back the Reds; and you've to come no farther – we'll take care of what's behind us."
>
> Sean O'Casey, *Sunset and Evening Star*

Christmas Eve; tomorrow or the next day. A city with an Irish accent. (The play is dedicated to "the men and women who fought through the great Dublin lockout in nineteen hundred and thirteen.") The working-class home of the Old Man and the Old Woman. The Old Man is a "paycock" in the family and a tame servant to the bosses. The Old Woman is under the heel of her husband and the church hierarchy. Their room is split by two long windows. In the one is a church spire with a silver star shining beside it. In the other, factory chimneys. This background remains through all changes of scene. Their younger son, Kian, has joined the fascist Saffron Shirts, while the elder boy, Jack, is active in the Communist workers' movement led by Red Jim.

The fascists, backed by the Purple Priest of the politicians and the Christian Front, are planning to celebrate the festival of peace by staging a *Kristallnacht* against the revolutionary workers, to be accompanied by a procession and midnight mass to excommunicate Communism and sanctify the take-over of state power by the fascists. For their part, the workers are conspiring to celebrate the feast of the Prince of Peace by putting an end to anarchy and oppression for ever.

The old couple are visited in quick succession by the Lord Mayor, the Purple Priest, and the Leader of the Saffron Shirts–all out to cajole or cudgel them into accepting the fascist seizure of power as God's answer to Communist anarchy. Threats are made against their son Jack, unless he gives up the red star and joins the Christian Front. The Leader has Jack's sweetheart, Julia, whipped, to show that he means business. Michael, her father, a militant trade-unionist, attacks the Saffron Shirt "Fuehrer." Kian shoots Michael.

Act II is set at the General Workers' Union headquarters on the same evening. At the instigation of the Purple Priest the cowardly careerists on the Council of the union have "deposed" Red Jim and nominated the Purple Priest as the new President. Now the latter issues his instructions, reluctantly backed by the Brown Priest of the Poor: root out Red Jim and his supporters. Jim enters with armed trade-unionists at his beck and call and deposes the deposers; *he* is now the committee.

Act III is again set in the flat of the old couple. Michael's corpse is lying on a bier surrounded by the rival insignia of crucifix, hammer and sickle, etc. A miserable deputation of physically and mentally crippled slum-dwellers comes in to accompany the body to the church. At the coffin Michael's daughter, Julia, pledges death to the priests and politicians who murdered him and victory to the workers' cause, inspired by his example. Jack and the Red Guards enter and take up positions round the body. Next comes the Purple Priest with his entourage and tries to have the corpse removed to the church, using the occasion for a renewed tirade against Communist "anarchy." The arrival of Red Jim and the workers' detachments puts paid to his plan. Michael's body is taken to the union hall.

Act IV. The Lord Mayor's residence. The Mayor tries to wheedle two lackadaisical workmen into completing the Christmas decorations in time for the official ball to celebrate the victory of the "Prince of Peace" over the revolutionary workers. The Old Man, dressed up in a Father-Christmas suit, has been set doling out weak tea to the assembled "deserving poor." A bugle-call. The workmen down tools and go. The factory hooters blow. The star, which has moved from the church to the smoke-stacks, turns red. Armed workers led by Red Jim take over the mansion and transform it into a military headquarters. Under the Christmas decorations they face the last fight, accompanied by the ballet music of Glasounov. The Purple Priest, Kian and others arrive under a flag of truce. From the other side: workers, and Julia in costume, with the body of Jack, who has fallen in battle. With them is the Brown Priest, now finally come over to the workers' side. The Purple Priest makes one last bid to intimidate them. Red Jim proclaims the passing of the cross and the coming of the star turned red. Kian, numbed with misery, remains with his dead brother. The news comes over the buzzer that the soldiers are beginning to join forces with the workers.

Perhaps the first thing that strikes one about this play is its historical allusiveness. Echoes of the great class battles of the century are unmistakable. There is the 1913 Dublin lockout and the dominant part played in it by Big Jim Larkin. There is the atmosphere of Germany in and around the time of the Nazi take-over. There is the experience of the Spanish Civil War, which was ending in defeat after a heroic struggle. There is the fight in Ireland against the fascist Blue-Shirts in the thirties. There is the role of the Catholic Church hierarchy which went hand in glove with the fascists in Italy, Spain and Ireland. And there is the all-transforming reference to the October Revolution of 1917 and the ensuing civil war, in which revolutionary workers succeeded in overthrowing the old order and turning the star red. In the last act the echoes of the storming of the Winter Palace and the transforming of the Smolny Institute into the military H.Q. of the revolution are anything but accidental.

O'Casey weaves all these threads together into a new synthesis of the kind he and the times needed. The aim is to make sense of the sacrifices and set-backs in the light of the historic and continuing successes of the working people in the Soviet Union. O'Casey seeks to put the recent struggle in a positive historical perspective–as a series of valid and necessary stages which must lead to final victory.

At the same time, in creating a model victory-situation which includes strong elements of actual situations which in life ended in defeat, he is indicating in true "Brechtian" spirit that things did not necessarily have to take the course they did. There was always an implicit alternative, certain factors which, if grasped and exploited resolutely, could have led to success. Every major battle fought in the class struggle contains the seeds of the final victory somewhere within it. Defeat is never preordained, even when the odds seem overwhelmingly against victory. With characteristic acumen O'Casey picks once again the most important point to make on the threshold of the titanic struggle of the forces of democracy against the forces of fascism, drunk on their initial successes.

In a real sense the play is a projection into that "tomorrow" in which the fascist hordes would indeed break against the bulwark of the first workers' state and its "Red Soldiers"–that Red Army which, once before, in the time of the White Guards and interventionists, had shown how it could transform an apparently desperate situation into its opposite.

Having established that this, in the general sense, is what O'Casey sets out to do, we have of course said very little about the dramatic and artistic quality of the play, and its effectiveness.

It is a commonplace of a certain school of criticism that O'Casey's art weakens in direct proportion to the clarity and directness with which his "communist opinions" are embodied in his work. Hogan says, "*The Star* is the closest to straight propaganda that O'Casey has written, and it is his poorest play."[1] Krause calls it a "bald political tract"[2] and betrays his distaste for all militant working-class literature when he writes that "the transparent plot follows the stock pattern of proletarian literature."[3] For them the play is a mock-battle, lacking in real dramatic tension, crude, black-and-white propaganda–"agitprop." The Lord

Chamberlain, however, seems to have had a higher opinion of the play's effectiveness, for he promptly banned it from public showing, and Macmillan's New York branch refused to publish it.

Indeed, the play is unusually full of drastically opposed symbolic images. In fact this system of crass and obvious contrasts is one of the basic structural principles of the play. In creating these antagonistic symbols O'Casey presses all the possibilities offered by the theatre into service: stage-set, colour, costume, insignia, gesture, movement, grouping and arrangement of figures, dialogue, linguistic character-istics, differing relationships to the cultural heritage, etc.

At one end of the symbolic scale we have the use of the flash-within-the-circle sign to designate the fascists (full of associations with Oswald Mosley's flash sign and with the badge of the Nazi SS), and opposed to this, the red star of the workers. The former sign arouses feelings of something constricting and itself constricted, while the latter suggests unrestrained beams streaming outwards in all directions. At the more complex end of the scale there are the polarised symbolic figures such as the Purple Priest (the embodiment of the ideology and practice of clerical fascism) and Red Jim (symbolic of the ideology and practice of the revolu-tionary proletariat).

The use of symbolic means to express drastic contrasts and contradictions, the paring down of the struggle of op-posites to the essentials, was no personal discovery of O'Casey's. In so making his play he was right in the main-stream of the international workers' theatre movement of the thirties. This was the theatre of the agitprop groups, of the "living newspapers," the political Christmas panto-mimes (*The Star Turns Red* is directly related to this), and the mass chants. The left-wing Unity Theatre, with which O'Casey was associated, played a leading part in develop-ing these techniques. He gave *The Star Turns Red* to the Unity Theatre, where it had its premiere on March 12, 1940.

The agitprop style and techniques brought into being by

the international workers' theatre were not a sign of immaturity or merely a "step" on the way to the true socialist theatre. This new approach, with its new subject-matter, was a unique and enduring contribution to theatre. The growing crassness with which the basic social contradiction between the imperialist ruling class and the workers expressed itself, demanded such "crass" dramatic techniques. Perhaps never before in the history of mankind had the forces of humanism and progress and those of savagery and repression stood in such massive and clear-cut confrontation. In such circumstances the categorical depiction of the basic contradiction can be a source of aesthetic appeal and of stimulation to take sides.

It would be wrong to assume that O'Casey used these traditions of the workers' theatre simply as window-dressing for his deeper analysis and meaning. What differentiated *The Star Turns Red* from the general run of its proletarian predecessors and contemporaries was indeed a greater depth and universality. But this was partly a question of developing and deepening themes and techniques already in the process of being opened up. The best workers' theatre was not content merely to act the illustrator to general socio-economic laws and contradictions or to act as a sort of simplified handbook of the strategy and tactics of the class struggle. The best productions did try to go beyond this and reveal the meaning and relevance of these struggles for the "soul" of man. That is, they sought to uncover the dialectics of the "public" and the "private" in man's social living. Working in the same direction, *The Star Turns Red* begins where the others leave off. One of the Unity members, writing in the *Daily Worker*, called it "the greatest thing we have ever attempted." [4]

O'Casey explores in depth this dialectic of the "general-social" and the "private" and reveals their mutual dependency and interpenetration. It is this that determines his particular combination of symbolic-generalised images, in which the socially typical is highlighted, and images in which the individual and particular are in the foreground.

In accordance with this strategy he opens with an extended, detailed image of the second type depicting the family life of the Old Man and the Old Woman. It is one of the most sophisticated images of this type in the whole of O'Casey's work. In his earlier plays, as we have seen, this theme of the mutual determination of the "public" (the great socio-political struggles, movements and personalities) and the "private," is all-pervading. In those plays, however, the "intimate," everyday sphere still monopolises the centre of the stage, physically speaking. The great national and international events are in this sense still "in the background" (a relationship determined by the kind of statement O'Casey was making about society). Now, in *The Star Turns Red*, O'Casey lugs these larger socio-political forces and figures right into the middle of the stage on an equal footing with the traditional "private" foreground milieu. This corresponds both to the "facts of life" in the new historical era and to the relatively different kind of points that he sets out to make.

In *The Star Turns Red* the great events, issues, and personalities literally muscle in on the "privacy" of the working-class household. There is therefore something symbolic in the "untypical" visits paid to the old couple by the Lord Mayor, the Purple Priest and the fascist Leader (the powers that be and those that seek to be). At the same time the appearance of the Great in this humble slum abode is concretely motivated. It is a point of crisis and decision and the forces of church and state are willing to descend to the obscure and lowly in order to win them to their side. *They need the people* and their backing. Their behaviour implies that ordinary, rank-and-file people are of decisive importance. They chose the household of the Old Man because he has shown himself in the past to be a true boss's and priest's man. He is the weak spot where they can apply the thin end of the wedge. That their cause is in a more precarious state than they would lead one to believe is seen in the wooing, blandishing language which they mix in with their threats: the Lord Mayor enters, talking effusively–"Good morning, good evening, my very deah friends!" (265) The Mayor's confusion is partly real, being the result of doing something daring and unusual, and partly calculating conciliatoriness. Having made his greeting fit both morning and evening he puts half of his large behind on each of the two chairs offered to him by the Old Man and the Old Woman in their genuine confusion.

The Purple Priest too applies the old "soft soap": "The peace of God that passeth all understanding be close to all and dwell in the hearts of all who are in this house tonight." (271) But he cannot, by his nature, entirely hide the iron fist in the velvet glove, and his minion, the Brown Priest of the Poor, is there to smooth the way, telling "his son" to do what the Church commands. In this respect the initial role of the Brown Priest is as a kind of Trojan Horse of the rulers among the people. At this point he illustrates in himself what they are trying to make out of the old couple—instruments against their own class, their own flesh and blood, for all this unusual effort is aimed against one thing—the little thing that makes the mighty tremble: the militant rank-and-file worker, Jack.

The forces breaking the supposed idyll of the home and family are not limited to these incursions from outside. The basic conflict of the era has penetrated massively into the core of the smallest social unit, the family, and split it apart. In words reminiscent of Juno Boyle, the Old Woman exclaims, "What about our own two boys, always at each other's throats for the sake of a slogan? [. . .] life's lost everything but its name." (248) What, in Juno, was an instinctively sound (if limited) reaction, has here, in the midst of this real struggle over real issues, become a sign of inadequacy and incomprehension. It is a fatal illusion to imagine one can build oneself a private idyll within one's four walls in the midst of an epoch of decisive social struggle. The elderly couple still cling to the traditional conceptions of social bonds in terms of blood-relationship. But these, as a viable basis for peace and harmony, are outlived and break under the new pressures. The seemingly inexplicable failure of the most sacred and self-evident "truths" causes pain and perturbation even in the apathetic Old Man so that he rises for a moment to true poetic eloquence in expressing the paradox of his two sons being deadly enemies. (249 to 250) The boys are, he says, trout in the same river, birds in one nest, deer in the same forest, etc.—and thinking but a single thought—mutual murder. But no words, however poetic (notice how curiously archaic these images are), can put Humpty Dumpty together again. New social loyalties must be and are being formed.

The paradox is that these two "average" representatives of the broadest masses, the old couple, have a much lower opinion of their own worth than that held by their 'betters." They have always played "your humble servant" and given thanks for being so graciously allowed to be of some little service to the masters. The play sets out to teach these ordinary folk that they are of decisive importance. If the old order can only stand with their connivance then it is clear that it can only be brought down with their participation. And if they can make or break one social order then it becomes conceivable that they can make a new one. Red Jim, Brannigan his lieutenant, and Jack are all workers too. They have freed themselves from the old, inadequate, purely private loyalties and established new, class allegiances: "I have brothers everywhere, Mother; but I have none in this house." (Jack, 249) We experience these men breaking the old world and beginning to make the new.

But it is the Old Man and the Old Woman who represent the masses at the grass-root level. Are the other more epic and symbolic characters not rather wishful thinking in view of the backwardness shown "at the bottom?" Are these revolutionaries conceivable as emerging from the masses as they actually are? What have the two levels got to do with each other?

Ignorance and mental enslavement to their pastors and masters is the salient characteristic of the old pair. This provides well-fertilised soil in which the Authorities can sow their counter-revolutionary seed. At the same time it is the soil which facilitates and partly produces a monster like

Kian. (Kian–Cain, the biblical figure who murders his own "kin," in this case his fellow worker Michael.) The Old Woman cries in her incomprehension–"Oh, Kian, my son, my poor, sense-forsaken son, what have you done!" (276) Her own son is suddenly a stranger to her, yet the family life from which he has sprung must bear a heavy responsibility for what he has become. Kian's chief characteristics– a fatal lack of class-consciousness and loyalty, his falling down and worshipping a supreme Authority (the Leader), his unthinking readiness to serve this authority to his own detriment, etc.–all these are easily traceable back to the same characteristics within his parents and family. He is their son, indeed, their recognisable progeny, the absolute escalation of one aspect of their lives. The way they are forced to live is a hotbed of fascism.

But there is more to it than this. With tremendous subtlety and economy O'Casey allows potential qualities to emerge in the old people which are totally contradictory to those so far mentioned. Consider how the Old Woman rebels against the god-ordained subservience to her husband:

Old Woman. I was just trying to think of something to stem the disorder that's sowing itself everywhere.
Old Man. Well, a barrage of holly and ivy won't avail much. But we've got the military, haven't we?
(The Old Woman does not answer.
Old Man (peevishly). Why don't y'answer? We've got the military, haven't we?
Old Woman. Yes; we've got the military.
Old Man. And the police, too, haven't we?
(The Old Woman does not answer.
Old Man. Can't y'answer when you're asked a question? We've got the police too, haven't we?
[. . .]
(The Old Woman does not answer.
Old Man (crossly). A minute ago you gave a thundering echo to every word I said; now you can't parade even a whisper before a man. (*Furiously*) We have the Saffron

Shirts and the Christian Front as well, haven't we, haven't we, haven't we?

Old Woman. Yes, yes, yes!

Old Man. What more do you want, then? They'll be able to preserve order, won't they?

Old Woman. Ay; but what kind of order?

Old Man. What kind of order! It won't be any of your holly and mistletoe order. Sound and sensible law and order—that's what it'll be.

Old Woman. And what's the good of order in the country if there's none in the home? What's the good of life if you have to get the military and police to mind it for you?

Old Man. What else are we paying them for? (247–248)

Beaten back again and again by her husband's bludgeoning into being his mere echo she never really gives up her refusal to knuckle under to him, the "supreme authority" within her little world. Her most serious insurrections occur, as here, when her primitive but deeply held class instincts are offended. Through her suffering she begins, like Juno, to free what is best in her. One of the demoralised mourners at Michael's bier calls Julia names for prophesying the end of the old gods and the dawn of the time of Christ the worker. This moves the Old Woman to tell the "fool" to let the girl be, let her proclaim her anger and so lessen the venom brewed within her by her father's violent death. "(*She stretches out her hands to Julia.*) Dear child, forgive the worker's hand that brought a hurried death to thy poor father." (316) The motivations and emotions concentrated here are extremely complex. There is a touch of self-interest, very secondary. The words "dear child" imply an ability to recognise her "kin" in a fellow worker, almost as if Julia was replacing her "dead" blood-child Kian. She is beginning to take the step, via a characteristic fellow feeling for someone suffering from the loss of a dear member of her family, to the recognition of the working class as her family. This is an awakening of the new class loyalty through, and not in spite of, or against, the *old* family feeling. The new incorporates the old and both are the richer for it. In her urge to insurrection against her old god, her husband, and in her dawning ability to see the whole working class as her family, she shows herself more than the mere biological mother of Jack.

Jack understands his mother, where others treat her as a confused gabbler. Jack learns from her what the people's deepest needs and longings are, and in what terms they conceive of these longings and their satisfaction. She muses on the star shining in at the window–could it be *the* star? What star does she mean, ask the Old Man and Julia. *Whose* star, asks Jack. She answers in a reverie, "The star of Him who is called Wonderful, Counsellor, Everlasting Father, the Prince of Peace." (255) Julia and the Old Man turn away in disappointment, but Jack presses her:

Jack (still interested). How does the star shine, Mother?
Old Woman. It shines as purest silver shines, all brightened by a useful and a loving hand.
Jack (turning away from looking at his mother). So it shone when it led the kings; so shall it not shine when it leads the people. It leads no more, and never shall till its silver turns to red. (255–256)

Now "Juno" does the star-gazing instead of the "Captain"–and to more purpose. Through his sympathetic understanding for his mother (also a product of their family life) Jack learns the lesson which this play as a whole brings home to its audience–the way to win the people is to engraft the new on to the old, on to what the people hold dear, what has the potency to move them emotionally.

It would be wrong however to see the mother alone as the family source of Jack. In certain directions the Old Man is more realistic than she is. (This shows through even in the above passage.) He is also less subservient to the church. His main occupation is doing the pools. In this senseless occupation he shows a sharp realisation of the need for those very qualities of character which he otherwise so conspicuously lacks: "Aaah! It would pay a man to have a mind of his own. Once get into the mind of others, and your own is a jungle of difficulties. The opinions of all these tipsters show that the only way to win is the best way to lose." (244) He too, has the courage to criticise, in words, supreme and sanctified authority. When pressed to "reason" with his son Jack he furiously retorts that the Purple Priest should do it himself—or his eminence (the Mayor, who is present) for that matter. In another place—"on any other question the Pope's as infallible as meself! Nice thing for a holy Pope to fix a red fringe on the Papal banner." (253) Note his equation of himself with the Pope. This satirises his view of himself as Lord of his little domain, but it also indicates that this ordinary worker is capable of conceiving himself as omnipotent, *as the next thing to God*. Although the Old Man's "presumption" is clearly more circumscribed and compromised than the Old Woman's, it is strong enough to show that Jack's sources are in both of them. Jack is this element in them developed to a new quality.

There are other underlying connections shown between the "private" and the "public" spheres. There is, in Act I, a lengthy exchange which seems on the surface to be more for comic relief than to contribute to the main themes. Julia and the old couple egg on Joybell, a complex-ridden, jolly flag-waving young Catholic lay brother, to make love to Julia. When Julia's provocativeness makes him finally lose control, they turn on him for what they themselves have encouraged; then the Old Man turns on Julia. At first the Old Woman defends Julia, but ends up taking her husband's part against her. In fact what is going on here on the ridiculous plane is the same as what we experience at times on the serious plane. In this scene they demonstrate their ability to revenge themselves on the "authorities" when they get one of their weaker vessels (Joybell) in their power; but their united front soon crumbles and they end up by "taking it out on the woman" and rallying round the established Authority (the husband). The main impression is of caving in, passing the buck, and turning on their own. Comical here, these characteristics appear as anything but comical when they are repeated in pure form in the behaviour of the spineless trade-union officials, those one-time "men of the people." These men incorporate one side of the popular character as illustrated in the Old Man and Old Woman–their sycophancy and play-safism, which move Brannigan to tell them that he'll show them it's dangerous to be safe in this world.

The way the people live their everyday lives partly produces the monster which betrays them. The "private" also determines the "public." Thus the working people contain within themselves the two possible alternatives. They themselves are responsible for what happens. In the "Dublin" plays their creative qualities are negated and alienated, remaining a potential only; here they are crystallised and embodied in heroes and heroines functioning in tune with history. The other destructive potential also "works itself out" from the masses, taking on the absolute, polarised form of the fascist supporters. The struggle of the two tendencies and alternatives within the people bursts out in dramatic, objective and decisive conflict.

In *The Star Turns Red,* as in the following *Purple Dust,* the cultural and philosophical heritage of the common people plays a crucial part. In the latter play the struggle for control of it is all over bar the shouting. In *The Star Turns Red* this struggle is still in full swing. The fight of opposing forces for control of the popular heritage is one aspect of the basic and specific conflict of this play.

The heritage of *Christianity* is in the centre of interest here.

The ordinary people in this play long for one thing above all: peace and order, escape from the threat and reality of anarchy. This longing they shared with the peoples of the world in 1938–9, when the possibility of peace was being threatened as never before. How is peace to be saved and guaranteed, and anarchy banished? Again O'Casey goes straight to the heart of the matter.

The Old Woman longs for something to stem the disorder that's spreading everywhere. She is willing to make any sort of compromise if, within the family, they can have "a little peace." The people associate peace and harmony with the traditional Christ, the Prince of Peace, the son of man, and with the festival of this Prince of Peace—Christmas and the star of Bethlehem. From these time-honoured symbols and traditions they hope that the promised peace will come, even at the eleventh hour. The innovation of the political Christmas pantomime or play provided O'Casey with an ideal basis on which to develop his theme.

Through their contacts with the working people the ruling class and its advocates know that the only way to win the people (and they must win them if they are to survive) is to appear to consummate these longings. The people's best champions also know (as we see Jack realising in conversation with his mother) that the people can only be won away from the old gods and mobilised for the revolution if the age-old unfulfilled promise of peace and harmony is made good in the process.

Who is the inheritor and executor of the Christian ideal of peace on earth and goodwill to all men? Who is the modern Prince of Peace?

The "peace" offered by the ruling class and its minions is presented in four stages in the course of the first act. First there is the fluttering Joybell: "Quite well, all well, and on the baker's list. And how's Mrs. What's-her-name's baby you take an interest in? All right again, eh, what? Yes. *Old Woman*. No, she's not all right." (258) Joybell is a caricature of the more sophisticated "peace"-pedlars, showing up the spent inadequacy of the old magic formulas. This approach will no longer wash with the people in their dire distress, but the idiot optimism which it creates has destroyed Joybell as a personality. He is both victim and tool, like the Evangelists in *Within the Gates*.

Next the Lord Mayor: "Isn't it grand, isn't it lovely, isn't it wonderful! Christ, the Prince of Peace, has conquered. The stay-in strike, arranged to begin to-night, is stopped before it started." (266) Joybell's approach, though still recognisable, is refined and concretised. Peace is identified with the (wished-for) defeat of the workers by the fascists and Christian Front. He tries to hypnotise the people by misusing their habitual conceptions of Christ, Christmas, etc. He comes, apparently, in the true Christian spirit, stretching out the hand of peace and reconciliation, offering them the advice to get Jack to leave the Communists and join the Christian Front before something happens to him. He demonstrates, then, what the old peace really means—capitulation, knuckling under, betrayal and class collaboration. Jack is not taken in: He the Mayor's friend? He'd sooner be the friend of Dermot of the Curses who sold his native land, or of Judas *who sold his Master*.

The third champion of ruling-class peace and order to enter the lists, the Purple Priest, swings the full weight of clerical authority behind the old magic. First comes the traditional blessing—The peace of God that passeth all understanding, etc., then comes the hammer—"*(in cold and level tones)* Peace to all but those who would mar the peace of this holy season with the hate of a deadly idea," etc. (271) Here their peace emerges in its true colours—as war, war against all who challenge the old order, the peace of the prison where joy and festival are cast out. Julia, he commands, must strip off the trappings of folly (her carnival costume) and don a garment befitting penance and prayer. Their way of celebrating the *festival* of the son of man is to turn those who should be the revellers into the reviled. This high priest's method is no longer persuasion, but terror—let them make their hearts humble and contrite before God begins with his sore wounding. They are not contrite, and the Purple Priest's God appears forthwith and puts his warning into effect (the leader of the Saffron Shirts).

The Fuehrer-leader stands at the other end of the scale from the simpering Joybell. Yet they are two levels of the same thing. In the Leader the nature of ruling-class peace and "order" is openly and brutally stated and demonstrated: "The State can have no enemies within its Circle.

We root them out, thousand by thousand, ten by ten, and one by one. If the warning isn't heeded, we come again. Neither drum nor trumpet tells of our second coming: we come silently, like a thief in the night." (274) Looking at Michael, murdered for rising in defence of his daughter, he says, "the violent shall be made meek." (276) This is the inner core of their peace—the "peace" created by intimidation and physical terror: the peace of the graveyard.

To lend this naked dictatorship authority and credibility the Leader has to appear as God, the Omnipotent, returned to earth. His prophets speak of him as such. The Old Woman describes her fascist son, Kian, as going about as if he were God Almighty's right-hand man. (248) The Leader appears as both old and new, so that the priest of the old god can easily function, with all his prestige, as the priest of the new. "Before God, for Whom we act, and in Whose name we speak," (279) the Purple Priest says to the shilly-shallying union officials, when browbeating them into regarding Red Jim as the source of havoc. The Leader is decked out with the attributes of Jehovah, the God of wrath of the Old Testament. Kian says the Leader's new order will overwhelm the living world! The Leader's entry is suitably godlike: "Let the door open; in the name of the new power, the great power, the one and only power—let the door open!" (272) He goes on to identify himself with such Jovian things as the sun in heaven and the hurtling of thunderbolts. He even uses the royal We. A Second Coming of the grim Jehovah of the Old Testament is all they can offer. They are incapable of even appearing to represent the second coming of the New Testament Christ, the Prince of Peace.

There is no real renewal here, although it is proclaimed as such. This is epitomised in the fact that *they* use biblical language more or less unchanged. The Purple Priest and the Leader are indeed the legitimate heirs of one side of Christianity—its institutionalised, state-sanctioning side, which has degenerated down to this. Nevertheless, they try to gain control of the whole of the people's Christian moral value system and manipulate it for their anti-popular ends.

In the yoking together of the church hierarchy, the fascists, and the bourgeoisie the relatively subordinate role of the spineless provincial bourgeois class in Ireland is embodied in the Lord Mayor. In this power elite the church is at least equal to the fascists. In fact they are almost indistinguishable. The "peace" of this clerical fascism is a formidable threat. The Purple Priest is able to impose it on the weak-kneed trade-union officials. The group of demoralised slum-dwellers who threaten Michael's bier (as the Down-and-Out threaten Jannice) show what a grip it has among the masses. Even the Red Guards guarding the bier waver when the priest offers them the peace of God and the church. But Jack confronts him with the alternative: "Your peace is not our peace: we seek a peace of our own–a peace abiding and a peace that's sure." (318)

The play shows the workers in the process of realising themselves as the true heirs of Christ, as the second, better coming of the Prince of Peace. In taking up arms against the forces of anarchy and enslavement, and for the dignity and joy of life, they both discover and create true peace. "Go, and let us fight in peace," says Red Jim to the Purple Priest during the last battle (351). Peace and joy, the essence of the Christmas festival, are attainable only through war–war on fascism. In this way *The Star Turns Red* brings flesh and blood to the struggle first embodied in the previous play. As Sarukhanyan says, "In it is reflected O'Casey's path from abstract humanism *(Within the Gates)* to anti-fascism."[5]

Revolution brings peace because it brings joy. Therefore the revolution, as the birth of this joy, the nativity of the Man-Christ, appears as a *festival*. It takes place under Christmas decorations, to Russian ballet music. Julia is wearing carnival costume. The movements are stylised as in a dance.

The fight is not for a bigger slice of the loaf–"we'll seize all that life can give," says the 2nd Workman (332). The grandiose scope of such aspiration and such action calls forth the characteristics of gods in them. Christ-God is brought down out of heaven and incorporated in them: "We are the resurrection and the life." (Jack, 317) "Ours is the kingdom, the power, and the glory." (1st Workman, 332) Christ is born again at Christmas—a nativity play with a difference!

Their claim to be the true Prince of Peace is personified in the largely symbolic-allegorical figure of Red Jim. Why was this necessary? The reactionary forces cunningly put forward their "God" in the form of an individual. The traditional popular conception of a god has always been of an omnipotent individual. If one is suggesting an heir to the old god then one of his aspects must remain that of an individual, if he is to convince. Furthermore, only if the workers' claim to omnipotence is given this personal form can the great argument between the rival claimants to the throne be staged.

The important thing about Red Jim is that he embodies the attributes of a new Christ rather than those of the old Jehovah. His very language is often that of the Christ of the New Testament, modified. He has that personal magnetism and power to inspire and transform people, to "resurrect" the dead and cure the incurable. He is a fisher of men, dragging them up from the depths and giving them a sense of their dignity. Much of this is epitomised in his relations with his somewhat drunk and disorderly lieutenant, Brannigan. He challenges him to give up the drink— "I want you, Brannigan, I want you." (304) Brannigan, under the spell of Jim's personality and of the revolution, promises, and Jim proclaims, "My comrade was dead, and is alive again; he was lost, and is found!" (304) His spirit has been capable of creating, almost solo, a whole movement, an army of "disciples." Some of them, it is true, have fallen by the wayside: the trade-union officials. In Jim's harangue to them his identity with Christ-God, the Creator-out-of-mud, manifests itself:

Red Jim (hoarse and raging). ... (To Sheasker) Who lifted you, you hearseman's get, from the job of worrying the poor to pay for their plywood coffins? *(Sheasker glares silently at him.)* I did! [. . .] *(To Brallain)* Who found you with hardly a boot on your foot, a ragged shirt flaunting a way out of a breach in your britches? Who took you up because he thought he saw a glimmer of a man in you, and made you into an Alderman? I did! The Union chose you, did it? The men elected you, did they? Who made the Union? Who made the men men? Who gave you the power you have? I did, you gang of daws! (302–303)

Christ-Jim must be understood metaphorically here, as, to a large degree, the spirit of the workers' movement.

The two conflicting claimants to the title of omnipotent authority and the Prince of Peace struggle for the body and soul of the working people as a whole. This takes the symbolic form of the struggle for the possession of Michael's body in Act III. This dramatic situation owes something perhaps to the tradition of the wake in Irish life and literature, and something to the tradition of the morality play. O'Casey already used it in the struggle for Jannice's soul in *Within the Gates*. Here it no longer offers the possibility of a subjective interpretation as a struggle *within* the character concerned.

The revolutionary forces win this tug-o'-war. At her father's bier Julia proclaims that the old priests shall fall and their dominion cease. But looking at Christ on the crucifix, she adds, "Against you, dear one, we have no grudge." (315)

In the last act the workers, won to the new Prince of Peace, carry out the historical exploit. The very stars are at their command, and turn red. We have come a long way from Captain Boyle's ridiculous "reaching for the stars" and yet there is some connection. What is best in Christianity has been won over and fights on the workers' side. This is symbolised in the final decision of the Brown Priest of the Poor to join them. He puts it in a nutshell: "The star turned red is still the star/Of him who came as man's pure prince of peace;/And so I serve him here." (351)

In his last great free-verse speech, Red Jim announces the inevitable conquest of all godly power by man. His lines here no longer echo the Bible but rather those of Shelley celebrating the unchained titan in *Prometheus Unbound*:[6]

We fight on; we suffer; we die; but we fight on.
Till brave-breasted women and men, terrac'd with
strength,
Shall live and die together, co-equal in all things;
And romping, living children, anointed with joy,
shall be banners and banneroles of this moving world!
In all that great minds give, we share;
And unto man be all might, majesty, dominion, and
power! (352)

O'Casey and Jim share in what the great mind of Shelley gave them, remoulding and concretising it. The hint of the slogan "All power to the Soviets" in the last line puts the finishing touch.

Thus O'Casey had no intention of demonstrating the actual "mechanics" of revolution, or rather the dialectics of its daily reality, as Brecht did in *The Days of the Commune*. These things are left shadowy, being sketched in only in so far as they are necessary for the development of his specific theme as described above. O'Casey was out to show the "what" of the fight against fascism and for the revolution, rather than the "how." What would be lost in terms of the people's hopes and desires if the fascists won through; what would be won in terms of these things if fascism were smashed and the workers took power. He shows how this revolution grows logically and by necessity out of these needs and traditions of the people. It is their natural fulfil-ment, not their negation. Things have reached the stage where this longing for peace, order and community must be finally fulfilled or for ever stamped out. The revolutionary working class are the only legitimate heirs of the past, pres-ent and future, because they are the only power which can meet this demand.

O'Casey shows Communism to be the only inheritor of what is best in the Christian tradition. In doing so he does not mystify the issues. It is not a revolution fought under religious banners on both sides, as was the English Revolution in the seventeenth century. It is a secularisation of the Christian ethos, a secularisation of "salvation." O'Casey knew that in countries like Ireland, where the Christian heritage had such deep and ineradicable roots, only a struggle which, in its terms of reference, could latch on to this tradition would be able to move the whole of the working people emotionally. In a letter to the editor of the Moscow journal, *International Literature*, O'Casey explains why he does not have Red Jim talk in Marxist terms: "Were Red Jim to speak as a Marxist, the audience here or in America –that is, if there ever be an audience–would take no notice; only the converted, those already Marxists would listen. Now I don't want to talk to those who are already (in) our way of thinking–they are already on the march; but I do want to get into touch with those who are lagging behind, especially those who (are) among the crowd of workers attached to the Catholic religion."[7] All this is clear enough, but not, apparently, to Heinz Kosok who, perhaps seeking to save the *Star* from Communism, says, "It would be easy to speak of a socialist-communist attitude on the part of the author were it not that an exceptional amount of Christian ideas and Christian symbolism has flowed into the play."[8]

A word in conclusion on two things which have often been a focus of criticism: the language, and the characterisation of Red Jim.

The language passes through various levels, from the colloquial almost-everyday, through heightened rhetorical passages with biblical and literary echoes, to free-verse declamations and song-poems. In its passion and violence of invective the language outdoes even that of his previous "revolution-play," *The Plough and the Stars*. Cowasjee objects that it is "unnecessarily violent and hysterical."[9] Does he expect people caught up in a revolution to talk in the same measured, mundane tone as in the drawing rooms of the well-made play? What of *King Lear*? In the "Dublin" plays the characters throw themselves totally into their speech because it is a substitute for significant action. Now the furious words are the expression and accompaniment of furious action. The potential energy boxed up in the eloquence of the earlier plays now flows freely. Later, in *Purple Dust*, all the eloquence is on one side. Here both sides have it still at their command. The Purple Priest is a worthy antagonist for the rhetoric of Jack and Red Jim. He has the whole battery of biblical metaphor at his finger-tips. Nevertheless the aridity of his cause is reflected in the rigidness and lack of creative modification in his use of the linguistic heritage. Jack, and especially Red Jim, modify the language of the Bible, which is only one element in their battery of linguistic means ranging from free use of the vernacular to creative reworking of the words of the great visionary poets. Shelley, who was misused by Davoren to help him hide from life, becomes a weapon in Red Jim's hands.

Do the workers carry the day because they win the rhetorical duels? Some critics have suggested this.[10] If this is the case then O'Casey falls into the very trap against which he never tired of warning his public: the belief that real battles can be decided by words. Surely, however, this play drives home his message: the rhetoric of the Purple Priest, effective as it is, is in the last resort of no avail against the universal power of the workers in word *and deed.*

Regarding Red Jim, there is a general feeling that he needs "humanising." Pauli suggests that the Maxim-Gorki Theatre production in Berlin did well in "uncovering individual features and significant contradictions in the figure of the revolutionary leader, Red Jim."[11] He agrees with Stolper[12] that Jim shows the "human" foibles of vanity, romantic attitudinising and enjoyment of the role of revolutionary glamour-boy. If our interpretation of the play and of Red Jim's function within its symbolic-allegorical structure is correct then such efforts at unearthing "foibles" in him are worse than a waste of time. The working in of such weaknesses would merely obscure Jim's essence as the personification of the revolutionary workers' character as the new Christ.

At the same time the play does provide opportunities for humanising Red Jim for he is, after all, a man among mortals and must convince on this level–Christ as the son of man at last.

In the most general sense this is done through his language, which is the colloquial and passionate speech of the people and their cultural traditions.

He is recognisable in Brannigan, and Brannigan in him. They share important qualities: courage, fighting spirit, enjoyment of confrontation, contempt for traitors and "the rules," the ability to take a situation into their own hands, and so on. But what is anarchy and partly brigandage in Brannigan is purified, through discipline and far-sightedness, into revolutionary leadership in Red Jim. The "foightin' Oirishman" is no longer enough, but he has essential stuff in him. Brannigan is a living bridge leading from the rank-and-file to Red Jim.

In contrast to his fascist antagonist Red Jim is in and of the masses, not over and separate from them. He is their moving spirit, inspiring each of them to reach for omnipotence, which is the inheritance of every one, rather than of some Fuehrer only, to whom we are mere worshippers.

Nevertheless the figure of Red Jim does present some aesthetic problems. In the last resort he is not shown concretely enough as emerging from the masses and the movement–as being also created by these, rather than creating them in a solo run. He is shown only at the "public" level, not at all in his intimate personal relations. In these respects the character of Jack, in relation to his mother, is more interesting. Could Red Jim not have been given more "body" in this direction without impairing him as a symbol and a metaphor? O'Casey never again ventured to place a *human* figure which functions mainly on the metaphorical-symbolic level so near the centre of a play. As things are it is difficult to avoid the impression of a revolutionary superman needing no collective leadership around him.

O'Casey's only direct experience of something approaching a revolutionary situation was during the Larkin-led Dublin Lockout of 1913, and it is possible that his unbounded admiration for "Larkinism," for the almost superhuman efforts of his hero, partly accounts for this weakness in the play. In 1913 the Irish Labour movement was militant but immature. There was nothing approaching a revolutionary party. So much depended on Larkin's personality. No seizure of state power is possible on the basis of a "Larkinite" movement, but this is exactly what O'Casey makes happen in the play. This leads to the overstraining and partial break-down of Red Jim as a dramatic figure. Later, in the person of Ayamonn Breydon in *Red Roses for Me*, O'Casey is able to do more justice to the real human richness of a man from the Larkin mould.

Notes

1. Hogan, op. cit., pp. 84–85
2. Krause, op. cit., p. 208
3. Ibid., p. 205
4. "Unity to Play New O'Casey Work," in the *Daily Worker*, Jan. 11, 1940
5. Sarukhanyan, op. cit., p. 64 (translation, JM)
6. Compare P. B. Shelley, *Prometheus Unbound*, Act III: "The loathsome mask has fallen, the man remains / Sceptreless, free, uncircumscribed, but man / Equal, unclassed, tribeless, and nationless, / Exempt from awe, worship, degree, the king / Over himself . . ."
   And act IV:
"To defy Power, which seems omnipotent; / To love, and bear; to hope till Hope creates / From its own wreck the thing it contemplates; / Neither to change, nor falter, nor repent; / This, like thy glory, Titan, is to be / Good, great and joyous, beautiful and free; / This is alone Life, Joy, Empire, and Victory."
7. Letter to Timofei Rokotov, April 17, 1939, in *Letters*, op. cit., p. 795

8. Kosok, op. cit., p. 169
9. Cowasjee, op. cit., p. 73
10. Pauli, op. cit., p. 133
11. Ibid., p. 257
12. Armin Stolper, "Arbeit an O'Casey," in *Theater der Zeit*, No. 18, 1968, p. 16, quoted Pauli, op. cit., p. 132

VII PURPLE DUST

Written 1938–40; published 1940; produced 1945 (Liverpool Playhouse)

> "It's meself is thinking, when all's over, the
> British Empire'll be a Nursery Rhyme."
>
> Sean O'Casey, December 1939

Two English businessmen, Basil Stoke, thirty, and Cyril Poges, sixty-five, have come to live in a mouldering Tudor manor house in the Irish village of Clune na Geera where they intend to live the country life and resurrect the glories of the past. With them are their mistresses, Avril and Souhaun, both Irishwomen, and two Irish servants, Cloyne, the maid, and Barney, the butler. The time is "the present."

Local workers are engaged to renovate the mansion. Among them, the 2nd Worker, Philib O'Dempsey, a dreamer and bitterly anti-English nationalist; his close friend, the working foreman Jack O'Killigain, just come back from fighting the fascists in Spain. From the start things go wrong for Stoke and Poges. Poges is kept from his "work" (working the stock-market by telephone) by the apparent vagueness and incompetence of the men installing his desk, light, telephone, etc., and by the continuous interruptions of the workers and their local cronies. Hens and cocks are offered for sale, a cow, too, which gets loose in the house and is taken for a bull by the terrified two. An immense garden-roller arrives unsolicited and smashes a hole in the outer wall; supposedly valuable vases are shattered; the beamed ceiling is perforated like a cullender by the Yellow-bearded Man who is up above trying, it seems, to install the electric light cable; Poges' antique writing-desk is vandalised in what might be a well-meaning attempt to get it through a narrow arched door.

One humiliation follows another for the two businessmen. O'Killigain wooes and wins Avril from Stoke, and O'Dempsey charms Souhaun from Poges. Stoke is thrown into the mud by a mettlesome Irish horse, while the invading cow reduces Poges to trembling inanity. The Communist O'Killigain openly mocks their philistinism and English chauvinism and drives Poges to the verge of apoplexy by predicting the imminent demise of the Empire. Their only ally is the local Catholic dignitary Canon Chreehewel, who accepts their help in downing dance halls and combating the influence of O'Killigain. This help takes the form of cheques payable to the church coffers–a method of cementing human relations which brings them less success when applied to Avril and Souhaun.

It is autumn when they arrive in Clune na Geera. During the action the wind and the rain increase. There are covert warnings that the river is going to burst its banks. The workers take precautions and await the waters with a strange exhilaration. Only Stoke and Poges notice nothing, until it is too late. The deluge breaks loose, smashes its way into the old house and completes the destruction started by time and the workmen. Avril and Souhaun make off, the one in a boat with O'Killigain, the other on a fiery steed with Philib O'Dempsey. Stoke and Poges are trapped and overwhelmed.

It is useful to begin with some critics' views on *Purple Dust*.

John Gassner says that, "Perhaps the chief example of poor timing was the appearance of *Purple Dust*, an uproarious travesty on the British, when England was enduring the blitz and was facing Hitler alone."[1] Our analysis will throw some light on the appropriateness or otherwise of the timing of this play. The view that it is about Irish Goodies as against English Baddies has been energetically propagated. Heinz Kosok gives it an ominous twist in the direction of "racial" incompatibility: "*Purple Dust* is concerned with [. . .] the fundamental opposition between two peoples, one which neither military victories nor political negotiations can eradicate."[2] Herr Kosok does, however, in another place, qualify his position. "The exposure of English characteristics has often led to *Purple Dust* being regarded as a satire aimed exclusively against England. This leaves out of account the fact that the Irish too, are subjected to criticism. The negligence of the workers borders on sabotage, their lack of due care not only irritates the Englishmen but leads to the destruction of valuable objects."[3] It is indeed a sobering thought that the Irish workers do not, on all occasions, live up to Herr Kosok's standards of Thoroughness and Efficiency. If the heavy-handed naiveté of this raises a smile the same cannot be said for Kaspar Spinner's elaboration on the theme: *"Purple Dust* [...] shows no sign of Marxism. On the contrary, it would be possible–on the evidence of the racial superiority of the Irish as embodied in the hero and his companions–to ascribe fascist motives to O'Casey."[4] Thus the Communist and anti-fascist O'Casey is put forward as a fascist traitor to the anti-fascist cause.

Contemporary reactions of the same type kept the play off the stage and prevented it from functioning in the immediate historical context for which it was written. Quoting George Orwell's predictable remarks on *Purple Dust*, O'Casey struck back: " 'England was the object of O'Casey's hatred.' To say simply that this remark is a lie is but to give it a good name; it is more, inasmuch as it throbs with malice, too. Certainly he [O'Casey, JM] had no liking for the England that was Orwell and his abune companions. But he had steeped himself in the culture and civilisation of the broad, the vital, the everlasting England."[5]

At first sight there would seem to be some justification for the assumption that the play is anti-English. Philib O'Dempsey, a positive character, proclaims, "Our poets of old have said it often: time'll see th' Irish again with wine an' ale on th' table before them; an' th' English, barefoot, beggin' a crust in a lonely sthreet, an' th' weather frosty." (120) Furthermore, O'Casey systematically debunks in Stoke and Poges certain things which have come to be regarded as "typical English" strengths–the ability to ride and shoot well, the stiff upper lip in the face of overwhelming odds, the ability to improvise and "rough it," an innate sense of fair play, treating every man on his merits, etc. But surely these are the very "qualities" with which the English *bourgeoisie* has plumed itself. Others take the best of them for granted, leaving out the huntin' and shootin'!

Getting down to the basic life-activity of Stoke and Poges one finds that there is nothing particularly English about it, even in form. It is the life-activity of capitalists everywhere—the extraction of cash profit. Poges may be ridiculous when expatiating on history and culture but when giving instructions to his London agent on the telephone he is efficient and realistic: "I want you to get me five hundred shares in the Welldonian Cement Co.; shares are bound to jump, the minute the bombing starts seriously." (188) For them the world spins round on the rim of a coin, as O'Dempsey says. Getting money is for them a means of making more money, not a means to make life better. It is the negator of life in their case, disabling those who practise it. This relationship to money on the part of Stoke and Poges is important because money and the attitude of various groups to it is developed as a unifying theme in the play.

It is not the fact that they are Englishmen, but that they are capitalist, colonial-minded businessmen with one-track life-functions, which O'Casey ridicules.

Their relations to the Irish workers are defined by their character as imperialist-minded exploiters. Poges says that "All the Irish are the same. Bit backward perhaps, like all primitive peoples, especially now, for they're missing the example and influence of the gentry; but delightful people all the same. They need control, though; oh yes, they need it badly." (136) There is nothing particularly English about this self-delusion, but it makes it impossible for those who hold it ever to understand and appreciate those they exploit, or cope with their rising self-assertion. Their human relations with them are totally impoverished, for they can only appreciate them as quaint playthings or mere tools. However it is not solely their relation as exploiter to exploited, as such, which severs them from the main body of humanity; at the secondary level their narrow-gauge life-function impoverishes and distorts their relationships to the whole world of objective nature and human culture.

The metaphorical tie-up between nature and society is very close and complex in O'Casey's work as a whole. Things healthy and dynamic are always in contact and in tune with the things and processes of nature. Things inadequate and unhealthy and out of tune with the "natural" course of events are always out of contact with nature. In *Purple Dust*, nature and people's relationship to it is worked up into one of the central metaphors and focal points of reference.

Stoke and Poges feel that somehow they have lost contact with nature, with the organic well-springs of life. This is a genuine motive for coming to Clune na Geera, as far as it goes. They would *like* to be "country gentlemen," involved (in a genteel, patriarchal way) in the life of the country. But their introductory song–"Rural scenes are now our joy:/Farmer's boy,/Milkmaid coy,/Each like a newly painted toy," etc. (122)–immediately establishes the falsity and hollowness of their view of nature and country-people. This is the only instance where they really use a part of the literary heritage, but it is a tradition which hinders rather than helps them to grapple with the realities–the played-out aristocratic "pastoral" tradition. The play reveals the roots of this view in the way the exploiting class lives and works and shows why they cannot learn from their experience but are doomed to inevitable shipwreck.

Stoke and Poges are physically detached from nature. They appear almost exclusively as indoor beings whose tools of "production" are sapless things like writing-desks, electric light, telephones and motor-cars (little, mobile "indoors"). In earlier plays the isolation of the people from the real issues of life was symbolised in their confinement to one room within a house. Here, in *Purple Dust*, the same image is used to indicate the "imprisoned" nature of the imperialists in decay. The timbering of the Tudor hall should, as O'Casey directs, suggest the bars of a cage.

Occasionally the pair do sally forth into the wide and windy world of outdoors. Such daring ends in defeat and humiliation at the hands of the representatives of nature–as when the local horse throws Basil. When nature, in its turn, breaks into their dusty cage, in the form of the farmyard animals, they are thrown into helpless confusion. They are out of tune with natural processes, the "natural course of events." These are hints of things to come, straws in the rising wind, and form a lead-up to the final "fantastic" nature image of the inbursting flood which overwhelms the financiers. The mustering of the elements is noted by everyone else, but not by them. They cannot recognise the signs and prepare themselves for the future because they have lost contact with nature. Thus the river-bursting-its-banks image at the climax is a perfectly natural one to end this play. Stoke and Poges have, on the one hand, lost their roots in nature, but, on the other, they still retain positions of economic and political power over life. So the metaphor of nature coming to the end of its patience with them (the waters exploding the confines of the old constricting river-banks) and revenging itself on them by flicking them off the face of earth, is in tune with the pattern of images developed throughout the play. To a public steeped in natural mythology the capitalists and their work must appear as running counter to the laws of nature.

So they begin to emerge as historically archaic figures, inadequate to the demands of a changing world.

Stoke and Poges spend a great deal of their time enthusing over philosophy, history and art. They are out to make contact with the heritage of the past. The problem of the relationship between the cultural heritage and the needs of the present is central to *Purple Dust*. As we have seen, it is something which preoccupied O'Casey from the beginning of his playwriting. In an important sense all the plays written between 1938 and 1945 are concerned with this.

The attitude of the two businessmen to philosophy and culture is self-contradictory in the same way as their approach to nature. There is a genuine desire to enrich their lives with these things, but their relationship to the cultural heritage is hopelessly impoverished and distorted by their function as capitalists, so that they cannot bring their aspirations into any sort of fruitful contact with life. The best they can achieve is an eclectic jumble of inaccurate and undigested bits and pieces—mere playthings to them in the same sense as are the rich personalities of those who "serve" them. Inasmuch as philosophy and culture have a function for them at all, it is to cast a spurious aura of civilisation over their mean-spirited money manipulations and so hide the true nature of these activities from themselves and others, as they disguise their car-garage in the form of a little, mock-Tudor cottage. Their culture is hollow because their life-work has no organic need for it; in fact a real humanist culture would get in their way.

The poverty of their working relationship to nature basically determines the inadequacy of their *artistic* and *philosophical* response to nature. Their introductory song, already quoted, owes its remarkable puerility to this. The same is true of their "natural" philosophy. Basil Stoke, who, as the "aristocratic" wing of the bourgeoisie, has "passed through Oxford," attempts to capture the essence of a primrose philosophically: "If we take the primrose, however, into our synthetical consideration, as a whole, or, *a priori*, as a part, with the rest of the whole of natural objects or phenomena, then there is, or may be, or can be a possibility of thinking . . ." (138)

This is what happens to philosophy when it is disconnected from practice. It turns scholastic and not only fails to enrich life but buries its beauty beneath a landslide of stifling words.

A lack of hold on reality, an inability fully to live in the present, begins to emerge. Art and philosophy, which, in theory at least, might have helped to compensate for the tenuousness of their practical activity, cannot fulfil this function because the quality of their reception of things cultural is itself determined by this very thinness.

It is with the national heritage that the two make the

greatest play, above all with the Tudor-Elizabethan era, the time of Shakespeare and the high Renaissance in England. Feeling subconsciously the thinness of their latter-day living, the imperialist businessmen turn nostalgically to an age when the life of their class was more full-blooded and colourful, seeking to regain something of the youthful vigour of their dawning ascendancy by donning the outward trappings of those more glorious days. In buying with their ill-gotten gains the Tudor house, they imagine they have acquired and resurrected the old spirit of "a great period. Full of flow, energy, colour, power, imagination and hilarity." (Stoke, 134) Stoke and Poges may hanker after these qualities in the abstract, but they are the very qualities which they can never achieve. The spirit of Shakespeare, the great, necessary heart of English culture, which must be defended and used in the fight against fascism, is as dead to them as they are to it. Beings whose relation to men and women is reduced to cash nexus, alienated from nature, and with such a poor hold on the present can never embody the wholeness, passion and immediacy of the men and women of the Renaissance, for whom theory and practice, insight and action, poetry and philosophy, poetry and action formed a seamless unity. What practical use can war-profiteers have for a heritage whose salient quality is humanism?–Or for the heroic heritage of Irish history and legend? For Poges takes a kind of antiquarian interest in the latter too.

O'Dempsey, the 2nd Workman, tells him of the exploits of Finn MacCool. A great man gone for ever, comments Poges with a show of hopeful regret. But O'Dempsey will not let him escape Finn that easily: "He's here for ever!" (175) His halloo can be heard on the hill and his spear-point seen shining among the stars, but not by those whose vision is encompassed by the edge of a gold coin.

The Elizabethan spirit and the heroic Irish heritage are to be kept safely in their place–in the past, a hook for sentimental nostalgia. Consciously or unconsciously Poges is here trying, unsuccessfully, to encourage the same castrated attitude in the Irish to their heritage as he has to his own, thus transforming something that is a potential "danger" into something binding the Irish to him in a sense of common, impotent nostalgia. (This was in fact the kind of relationship to tradition that O'Casey criticised in the Irish people in his "Dublin" plays.) Poges puts it clearly: "Come, come; we mustn't be always brooding upon the present and the future. Life is too much with us, O'Killigain; late and soon, getting and spending, we lay waste our powers." (135) Here Poges tries to use, or rather misuse Wordsworth's sonnet, which in fact demonstrates the poet's preoccupation with the continuity of past present and future. But the words of the sonnet take their revenge on Poges, so that with unconscious irony he is made to reveal his true nature—even though he avoids the astonishingly apt next line of the poem: "Little we see in Nature that is ours."

So the capitalists capsule off present and past from one another. They are incapable of living in either the present or the past. They have no real past because they have no real present. Their lack of a productive grasp of their cultural heritage further impoverishes their present. They have no present partly because they have no past. The possession of a future, however, demands both a real past and a real present with a developing line of continuity between them. Therefore they are people without a future. Poges' distaste for the future expressed in the above quotation is symptomatic. In their case the seamless coat of past present and future is torn in three and its colours fade. They are the outcasts of history, at home nowhere. This is also symbolised in their geographical homelessness. They have left England where they no longer feel at ease (though neutral Ireland may also appeal to them as a place where they can safely stay and draw their war-profits without the danger of their becoming victims of their own weapons). They make for Ireland in search of a "refuge" and a new life as so many social outcasts and sturdy bastards had done since the fateful time of Strongbow. But in Ireland, where their conquering forefathers usually ended by being conquered and absorbed into Irish culture, these latter-day "Tudors" remain rootless aliens.

Are these outcasts to be entrusted with leading humanity against Hitlerism?

Once again one sees how apt the final "fantastic" image is—the River of Time. Why it should be a river, has already been noted. That *Time* should up and annihilate them, aliens as they are to all three phases of time, is logical. Furthermore: this final deluge is portrayed in terms of legend and ballad—riders, boats and wild waters. It springs from that cultural heritage which they cannot master. They cannot contemplate that life should assume ballad-shape, they fail to recognise the signs of the times, and ballad-life wreaks vengeance on them.

But why are there *two* capitalists? There is the obvious answer—to generalise, to avoid the assumption that one is faced with certain purely individual idiosyncrasies. But there is more to it than that. Juxtaposing the two allows O'Casey to bring out the underlying sameness beneath the surface differences, and, on the other hand, their basic lack of harmony or ability to unite in a productive human way, which lies beneath their superficial unison. Whereas Basil Stoke reputedly "passed through Oxford" and claims to be a twig of the true aristocratic branch, Cyril Poges likes to see himself as the rough diamond, the self-educated, self-made man. Both are revealed as, at bottom, the same: parodies of men, men in bits, self-alienated and alienated from the world and time. Because they lack integration and universality they need no other person to complement them—although at first sight this may seem a paradox. Their real social-human needs are reduced almost to nothing, and so each is sufficient unto himself, the essential bourgeois individual. They exist alongside each other without enrichening one another. Being mere duplicates of each other, they lack all true individuality. Having no motive for cooperation, in human terms, and having only their alienation in common, like hollow vessels they grate on each other.

Thus one of the underlying preccupations of earlier plays

187

such as *Juno and the Paycock* and *The Silver Tassie* reappears here strongly and in a different context: the disastrous effects of the disintegrated personality with its falling apart of the imaginative-intellectual capacities from the practical and bodily life-activities. In the earlier plays this problem was examined in the context of the Irish working people, where it assumed a strong note of tragedy because it hinders them from mobilising themselves to play their necessary part in history. Now, in *Purple Dust,* it is the exploiters who are crippled in this way. Stemming from the very nature of their life-activity, it is inevitable. These people have no positive historical role to play in the modern world and their disintegrated personalities are both cause and effect of their necessary downfall. Because they have no future their problems can never have tragic implications. The contradiction between what they think they are and what they really are is insoluble. This makes them totally ridiculous, comic figures, unlike the split and self-deluded characters from the common people in the "Dublin" plays, who can and must overcome these contradictions.

How should one play these types? Ingeborg Pietsch takes the line (and she is not the only one) that it is possible and important to bring certain "potentials" to light in the two capitalists. She concludes: "In general it would be difficult to find figures in O'Casey's plays, who are totally surrendered through satirical portrayal."[6] O'Casey himself concedes that Stoke and Poges may even be likable at times, then polishes them off: "But Time and Change do not care a damn for these lovable things, neither can the playwright care either. All that they are, and all they represent, must go."[7] This quotation makes two things clear. First, it underlines that O'Casey had no intention of satirising "the English" in these two—or did he think all the English would be swept off the face of the earth? Secondly, it shows that he held their chief characteristic to be *lack* of potential, and our analysis has borne this out. What function could the uncovering of "potentials" have in the characters of Stoke and Poges? To look for potentials or productive con-

tradictions here is to have failed to grasp the whole underlying aim and strategy of the play in the context of the class
struggle.

And yet, Stoke, and especially Poges do have one feature
which, in another constellation, would be potentially positive: their basic desire for a colourful, jolly life. This saves
them from the savage satire and bitter hatred which O'Casey metes out to the life-denying joy-detesting clerics and
fanatics in the later plays. The two businessmen are ridiculous, but not detestable. Another reason for this relaxed
view of the exploiters is that, in the context of the play, the
life-and-death contest has already been decided, and they
have lost it. They are superannuated, still there only due to
the temporary forebearance of time, nature and the working people. They are laughed from the stage of history.
They are ridiculous and not hateful because they try to
regain humanity from a position which automatically ne-
gates humanity. In so far as they try to do it by turning
back the clock there is also a faint Quixotic touch to them.
Through the insurmountable antagonism between the urge
to a richness of human relations and their function as imperialist exploiters being presented as an inner contradiction within personalities, the life-denying essence of the
drive to cash profit as the destroyer of positive human potential is brought home.

Before leaving the capitalist side of the conflicting forces
in *Purple Dust* a word is necessary on Canon Chreehewel.
His very existence refutes the claim that the play is about
Irish Goodies versus English Baddies. The Canon is a Bad-
die, and Irish. Poges pretends to disapprove of the Catholic
dignitary as one of those who keep the Irish in leading-
strings, but on the quiet he gives him cheques for the work
of the church. After he has been knocked about a bit Poges
calls in the Canon and his help to curb the loose and dangerous ways of the local commoners, especially that serpent
in the garden, Jack O'Killigain and his communistic ideas.
All this embodies the continued undercover alliance (the
two meet confidentially) between British capitalism and the

reactionary clerical oligarchy who rule the "Irish Free State" in their interests. These on-the-spot rulers do the dirty work which the British ruling class can no longer afford to carry out in person. As Poges says to him, he (Poges) is what is called a foreigner down here and couldn't afford to interfere with O'Killigain directly.

The money theme integrates this episode into the thematic fabric of the play. The Canon is Irish, and is like the workers and the two women in so far as he is trying to get as much money out of the two old relics as he can while the going's good (from his Irish perspective he too, sees that their days are numbered). He is like the other Irish, and unlike Stoke and Poges, also in that he is extracting and using money for a concrete purpose beyond itself. Unlike the other Irish, however, he does not use this money to make life merrier, but in a crusade against joy. So we see that "Irishness" is not inevitably a good thing in itself.

O'Casey underlines the Canon's Irishness by broadening his Irish "brogue" as he warms to his theme. Canon Chreehewel may share important attitudes and interests with his English capitalist backers, but when it is a matter of the future he shows an important difference. As an experienced functionary of the Catholic Church he has his ear much closer to the ground. He has his weather-ear cocked for signs of the approaching storm. He bids a hurried goodbye: "I must be off. Bad sign. The soft rain that's falling may change to a downpour, and I've a long way to go." (193) He is adequately dressed for the weather. He is taking precautions. Like the Irish, and unlike the businessmen and what they stand for, he and the church he stands for have developed and retained a capacity for survival under difficult and changing conditions. He will weather the storm, most likely, as so often in the past. Here O'Casey is issuing a warning to the working people. Even after the Flood this Catholic hierarchy could need watching.

The main organisational principle of this play is the systematic pattern of contrasts between two different qualities of humanity—that represented by Stoke-Poges, and that represented by the Irish workers. There are three focal points of conflict—around renovating the house; for intellectual and cultural hegemony; the struggle for the two women, Avril and Souhaun.

At almost every point the qualities displayed by the Irish workmen are diametrically opposed to those of Stoke-Poges. Are these the qualities of the "Irish," or of Irish *workers*? Let us begin with the contrasts and conflicts generated round the renovation of the Tudor manor house.

Right at the start they reveal attitudes which are those of *working* people. O'Dempsey, for instance, pours scorn on fools who leave the comforts of civilisation to come and live in a place like a disused morgue. These workers are much too embedded in the struggle to make ends meet and in their activity as builders who make life more convenient, to have anything but a healthy respect for the blessings of civilisation—to which belongs money, when properly used. Money to them is a means of getting themselves some of these benefits. Souhaun, says the 1st Workman, deserves God's goodness for luring some of the dodderers' cash to where it's needed.

This appreciation of the use-value of money they have in common with the two women and in opposition to the money-men. In order to get back as much of the capitalists' ill-gotten gains as they can while the going's good they show no initiative in renovating the despised old house quickly or efficiently—especially as it represents one of the worst times in the history of their oppression.

But does not their destruction of the house go beyond pure inefficiency or go-slow tactics? Isn't the chaos the product of those supposed "traditional" *Irish* characteristics—slovenliness, ignorance, the inability to agree or combine for a practical end, etc.? There is certainly evidence to support the existence of a critical element in O'Casey's portrait. In the first scenes the workers show not only realism, but also prejudices. The 3rd Workman complains that O'Killigain is for ever spouting subversive talk against the Church and the composure of the community. O'Dempsey is against the

English as such and all their works and he is initially shocked at girls "born in Ireland, an' denizenin' themselves here among decent people!" (125)

Above all there are the "absurd" scenes of chaos doubly distilled—the men apparently vying with each other to sell Poges things he doesn't want (their hunger for money getting the better of their loyalties?) or the scene where the two servants, Barney and Cloyne, fail to light the fire:

Cloyne. It might be worse.
Barney (striking a match to light the paper). We're goin' to be worse, I'm tellin' you.
Cloyne. We can't be worse than we are.
Barney (as the flames of the paper die down). There's no chance o' kindlin' here. Why did you say, then, that we might be worse?
Cloyne. Well, so, indeed, an' we might.
Barney. How can we be worse, woman, when we're as bad as we can be?
Cloyne. Simply be bein' worse than we were.
Barney. How can we be worse than we were, when we're as bad as we can be, now. (161)

The fire is never lit. The place remains as cold as the morgue that it is. This classical piece of absurdity in the "Irish" vein where logic is split with such dedication that it disappears altogether, where playing with words diverts one from getting anything done, harks back to the early critical plays where O'Casey was, in first line, lashing the fecklessness of his working people. But here, as the chaos builds up, one becomes conscious of a new, an alternative view of the old characteristics. There is a mounting suspicion that the sabotage of the house, the plans, the two capitalists themselves, and, in a somewhat different way, of the two women is not purely spontaneous but perhaps an organised conspiracy. There is no obvious proof, but one should hardly expect this from such past masters of the art as the Irish working people. After all, they have had seven or eight hundred years of clandestine struggle, especially in their Whiteboy type of rural "underground," in which to perfect it. The fact that underground conspiracy and sabotage have always been part and parcel of the everyday living of the Irish masses should, by itself, alert us to certain possibilities in a play dealing with this type of material.

Let us take a closer look at a typical scene. Cloyne brings Poges his *Financial Universe*. Just as he is about to look at it a great cackling, crowing and mooing is heard from without and Barney appears at the left entrance.

Poges (with the paper half spread before him). What the hell's that?

Barney. There's a man outside wants to know if you want any entherprisin' hins?

Poges. Any what?

Barney. Any hins, entherprisin' hins?

Poges (impatiently). What the devil would I want with hins enterprising or unenterprising?

Barney. He says it's all over the counthry that you're searchin' high an' low for entherprisin' hins.

Cloyne (appearing at the right entrance). There's two men here wantin' to know if you'd buy some prime an' startlin' cocks, goin' cheap?

1st Workman (appearing beside Barney, and shoving him aside to get in front). Excuse me, sir, but there's a friend o' mine just arrived with a cow that ud do any man good to see [. . .]

Poges. Hins, cocks, and cows! *(To 1st Workman)* What the hell do you take me for – a farmer's boy, or what?

Souhaun. It's all out of what you said about having hens and a cow in the place. *(To Cloyne)* And you, you little fool, must have gossiped it all over the district!

Cloyne. The only one I mentioned it to was Mr. O'Killigain. (141–142)

Poges, goaded to fury, sends Barney and Cloyne out to pack the poultry-sellers about their business. After they are gone he settles down to forget the world and its worries.

But he is kept on his toes by the 1st Workman who has been persistently pulling at his sleeve.

1st Workman (earnestly, almost into Poges' ear). Listen, whisper, sir; take the bull be th' horns, an' get the cow, before she's gone. An' as for entherprisin' hins, or cocks that'll do you credit, leave it to me, sir, an' you'll go about with a hilarious look in your eyes.

Poges (catching 1st Workman by the shoulders, in a rage, and pushing him out of the room, and down the passage). Get out, get out, you fool, with your hins and cocks and cows!

Souhaun (quickly–to Avril, when Poges has disappeared round the entrance). Go on up, and flatter and comfort your old fool by ridiculing my old fool; and, when he's half himself again, wanting still more comfort and flattery, wheedle a cheque out of the old prattler.

Avril (jumping up). Splendid idea! *(She runs off out.* (143–144)

Poges comes back in and settles down to the *Financial Universe*, but not for long: "*(1st and 3rd Workmen peer around corner of the left entrance; then they come over quickly and smoothly to where Poges is buried in his paper, the 1st Workman standing on his left hand and the 3rd Workman on his right. 1st Workman (persuasively–to-wards Poges' paper).* Listen, here, sir: if it's genuine poul-thry you want . . ." (144)

Several significant things emerge here (whereby the stage directions are particularly enlightening). It is impossible to avoid the suggestion of something precisely aimed and systematic in the disruption of Poges' attempts to take up his "work." There is a strong indication of a synchronisation of roles, a division of labour, of a new "team" or person taking over as soon as the previous shift leaves the scene for a breather–thus making sure there is no breather for the person being grilled (Poges). There is also the feeling of a whole community dovetailing its efforts in a universal mobilisation, those unseen and outside delivering the necessary ammunition, and those inside acting as their executives. All these conspiratorial elements are clearly pointed up by the insertion of the "open," clear-cut conspiracy between Souhaun and Avril into the midst of the scene This "suggests" a similar understanding of the scene as a whole, and others like it.

In connection with roles and division of labour, the specific function of the 1st Workman is interesting. O'Casey emphasises that he has "a foxy face," (119) i.e. his chief characteristic is cunning. He functions as a kind of fifth column, sabotaging Poges from within, sapping his morale. He does this by appearing particularly subservient–a kind of confidant insinuating ideas and associations. This psychological warfare of his includes a subtle playing on Poges' nostalgia and inability to connect with the present, which plunges Poges into a state of black melancholy:

> *1st Workman...* Worn away we are, I'm sayin', to shreds and shaddas mouldin' machines to do everything for us. Tired, is it? Ay, tired an' thremblin' towards th' edge of th' end of a life hardly worth livin'!
> *Poges (gloomily pacing up and down).* Not worth living, not worth living. (170)

The method of playing up to the English "gentry's" delusion of what an Irishman is, in order to steal a march on him, is strongest in this 1st Workman, who, when talking to Poges, puts on an exaggerated stage-Irishman's brogue– "Arra, be God, indeed an' they do, sir." (168) This tactic of using the exploiter's self-constructed misconception of one's character against him has been, and is, a method of resistance developed by all colonised peoples and exploited classes. Because it has had so long to mature in Ireland it has become second nature to the Irish working people and functions more or less spontaneously–as does so much else. Here, in this situation, however, a marshalling hand of a new kind–O'Killigain–is clearly at work, often behind the scenes. ("The only one I mentioned it to was Mr. O'Killigain.") In the early episodes this International-Brigader sets the tone for the others, clarifying their instinctively healthy reactions for them, giving them their cues. His simultaneous flirting with Avril, Souhaun and Cloyne at the outset is not just a demonstration of his versatility (though it is this) but also a broad and considered offensive to woo people from the businessmen and organise the front against the latter. O'Killigain's role as nerve-centre is only hinted at, and he needs only to hint at certain things. A little unobtrusive guidance is all that is necessary. Even the dependents Barney and Cloyne are integrated into the campaign (see above). The conscious character of the sabotage is, in fact, best seen in the episode where Cloyne pretends to be frightened of the "bull" (she must be pretending—an Irish village girl certainly knows the difference between a cow and a bull). Falling on her knees at the sight of the "bull," she clasps Poges round the legs, preventing him from fleeing. At the opportune moment Cloyne jerks Poges' legs from under him so that he crashes to the floor, (165) and his exposure is complete.

In all this, then, we are given an alternative view of that "Irishness" which O'Casey criticises in the early plays. Here the alternative, positive possibility, hinted at before, comes into the foreground, so that what previously appeared mainly as a stumbling-block now emerges as a unique and infinitely flexible weapon, when encouraged and moulded in te right way. Nevertheless, the possibility of construing it critically still lurks in the background, so that one is kept guessing until quite near the end whether there is method in their madness or not. All doubt is finally removed with the blatant smashing of the quattrocento desk as a kind of festive prelude to the deluge.

A kind of field of tension is created between the conspiratorial and the chaotic possibilities of interpretation. This engenders an active analytical interest in the characters on the part of the public. The new view has to be worked for and discovered. It has to establish itself through and in competition with the conventional and therefore easily accepted position that the Irish are either confused dolts or ineffectual visionaries, or both. Something to keep the audience on their mental toes.

At the same time, the simultaneous existence of the two possibilities of interpretation, in juxtaposition and interplay, help to bring out the precariousness of its positive application, as something which has to be continuously fought for in the teeth of the other tendency. The play demonstrates that the person to do this, to purify the mixed ore that is in the people into flexible metal, is the anti-fascist fighter, Communist and humanist of the O'Killigain stamp.

What we have in all this is the "absurd" as a weapon in the class struggle. How much more subtle, productive and poetic is this dramatisation of the "absurd" in life than in the flat, mean-hearted and repetitive situations of the Absurdists of the Beckett-Pinter brand. Attempts to claim O'Casey as one of the precursors of the Absurdists are absurd.

But why do the workers carry on this strange kind of war against Stoke and Poges and all their doings?

There is, of course, the immediate politico-historical reason. The Days of Good Queen Bess might have been glorious days for English culture, but for the common people of Ireland and their national cultural heritage the Tudor period was an infamous orgy of bloody annihilation carried out in the interests of English capitalism. The efforts (hopeless as they might be) of the two English businessmen to resurrect that "glorious epoch" in modern Ireland, in the process of freeing herself, was bound to be looked upon by the Irish working people as an insult born of insensitivity. The somewhat paradoxical "vandalism" of the workers towards the various relics of that time is partly explained by this.

But there are deeper and more strategic reasons for the workers' campaign against the bosses, and the form it takes. This is determined by the specific nature of the challenge which the capitalists present to their intrinsic quality of humanity.

Because their life is a working and struggling in the present these Irish workers are at one with nature, indeed they are portrayed as an integral part of it. Their daily work is with the materials of nature. They are of "outside." They are always coming in from outdoors and the subtle bands of the great conspiracy tie them to people like the roller-seller and the lorry-men, who are completely outside and never appear in person. Their poetic speech reflects their identity with nature. O'Dempsey says his lineage began "a day or two afther th' one when the sun herself was called upon to shine." (204) Wild nature holds no terrors for them: the "wild" Irish horse which threw Basil Stoke responds willingly to the guiding hand of O'Killigain.

Men of this type must hate and reject those who seek to shut nature (life) out, "seekin' a tidy an' tendher way to the end. Respectable lodgers with life [...] behind solid doors with knockers on them, an' curtained glass to keep the stars from starin'!" (177) Their ears are opened to the signs of the times. They are wise because they are in tune with the natural course of events. Wisdom, says O'Dempsey, is not in a desk, but out in the life of all things living and moving under the sky. Thus their anger at and rejection of Stoke and Poges is part of that of nature as a whole. So their being and behaviour assume symbolic-metaphorical significance alongside their concrete-historical plane of existence: they are nature finding a human voice.

Their campaign rises to a crescendo with the rising rhythm of the elements. When the Canon mentions O'Killigain's name "The wind and the rain are plainly heard." (190) They destroy the things which are anathema to this kind of nature—the old and outlived and the pernicious indoor things like the desks of the exploiters. Nevertheless, when O'Killigain says to Avril, "It is for us to make dying things live once more, and things that wither, leaf and bloom again," (130–131) this is no mere decorative talk, but a fitting and precise description of their social role and of their "metaphorical" role as a force of nature. Much of the floweriness of the workers' language in *Purple Dust* is the expression of this aspect of their inner essence. Above all, the great culminating natural image of the flood, of the river bursting its banks, arises logically and *naturally* out of this context, and is its fitting culmination. The workers cannot be overwhelmed, in fact they foster the deluge, and welcome it. In it they are in their element.

Because the workers live and struggle fully in the present, and because of their organic connection with nature, they are able to respond to and use their historical and cultural heritage in a fruitful way. Their ancestors, the heroes and bards of old, created their history and culture in the same close communion with nature as they themselves. In most of their images nature and the heroic heritage are fused. Avril says that O'Killigain's words comparing her with Helen of Troy are as ready to him as the wild flowers. For Philib O'Dempsey the heroes are *born* of nature: "Then every rib o' grass grows into a burnished fighter [. . .] with the branch of greatness waving in their hands!" (175)

The way they live and struggle in the present needs the nature-steeped heritage to express itself. Their present is a contest which they enjoy to the full. The figure of the Yellow-bearded Man, who is up above "mending" the ceiling, brings this out clearly. He bemoans his fate–to be for ever up and out of sight of the world and its wonders. Wonders indeed: present events are given legendary proportions, before they have time to cool, in the creative fantasy of the people, as when O'Killigain's wild ride with Avril becomes, in the telling, a ballad-event, with Avril up beside him like Lady Godiva, naked and unashamed. This is an imagination fed by legend.

In the figure of Philib O'Dempsey and his relationship to O'Killigain, this mutually enriching interflow between life and heritage and between past and present is given direct personal expression. O'Killigain calls his nationalist friend "a wandherin' king holdin' th' ages be th' hand." (132) Philib is the nationalist and dreamer–a more sympathetic study of the Padraic Pearse type than that associated with the Voice in *The Plough and the Stars*. When he confronts Poges two irreconcilable views of the relationship between past and present, between heritage and now, clash head-on. After Philib has told Poges of the mythical heroes, the latter says sadly, "And there it ends!" To which Philib answers, looking at Poges, "I'm thinkin' it might have been well for some if the end an' all was there . . ." (175 to 176) For Philib and his like the past is an unfinished process, a tale begun that's not yet ended, the reminder of a responsibility handed down to the present, something to be lived up to. This identity of past and present leads effortlessly and by necessity into the future. A future as legendary and heroic as that which is fast approaching must be easily recognised and welcomed by men like Philib as his own birthright. In his legend-nourished imagination he can shuttle at will from the present to the future and back: "Come, then, an' abide with the men o' th' wide wathers, who can go off in a tiny curragh o' thought to the New Island with th' outgoin' tide, an' come back be th' same tide sweepin' in again!" (to Souhaun, 205)

He and Jack O'Killigain are inseparable friends. O'Killigain loves him for his wholeness, his wearing of past present and future as a seamless garment. For all his own richness of personality O'Killigain needs O'Dempsey and his visionary quality. In his relationship with Philib his vital link with the mass of the working people is personified. But Philib also needs O'Killigain. It is the latter that guides his dreaming into fruitful channels for today and tomorrow, pushing him, with his repeated "And there are others," to trace the line of heroes from the past into the present. There are signs that the emotional nationalist O'Dempsey might fall into contempt for the present, were it not for O'Killigain, International-Brigader and Communist, who, in his actions, becomes for O'Dempsey, the present link in the unbreaking chain of heroes. He reveres O'Killigain for this.

So in contradistinction to the Stoke-Poges pair, each one of this pair is incomplete in himself—for all his inner richness, or rather because of it. They complement each other. Universality of personality is not the abstract bourgeois individual, but richness of social relationship. In the "Dublin" plays O'Casey had castigated the fruitless, hero-worshipping, enervating dreaming of his people, their barren "sense of history" and living in the past. Here, once again, the thing which was before seen from a critical perspective casts off its alienated context, and the "alternative possibility" no more than a faint potential in the old context, now comes into its own. Under the guiding, disciplining hand of the new revolutionary realist (O'Killigain) this sense of history gains continuity, and dreaming becomes a weapon for changing the world. Dreaming tempered by realism; realism permeated by imagination: this great synthesis is embodied in these two workers and their relationship to each other. Republican nationalist and Communist internationalist—this is the grand alliance, here lies a real nucleus of leadership in the fight against imperialism and fascism.

It is understandable that such universal men, moving at will from present to past and future, alive and at home in all of them, should feel an irreconcilable enmity for fragmented men like Stoke and Poges, tearers of the seamless garment, outcasts of time and place. These workers are the only heirs to the future. When they have destroyed fascism they will return home and claim their rightful inheritance. These Irish workers can have nothing to fear from the rising river of *Time*. They swim in time like fish in water.

There is another sense in which O'Killigain completes O'Dempsey. Universality in O'Killigain also means the effortless unity of word and deed, art and life, philosophy and art, philosophy and life. In this way that quality of living-in-the-present, common to all the workers, is most intense in him. O'Dempsey is quite right in seeing in him the living representative of the great Irish tradition, for this man who fought fascism in Spain is scholar, poet and hero-warrior in one.

Near the beginning he sings two songs. In contrast to the futility of the parallel Stoke-Poges ditty they embody his true life-philosophy. Poetry and world-view are fused. And the programme contained in the second, a song in praise of life and love-making, he has just been putting into practice by wooing all three women at one time. The transitions are seamless and immediate. He will brook no obstacles. Take his wooing of Avril. She says he must sing her a few of his own songs "sometime."

O'Killigain. Now, if you'd like to listen, an' you think that the time is handy.

Avril. Not now; we might be disturbed; but some evening, somewhere away from here.

O'Killigain. I will, an' welcome; some of them, too, that have been set in a little book, lookin' gay an' grand, for all the world to see. Come; listen—*(in a mocking whisper)*—and brave the wrath of the gouty, doughty Basil Stoke.

Avril (with a toss of her head). That thing! *(With bitter contempt)* A toddler thricking with a woman's legs; a thief without the power to thieve the thing he covets; a louse burrowing in a young lioness's belly; a perjurer in passion; a gutted soldier bee whose job is done, and still hangs on to life!

O'Killigain (embracing her tightly). Tonight, or tomorrow night, then, beside the blasted thorn three.

Avril (with fright in her voice). The blasted thorn tree! Oh! not there, not there—for evil things sit high, sit low in its twisty branches; and lovers, long ago, who leaned against it lost their love or died. No, no, not there: a saint himself would shudder if he had to pass it on a dusky night, with only a sly chit of a moon in the sky to show the way.

O'Killigain. Oh, foolish girl, there never can be evil things where love is living. Between the evil things an' us we'll make the sign of the rosy cross, an' it's blossomin' again the dead an' dhry thing will be, an' fruit will follow. We are no' saints, and so can abide by things that wither, without shudder or sigh, let the night be dark or dusky. It is for us to make dying things live once more, and things that wither, leaf and bloom again. Fix your arm in mine, young and fair one, and face for life.

Avril (after a little hesitation). Undher the thorn three then, with you. (130–131)

Throughout the play there is a tendency to a "Shakespearian" quality of speech. But the Shakespearian linguistic situation is reversed. The representatives of "higher society" now speak prosaically, with little colour or vigour of rhythm, while the talk of the "lower orders" is now in iambics and blank verse. The speech in this particular scene is exceptionally highly wrought and rhythmic. When Avril catches the spark of eloquence it takes the form elaborate abuse with clear lines going back to Shakespeare. The integration of philosopher, poet, lover and man of action which emerges here is truly Shakespearian. When Stoke enthuses over the early-Tudor end wall, O'Killigain taps the bit of wall which he is leaning on—Middle Tudor, he says, no doubt about it. (134) This can be construed as a reference to himself. All those Elizabethan qualities which Basil has just been enumerating are O'Killigain's qualities. So the worker O'Killigain (and to a lesser degree O'Dempsey) effortlessly achieves what Stoke-Poges so laboriously fail to achieve—to make the Elizabethan spirit live again. (It is for them to make dying things live once more.) O'Killigain, then, and not Poges, is the true "self-made man," the reincarnation of the man of the Renaissance at a higher level. Only the workers are adequate to that "Elizabethan" spirit which alone is adequate to the job of defeating fascism and building a new future. In this way a spirit which is associated with the *English* people at an important stage in their development appears as a quality of *Irish workers*. The irreconcilable "difference" melts. The workers of one nation can begin to recognise their best selves in those of the other. On the other hand, those who presume to be connoisseurs of things Elizabethan (the two men-of-affairs) fail to recognise the real, living thing when it appears under their very noses in the persons of the workers, accounting them so much dirt. These people are blind because, in their hearts, they don't really believe the Elizabethan spirit could ever rise again.

Because O'Killigain and his comrades embody the living essence of the Renaissance spirit they are bound to be profoundly opposed to those who try to counterfeit this spirit. People who do the latter with the aim of using this heritage to perpetuate their privileges rather than to liberate mankind are especially obnoxious to them and must be put in their place.

Purple Dust gives us a portrait of the new universal human being. He appears not as a humanist luxury devoutly to be desired but, like his predecessor in the Renaissance, a practical necessity in the process of the people's self-liberation. And he is clearly identified with the Communist internationalist and active fighter against fascism.

The struggle for the two women is the focal point where the general conflict becomes a specific struggle for the "possession" of humanity at large.

Initially the two belong fully to neither one side or the other. An underlying feeling of community with the Irish workers (they were born and bred in the same district) struggles within them with the wish to preserve and consolidate their status as "ladies" of wealth and position, a cut above the workers. The two figures are a battle-field where health and corruption, absurdity and meaning fight it out for the body and soul of humanity.

Money-corruption has a very real grip on them. This is possible because, in being pulled into the human vacuum of the Stoke-Poges world, they have been cut off from their *natural* roots. Money then becomes the only means for them to add colour and enjoyment to life. And this is how they use money—like the other workers and unlike the capitalists. Now, coming back to Clune na Geera, they come back into the gravitational pull of that natural world whose most potent expression is the workers' collective, and they are inexorably re-absorbed, their basically healthy impulses re-activated. Alternative channels for full-blooded living are opened up—a whole universe of vigorous life where they can, for the first time, really put money to good use. Even after they have been got at by O'Dempsey and O'Killigain or possibly because of this, they continue to milk the two money-bags for all they are worth. For O'Casey this is not opportunism but just good sense. In the context of the workers' sabotage the money-extracting on the part of the two women takes on the character of a piece of conspiratorial team-work through which they become integrated into the general conspiracy (see p. 194 above). Like the other workers they derive tremendous *fun* from this contest of the classes.

O'Killigain and O'Dempsey consciously set out to win back the two women to the natural community. They are best equipped to bring out the latent qualities uniting them with the workers. In his first wooing O'Killigain's eloquence at once sets fire to Avril's own. In their case too, O'Killigain aims and sharpens their own instinctive methods of retaliation which have been recalled to life by the behaviour of the workers as a whole. They are of course especially effective in that part of the conspiracy which is aimed at the capitalists' belief in themselves as the carriers of culture. In their gleeful vandalising of the "Annamese" vase and the "Cambodian" bowl their own instinctive common sense and O'Killigain's encouragement are fused together.

The two women enter with the bits, while the 1st Workman, who has been "on duty" demoralising Poges "slinks off" leaving the field to the next shift. Souhaun tells Poges the bowls were worthless trash.

Poges (with quiet emphasis). And who gave you that information?

Avril. Couldn't anyone, not a fool, see what they were the minute they saw them?

Souhaun. The minute Mr. O'Killigain set eyes on them, he said that they went from Derby in thousands to Singapore and Saigon for suckers to buy them! (172)

Having said all this it must be emphasised that a similar kind of ambiguity to that surrounding the general behaviour of the workers also persists round that of the two women.

The alternative possibility that a large part of their behaviour might after all be the result of clodhopping ignorance is kept slightly open almost to the end. This, in my view, performs the same double function as already indicated.

So the mass of ordinary people, like these two women neither good nor bad, not necessarily proletarian but certainly not capitalists, will turn their backs on the corrupt society of finance capital and go with the workers and the revolution. They will do so not so much for the negative reason that the capitalist class has nothing left to offer, or even because the workers' champions have the better or more poetic arguments, but because it corresponds to their deepest nature to do so. In these revolutionary workers they recognise the quintessence of themselves; only through and with them can they become fully themselves.

Although placed in the present, this play is itself a fantasy in which past present and future meet and commingle. It is among other things a parable or allegory for the whole attempt of successive English ruling classes throughout history to "rule" the Irish on the mistaken assumption that they (the English overlords) represented a higher culture. But it is also a projection into the future in that it shows the strategic historical perspective—the natural, logical and inevitable downfall of capitalism and the take-over by the working people. It is this generous strategic view which enables it to take the real, contemporary and bitter struggle "for granted" and to laugh the played-out oppressors from the stage. This is why, despite its basic conflict—the confrontation of capitalists and workers—it remains pure and unadulterated comedy.

Notes

1. John Gassner in "The Prodigality of Sean O'Casey," in *Modern Judgements*, op. cit., p. 112
2. Kosok, op. cit., p. 352
3. Ibid., p. 185
4. Kaspar Spinner, *Die alte Dame sagt: Nein! Drei irische*

Dramatiker: Lennox Robinson, Sean O'Casey, Denis John-ston, Berne, 1961 (translation, JM)

5. Sean O'Casey, *Sunset and Evening Star*, in *Autobiographies II*, op. cit., p. 545

6. Ingeborg Pietsch, "Über Probleme der O'Casey-Rezeption in der DDR," in *Material zum Theater*, Nummer 30: Sektion Schauspiel, Heft 10, Herausgeber: Verband der Theater-schaffenden der Deutschen Demokratischen Republik (translation, JM)

7. Sean O'Casey, "Purple Dust in their Eyes," in *Under a Colored Cap*, op. cit., p. 264

VIII RED ROSES FOR ME

Written 1941–2; published 1942; produced 1943 (Olympia Theatre, Dublin)

> "And as time requireth a man of marvellous mirth and pastimes; and sometimes of a sad gravity: a man for all seasons."
>
> Robert Whittington

The Star Turns Red explored certain possibilities inherent in the Dublin lockout of 1913. These one might call the "epic" or "objective" possibilities of social and political revolution. In *Red Roses for Me* O'Casey works up a different but complementary model on the basis of a similar real-life situation, this time with the emphasis on the lyrical dimension. Red Jim is already "made" and functioning as a public figure; Ayamonn Breydon we experience in the making, moving from the private to the public, the personal to the social. *Red Roses for Me* tackles the open questions: what sort of personality must a working-class leader possess? How does it come about? What is the chemistry of the relationship between this personality and the masses?

It has often been said that Ayamonn Breydon is the most autobiographical of O'Casey's heroes. In fact O'Casey uses some aspects of his own character and history, plus his imagination, to elaborate a figure who, while not based directly or solely on the character of Jim Larkin, is a poetic metaphor of something essential to the Larkin spirit.

At Easter 1916, according to O'Casey, the leadership of the national movement was not adequate to the needs and strengths of the masses. This leads to tragedy in *The Plough and the Stars*. But 1913, as O'Casey saw it, was a situation with real revolutionary potentials because in it the leader (Larkin) was adequate to the masses, and the masses to him. He was of them and from them—one with them. The new revolutionary spirit born in the great struggle, the dawning sense that the world belonged by right to them, that they were Humanity, found its quintessential embodiment in the personality of Larkin. This is why O'Casey gives him the title of Prometheus Hibernica in his autobiography.[1] What was the secret of Larkin's universal appeal? This is what the dramatist investigates in *Red Roses for Me*. It is not only a complementary play to *The Star Turns Red*, but the counter-play to *The Plough and the Stars*, a model of what the relationship between leader and masses must be like if success is to be achieved. It plays through the alternative possibility inherent in Irish history itself, the one which must be recognised and developed under contemporary conditions.

It is clear that the portrayal of the hero, his inner life and intimate personal relationships, must loom large under these circumstances. This lyrical emphasis has its consequences for the forms taken by the dramatic conflicts. It is more difficult here to put one's finger on a sharply defined central conflict running through the play as a whole. Nevertheless, the fabric of the play is interwoven with a complex system of conflicts, contradictions and dramatic contrasts so as to create an artistic unity which, in its novelty, must make one rethink all preconceived notions about the nature and boundaries of theatre.

Act I opens in a Dublin slum flat "a little while ago." Ayamonn Breydon, a young railwayman, rehearses a scene from Shakespeare's *Henry VI* with the help of his mother. It is to be performed as part of a "minstrel" show in aid of the workers' strike fund. The transport workers and others threaten to strike if they are not granted a shilling a week rise.

Ayamonn tries his hand at a whole variety of arts—painting, song-writing, acting. He is a practising Christian and vestryman in the Protestant Church of St. Burnupus. Sheila Moorneen, his girl friend, the daughter of a policeman, is a strict Catholic. His mother is against the match. Sheila has no understanding for Ayamonn's aspirations and badgers him to be "sensible" and think of their future.

Ayamonn's flat is a mecca for his friends. There is old Brennan o' the Moor, a retired house-painter turned petty landlord, who now divides his time between singing ballads for pennies in the street and worrying whether his money is safe in the vaults of the Bank of Ireland. He and Ayamonn make up the music and the words respectively to the song "Red Roses for Me" which is also to be performed at the show in aid of the strike fund. Then there is Roory O'Bala-caun, "a zealous Irish Irelander." He brings nationalist magazines that his friend Ayamonn has asked him for. Mull-canny, militant Darwinist, contributes a rationalist book. Roory and Brennan, rabid Catholic and rabid Protestant, bury the hatchet only when faced with the common enemy in the person of Mullcanny, mocker of all things sacred. The miserable slum-dwellers come and tell Ayamonn that their holy statue, the Lady of Eblana's (Dublin's) Poor, has vanished from her niche in the hall. The thief was Bren-nan. He repaints the tarnished effigy and secretly sets it up again.

Sheila delivers a message from her other admirer, Inspec-tor Finglas: if Ayamonn will turn blackleg he'll be made foreman and their future will be assured. His friend, the Protestant Rector, brings him a warning from the same source: the strikers' meeting will be banned and force used if necessary. Ayamonn advises the workers to ignore the ban and agrees to speak at the meeting.

It is late afternoon on a cloudy day (Act III). The slum-dwellers lounge listlessly on a bridge over the river Liffey. Nothing seems able to rouse them—neither Brennan's sen-sual love-ballad nor Roory's exhortations to remember the great feats and fights of the past, enshrined in patriotic song —until Ayamonn arrives and, making use of the mantle of splendour thrown over Dublin by the setting sun, succeeds in inspiring them to a new hope and vision. The sunset fades; the people on the bridge seem to sink back into apathy.

The last act is set on a warm Easter evening in the grounds of St. Burnupus Protestant Church. Ayamonn ig-nores the pleadings of his mother and Sheila and the veiled threats of Finglas, and goes with the workers. His mother and the Rector now rally to him. Sounds of fighting off. Various people, fleeing, seek sanctuary in the church, including two railway foremen, Foster and Dowzard, blacklegs, rabid Orangemen and church vestrymen. Ayamonn falls fighting and sends a last message to the Rector: he wants his body to lie in the church that night. The corpse is brought. Sheila rejects the blandishments of Finglas at the last moment and puts a bunch of red roses on Ayamonn's breast. The Rector defies the threats levelled at him by Foster and Dowzard and has Ayamonn's body placed in the church. Brennan softly sings their song, "Red Roses for Me," at the church door.

With O'Casey it is always best to begin at the grass roots, that is, with his picture of the ordinary rank-and-file people. They are defined by inner contradiction, by the clash of opposites, i.e. each of them is a minor drama in himself.

Mrs Breydon is a woman of deep humanity and warmth. Behind her stands the personality of O'Casey's own mother. She is what Juno could become (there is no mention of a father in this family). Her ingrained urge to mother those around her extends beyond her family to all those in distress within her little scope. She is the good Samaritan of the district, loved and trusted by her Catholic neighbours. Her willingness to sacrifice herself for others is such that Ayamonn is constrained to comment that she thinks more of other homes than she does of her own.

These are the very qualities which she has generated in her son. They are central to his make-up.

She is also physically courageous when courage is needed to preserve life. It is she who intervenes when the mob threaten to murder Mullcanny for mocking man's godly descent. She needs and responds to beauty. While saying that she manages to get on quite well without the artistic activities that her son engages in, she moves over to the window and gently touches the fuchsia she has in a vase. These qualities too, she hands on to her son.

But these positive things in her are contradicted, limited

and distorted by other characteristics. Mrs Breydon's class-consciousness throughout most of the play is embryonic. Her outlook is narrowed by a sectarian, highly divisive Protestantism. The conflict which characterises her attitude to the Catholic Sheila is epitomised in her "fractured" reaction to the repainted statue. Its new beauty makes her cry out, but she orders Brennan to hurry it out of her sight for it's not a thing for Protestant eyes to feast on. Like Juno she fears her beloved son is sacrificing himself for some imponderable principle. The difference, as with Jack in *The Star Turns Red*, lies in the principle and the context. Juno's fear and distrust of her son's "principles" was right; Mrs Breydon, doing the same thing, from the same spontaneous standpoint, is wrong, because the cause to which Ayamonn dedicates his life is vital to the interests of the working people. As O'Casey once put it in a letter—"it is good to die for one's friend, but foolish to die for one's enemy."[2] Thus Mrs Breydon is not purely a positive extension of Juno. In this particular instance it is the second, negative possibility, inherent in an attitude of Juno which seems, at first, to have the upper hand. Because of this Mrs Breydon is not able to achieve the *social* effectivity which her positive qualities ought to bring her.

Brennan o' the Moor is a talented musician with a deep responsiveness to the sensuous beauty of life and poetry. He demands gangway for poetry and music on to the centre of life's stage. When he brings a shy young singer to present the song, "Red Roses for Me," he buffets Sheila and Ayamonn to the side-lines—"Outa th' way, there! [. . .] Farther back, there, farther back!" (244) Music and song for him are not something to be capsuled off from the struggle, but are a means of organising and rousing the people. He has written the music for this song so that it can be performed in aid of the strikers' fund. On the Liffey bridge in Act III his main impulse in singing his love-song is to use beauty to resurrect a responsive chord in the breasts of those sunk in despondency. When he takes a last farewell of his friend Ayamonn he does it with a song.

This, above all, he has in common with Ayamonn. Ayamonn needs Brennan for this component of his own make-up. And there are other signs of Ayamonn in the old man. He is not easily led into petty squabbling but is at pains to be on easy terms with all sorts and manner of people. He also possesses qualities which Ayamonn needs but initially does not possess—realism, for instance, regarding the hard facts of existence. When Ayamonn romantically announces that Sheila is not interested in money, Brennan counters: "Eh? Arra, don't be talkin' nonsense, man! Who is it daren't think of what money can buy?" (241–242)

But there are important features in Brennan which run counter to these qualities. His connection to cultural tradition is spontaneous and illiterate, purely in the folk-song line. He envies Ayamonn his wide reading and wishes he was young enough to bury himself in all the great books of the world. This lack hinders Brennan from forging his music-making into a weapon for real social activation. He is, in his way, rather like old Luka in Gorky's *Lower Depths*—a sentimentalist seeking to slur over real problems and conflicts with well-meant but dangerously facile traditional "comforters." This lies behind his trick with the Virgin's statue. It is also expressed in his attempts to pour oil on troubled waters with the repeated stock phrase, "Lady present, lady present, boys!" There is an underlying fund of narrow Protestant bigotry and general religious prejudice and superstition in him, which, when provoked by the Catholic Roory or the rationalist Mullcanny can make him entirely forget his efforts to bring people together in harmony: *"Brennan (lapsing, in his excitement, into a semi-Ulster dialect). We dud ut tae yeh in Durry, [th' Protestants]* [3] *sent your bravest floatin' down dud in th' wathers of th' Boyne [. . .] Thut was a slup in th' puss tae your Pope!"* (259–260) Bigotry, once set in motion, can transform this gentle, humane artist into a savage.

Brennan's respect for money is continually tipping over into a monomaniacal concern with the security of the Bank of Ireland, that is with the preservation and multiplication of his capital. The Bank is a kind of King Charles' Head with him, a canker eating into his humanity and impairing his dignity. Brennan is a centaur personality—still the plebeian street-singer from the old bardic-vagabond tradition, and already petty capitalist and exploiter. This gives rise to an ambivalence in his attitude to the workers' cause. When the possibility of revolution seems real he appeals to the Rector for reassurance that the "community at large" is in no danger and that the iron-doored vaults of the Bank of Ireland will hold back the ravenous pack. His lack of clear definition and staying-power as a fighter, like his sentimental wish for superficial harmony, all stem from his new position as a small property-owner. The working people know him as a slum landlord and distrust his motives. They may like him, but they cannot respect him. Thus his potentially activating qualities too, are deprived of the social impact they should have.

Historically Brennan is a man at the cross-roads. He can take either of two paths. He is the type of small-time bourgeois who came into their own with the establishment of the Free State in 1922. O'Casey is reminding us and them, from the vantage-point of 1942, that there was a plebeian-democratic political and cultural root in their past, which they would all too often rather forget about, that these people had it in them to take a different path from the one taken so far.

Roory O'Balacaun, the ardent nationalist, is steeped in the lore of republican Fenianism. The battle-songs of this tradition are crucial to his apprehension of reality. This patriotic musical "folk-lore" is to him a slashing sword, a weapon to revolutionise the masses. But at the same time he is "one o' th' men meself" (245) and identifies the new rising of the workers with those older risings of the "Fenians": "Th' Fenians are in force again, Ayamonn; th' Sword o' Light is shinin'!" (253)

It is this aspect (the fusion of class militancy with the traditions of militant republicanism) of the rich tapestry of Ayamonn's character that Roory feeds, and he too, is Ayamonn's friend. He it is that brings the nationalist magazines which Ayamonn reads regularly. The two of them combine their voices in a Fenian war-song: "Our courage so many have thought to be agein',/Now flames like a brilliant new star in th' sky . . ." (253)

But Roory's effectiveness too, is neutralised by inner contradictions. He is an ignorant unread man whose appreciation of culture begins and ends with this Thomas-Davis type of patriotic song–the opposite pole to the "pure" love-songs of Brennan. Roory sneers at the wider artistic and intellectual aspirations of Ayamonn and Mullcanny, telling them that he has no time to waste on books. His intellectual horizon is narrowly provincial. Anything new is foreign and "English" and therefore suspect. He lacks all urge to intellectual enquiry and accepts traditional values unquestioningly. At the core of this philistinism lies an idiot Catholicism as narrowing, exclusive and divisive as Brennan's brand of Protestantism:

Brennan (contemptuously). I refuse to argue with a one who's no' a broad-minded mon. Abuse is no equivalent for lugic–so I say God save th' King, an' tae hull with th' Pope!

Roory (indignantly). You damned bigot–to hell with th' King, an' God save th' Pope!

Mullcanny (to Ayamonn). You see how they live in bitterness, the one with the other. (260)

Exactly. These people, as they are, *tend to cancel each other out*. It was these negative sides of Irish Catholic nationalism that won through after 1922. In Roory, as in the case of Brennan, O'Casey is showing us that there was (and is) an *alternative possibility* inherent in Irish nationalism, if it would go hand in hand with labour. The play is a model, derived from the 1913 events, of how things could and should go.

Paudrig[4] Mullcanny is a militant rationalist. He derives his highest pleasure from mocking the most dearly held religious illusions and superstitions of his fellows. When they proclaim the "diamond-core of an everlastin' divinity" (Roory, 267) in the soul of man, Mullcanny counters that human beings are nothing more than time's promoted reptiles. Paudrig is the unflinching enquirer, the querier of hallowed "truths," the scourge of all mystification. It is he who proposes one of the central postulates of the play: "Couldn't you all do betther than wasting your time making gods afther your own ignorant images?" (249) And he is ready to put his livelihood and even his life at stake in order to emancipate the minds of the people. Ayamonn relates how Mullcanny gave up his job rather than what he believed in. He barely escapes from an infuriated mob who want to lynch him for saying that men are descended from monkeys, and, having taken refuge in Ayamonn's flat, continues the "polemic" with Roory and Brennan while crouching on the floor to avoid the stones coming through the window. There is nothing of the coward in this man.

These are the qualities which Ayamonn so much values and needs in Mullcanny. Ayamonn is his fearless protector, proclaiming that anyone who adds another colour to the brilliant spectrum of the truth is always sure of a roof to his courage in the Breydon dwelling. Like Ayamonn, Mullcanny is a dedicated reader. He goes to some lengths to obtain Haeckel's *The Riddle of the Universe* for his friend. He is the feeder of this quality in Ayamonn. The latter would not be so attracted to Mullcanny if he did not possess an underlying sensitivity to the sensuous beauty of art and life. The ungracious young man must grudgingly admit that what he'd heard of the "Red Roses for Me" song wasn't bad. He scorns those who go about "with noses long as a snipe's bill, sthripping the gayest rose of its petals in search of a beetle, and sniffing a taint in the freshest breeze blowing in from the sea." (247)

Yet the total composition of Mullcanny's character is such that these valuable qualities are largely self-defeating. There is nothing of the full-blooded yes-to-life, of which he is capable, in his mechanistic-materialist philosophy of man and society. He makes no attempt to liberate what is true and poetic in the people's view of humanity (themselves) from its outdated and mystical form. Instead he makes a mockery of their dearly held belief in humanity's "divine spark." Like the Atheist in *Within the Gates* he kicks man out of that place at the centre of the scheme of things which Christianity (in theory) gives him, and demotes him to the status of a modified beast. He can never hope to get through to the masses with this anti-poetic pure negation. Their furious rejection of him is understandable, for he is in fact undermining their precious and precarious underlying urge to fight for a life worthy of *human* beings, and not animals—as their existence is at present.

The Rector is not one of the people in the strict sense. Their misery frightens him because he feels incapable of really helping them. Nevertheless, there is something in this man too, that answers to a need and a quality in Ayamonn, and the reverse is also true. He is a Protestant churchman, but his Protestantism has none of that narrow bigotry which reaches its quintessence in the Orangemen Foster and Dowzard. His creed is marked by tolerance and breadth of understanding and acceptance; the Rector is a catholic Protestant. He is accused of "papistry" because he seeks to introduce a touch of colour and life into the grim church in the form of the Easter daffodils. He refuses to get involved in the petty bickerings between sects. He is dedicated to the search for truth, according to his own lights.

It is this that he honours in Ayamonn. Like his "dear friend" he is one who cannot be intimidated. For the sake of what he believes to be the truth he is willing to risk his position in the church.

It is the universality of the Rector which makes him and his parish church a focal point in the time of crisis after Ayamonn himself is removed from the scene. Yet his universality, as he knows himself, is only a partial and passive thing compared to Ayamonn's. The Rector shelters the people, as Ayamonn did (still more all-embracingly) in his flat, but he cannot inspire them and lead them as Ayamonn does. He is the outsider-sympathiser, the bringer-of-warnings to those who actually go out to battle. This limitation is both objective and subjective. His bourgeois position and background prohibit him from finally grasping the nature of the working people as the heirs to all that is human. He cannot get beyond a vague apprehension of what is at stake. Standing on the Liffey bridge with Inspector Finglas, he says, "Ayamonn Breydon has within him the Kingdom of Heaven. *(He pauses.)* And so, indeed, may these sad things we turn away from." (280) And at Ayamonn's death –"Oh, Lord, open Thou mine eyes that I may see Thee, even as in a glass, darkly, in all this mischief and all this woe!" (307) As a pillar of the church, he, like Brennan, has a stake in the preservation of the status quo. When the latter asks if the present disturbance will shatter the community he answers, "I hope not." The result of this inner contradiction is that, at the very moment of decision in the class conflict (Act IV), he retires to the vestry to drink tea.

The two Railwaymen in Act II and the three Workmen who move quickly across the scene in Act III have an important part to play in O'Casey's scheme. He added the episode with the workmen in Act III after the play was first published, and extended the railwaymen-scene in Act II in the late revisions. These men are only lightly individualised because their function is to indicate the collective energy of the emerging militant proletariat. They embody that new aggressive self-assurance and determination to act at all costs which defines Ayamonn himself: "*1st Railwayman (a little impatiently).* We've been warned often enough, sir; we're sick of warnin's; let them who come out to fight us, now, be warned, too!"[5] Whenever they appear a decisive step forward in the mounting struggle is indicated. It is their entry on to the centre of the historical stage as a dominant social and political force which permits Ayamonn to mobilise all that is best in himself and in others so that he can begin to take decisions and actions of crucial practical effectiveness without the least sign of hesitation. They ask Ayamonn what he would do with the notice proscribing the strike. He puts it in the fire. That is what they expected him to do.

The slum-dwellers are a remodelling of those strata of the "lower depths" already depicted in the collective images in previous plays. In a play like this one, which above all *depicts the process of the revolutionisation of the masses*, a more contradictory and therefore dynamic image of these "sunken" strata became imperative. The collective portrait of the masses as slum-dwellers functions at two levels. First, it is a model of a specific part of the people– the semi-proletarian urban strata, consisting of hawkers, casual workers, long-term unemployed, etc. As such they are something relatively different from the proletariat proper. The latter was new and numerically still small. It is the "slum-dwellers" who represent the traditional mode of existence of the mass of colonial urban working people. To move the masses in a situation like that of Ireland you have to know how to move these people! Their depiction at this first level is therefore essential to the play, given its theme.

At the second level they epitomise certain basic aspects of the working people of Ireland as a whole, and therefore encompass within their image all the other characters and groups from the common people shown in the play. The binding substance between these two levels is that traditional plebeian-Catholic quality of consciousness developed by the old-style urban masses (level one), which still puts its stamp on the attitudes of the working people as a whole.

Ayamonn bases his song, "Red Roses for Me," which is in praise of the unique loveliness of Kathleen ni Houlihan, on a contrast between enshrouding darkness and a brilliant point of colour: "A sober black shawl hides her body entirely,/Touch'd by th' sun and th' salt spray of the sea;/ But down in th' darkness, a slim hand, so lovely,/Carries a rich bunch of red roses for me." (246)

If one pays careful attention to the symbolic use of colour-combination and brightness-darkness in this play it becomes clear that O'Casey is not necessarily indicating an *ideal* national type of beauty here, to be attained only at a later date through struggle; rather he is affirming a type of beauty characteristic of the people *now*—at least in an embryonic stage, a beauty which itself must become instrumental in bringing about the *victory* of beauty. Thus the colour-proportions in Ayamonn's song and those indicated in the image of the masses already have the beginning of an analogy in them. The slum-dwellers have set, mask-like faces. The men are clothed in drab brown, the women in a dull grey, but each of them has a patch of faded colour somewhere about their garments. It is the cultivation of the dulled ember of colour, the fanning of it from an unrecognised remnant into a veritable sun, which the play shows. In the course of the struggle these little patches flourish into "red roses" in the form of the sun-badge. At another level of symbolism the colour-patches represent the militant proletarians within the people's community—the potential which is fully developed in Ayamonn himself. If he is that patch of colour at first, he later blossoms into the sun-badge. He and his like are the bunch of red roses in Kathleen's hand. The royal robes worn by him and his mother during the rehearsal at the beginning are a kind of anticipation of the day when the modest patch will have become transformed into a gorgeous whole.

I have analysed the characterisation of these "secondary" figures at some length because they all point towards the central figure, Ayamonn. This is perhaps the most basic organising principle of the play. He is the focal point where their individual colours merge into one brilliant and variegated synthesis. He is not, as Kosok maintains, "a synthesis of all the mental attitudes dealt with in the play,"[6] but a confluence of all those best and most necessary qualities which are otherwise extant only in a scattered, self-contradictory state.

I have tried to point out how each of Ayamonn's friends, with the exception of Sheila (see below), contributes something specific and essential to him, without which his totality would be incomplete. Thus in an important sense he is created by the community of the working people around him, an emanation of their revolutionary essence. In him they are able to recognise their own best selves in pure and unfractured form. Through his prism they are enabled to see themselves in others and others in themselves. The importance of this for the development of their class unity and the consciousness of their paramount claim to the title of Humanity needs no underlining. This universal man is the personified embodiment of that alternative, better possibility struggling to free itself in the masses themselves. Out of themselves they can provide all the raw material necessary to revolutionise the situation.

Their need of Ayamonn is made manifest in the fact that his flat has a magnetic attraction for them all. They begin to form promising constellations there, whatever their personal differences and petty quarrels may be. Ayamonn's flat and what it stands for is a more truly "catholic" church than the good Rector can provide in Act IV.

On the other hand Ayamonn needs them equally. His universality of character is a parallel to what he says about his artistic activities—"my life needs them all." (229)

Given this underlying theme of the play the "domestic" setting of the first two acts is right and proper, and essential to the larger social dimension of the great events taking place around it.

There is a glimpse of something true behind Finglas' defamatory remark that Ayamonn is "a neat slab of a similar slime," (280) yet it is inadequate even allowing for the insult. Ayamonn is not simply an arithmetical sum of the positive sides of those around him. In the others these qualities are always partly negated and distorted. In Ayamonn they are liberated from these contradictions. They combine and complement each other in such a way that the possibility of an intrusion of the negative features is cancelled out. Through this chemistry they are raised to a qualitatively new synthesis. They are, in Hegel's untranslatable terminology, *aufgehoben*.

Thus Ayamonn's need for beauty and art is not identical to his mother's need for beauty, as indicated in her tender solicitude for the flowers on her window-sill. The former is a development of the latter, but vastly more sophisticated and universal. The same is true of the relationship between his mother's willingness to sacrifice herself for neighbours and Ayamonn's passionate class loyalty and his willingness to sacrifice that which he values so highly—his life. Ayamonn's truly catholic breadth of understanding and acceptance is still clearly related to that of the "catholic" Protestant Rector, but it is far more all-embracing and concrete because it is free of the restricting elements present in the Rector. This process is often traceable in concrete detail. I have mentioned, for instance, how Brennan admonishes Ayamonn for underestimating the importance of "mere" money. Yet when Inspector Finglas says of Ayamonn that it wasn't a particularly noble thing to sacrifice one's life for a shilling, Sheila is constrained to reply that "Maybe he saw the shilling in th' shape of a new world." (310) So Ayamonn returns to Brennan's respect for what money can do at a far higher level of social awareness.

Perhaps the most important example of Ayamonn's ability to pick up aspects of the people's world-view and "refine" them is his profound belief in the poetic spark of humanity at the heart of the downtrodden. This is expressed in all his doings and in that much discussed tendency to extravagance in his speech. Ayamonn's belief in this spark is epitomised in the half-hidden bunch of red roses held by Kathleen in his song. It is the driving force behind his rousing of the people on the bridge. At a certain level of generalisation he holds this belief in common with all his religious friends (he himself is a practising Christian). The others conceive of it in the traditional religious sense of a "diamond-core of an everlastin' divinity" in man. They cling to this in the teeth of all the misery and alienation in which they are sunk. Mullcanny is cast into the wilderness for mocking it. Like Jack with his mother in *The Star Turns Red* and unlike Mullcanny, Ayamonn understands that there is something profoundly true and essential in this achievement of Christian culture, which must be cultivated if the working people are to win the self-confidence necessary to take over the world. However, under existing circumstances, where human dignity is denied and trampled upon, this assertion of man's godlike quality has degenerated into an empty parrot-cry which in fact helps to veil and perpetuate the existing misery. Worse–things have come to such a pass that the people are in danger of finally losing this belief in the "divine spark." The woman Eeada, sitting on the Liffey bridge, says drowsily, "This spongy leaden sky's Dublin; those tomby houses is Dublin too–Dublin's scurvy body; an' we're Dublin's silver soul. *(She spits vigorously into the street.)* An' that's what Eeada thinks of th' city's soul an' body!" (276) The alienations of capitalism and the teachings of the traditional churches have been responsible for this crisis of the soul. By a theological sleight-of-hand the latter have actually removed the "divine spark" to a place safely outside man, outside society, while still paying lip-service to its existence in the human soul. Thus the people worship this glory not in themselves but alienated from them in the church, its God, Saints and Holy Virgin.

Ayamonn sets out to free the human-divine spark from its alienated and mystified "exile" and return it to the people, so that Roory's assertion "We stand on the earth, firm, upright . . ." (267) will cease to be a ludicrous parody of the facts.

In this connection I would like to compare two actions which contain underlying parallels and contrasts: Brennan's painting of the holy statue and Ayamonn's "painting" of Dublin on the bridge.

The statue with its castellated crown is a traditional personification of Dublin. Brennan's small-scale act resembles Ayamonn's large one in that Brennan too, seeks to return to this "Dublin" her former regal splendour. It is a humane impulse and encouraging from a dogged Protestant. Kosok says that "The restoration of the statue hints at the possibility of a transformation in the life of the slum-dwellers [...] If the deliverance of the city is to follow, it too, will not be handed down as a miracle from on high but will also have to be brought about by human beings."[7] Admirable sentiments, but an inadequate interpretation. Certainly the people rejoice at their "protectress'" return. But the stage directions tell us that they come half-backing into the room, softly chanting a hymn, with the old look of resignation still on their pallid faces, staring backwards at the effigy (which is *outside* the room). (In this play Ayamonn's room—and the stage in general—often symbolise the arena of life.) They sing a prayer to the effigy in which they plead for the minimum: The "chance to live lightly/An hour of our life's dark day," and to be shown "thro' th' darkness, descending,/A cheerier way to die." (268) At once they begin to weave supernatural myths around the saint's return. Thus, far from grasping the transformation as being the work of human hands like their own, they attribute it to miraculous intervention. Instead of inspiring and encouraging them with the insight that their destiny lies in their own hands it confirms the mystification. The hope, the divine spark, remains outside them and their lives. Mrs Breydon is right in saying of Brennan that "He meant well, poor man, but he's done a dangerous thing." (256) He has strengthened the opium with which the people are comforted. Nevertheless, his action contains within it the embryo of Ayamonn's.

It may seem that Ayamonn's exploit on the bridge is the answer to the people's prayer to the statue, for he declares what they are experiencing to be "a passing hour of loveliness." (289) It is certainly a development of Brennan's idea, but it is the difference that matters. Ayamonn, their trusted fellow worker, uses perfectly *natural* means (the colours of the sunset) to help the people see their *actual* city and themselves in a *new* light: "Something funny musta happened, for, 'clare to God, I never noticed her shinin' that way before." (1st Man, 288) The city's "hidden splendour" (287) is revealed as *their* doing, *their* responsibility: "She's what our hands have made her. We pray too much and work too little [. . .] but her glory's there for open eyes to see." (Ayamonn, 285) The great exploit of the gathering struggle gives him the base from which to appeal to them to make the city really and fully their own at last and so liberate its hidden and potential beauty. Ayamonn begins by proclaiming–"Rouse yourselves; we hold a city in our hands!" (285) While a little later he says that the city is in God's grip. Thus God and the working people are identified, and so he de-alienates the divine spark and returns it to the people, at the same time fanning it up into a blaze. A process of demystification takes place, in which the deep-rooted popular concept of the "divine" is modified and built upon rather than confounded. It is "Brennan" combined with "Mullcanny" (the demystifier) in which the weaknesses of both are cancelled out.

Whereas Brennan's act confirms the people in their passivity, Ayamonn's activates them. In partnership with nature and the spirit of the strike he actually demonstrates before their eyes, through a kind of act of transformation, that men and women like themselves can change the world, and challenges them to take part in changing it. He shows them a perspective–"Young maiden, another world is in your womb." (287) What he shows them is not the cheerier way to die of their prayer, but a cheerier way to live, in which they will take possession of the earth. He succeeds. The visionary moment fades in its intense clarity, but leaves a vital residue. This is why Katharine Worth is very wrong indeed in saying that "The gods have come among the company as the fairies come into the pantomime to work miraculous–but fleeting transformations." [8]

These, then, are some of the uses of the universal, integrated man in the revolutionary struggle. Brennan and Roory both try, using the means at their disposal, to rouse the people on the bridge from their lethargy. They are rejected. They are too one-sided in themselves to save the situation. On the one hand they fail to combine the old visions, which in their traditional guise have lost their potency, with a new point of reference. On the other hand they have not lived in a way which has gained the people's confidence and respect. Ostrovski writes of the revolutionary–"He must so live [. . .] as not to be seared with the shame of a cowardly and trivial past: so live that, dying, he can say: 'All my life and all my strength was given to the finest cause in the world–the liberation of mankind.' "[9] This sums up the Ayamonn we get to know in the first two acts. His "private" sphere has been a preparation for this stepping on to the public stage.

But this dialectical process is also demonstrated in the opposite direction. Ayamonn in the first two acts is already the universal "exchange" of the others' best selves. But, on the whole, he does not yet succeed in bringing them together. In fact, for all his breadth and attractiveness of personality, he actually loses Sheila. There are reasons for this which are connected with the development of Ayamonn's personality, as we shall see, but it is objectively determined too. The sombre tone of deepening resignation among the slum-dwellers reaches its nadir at the end of Act II and the start of Act III. Against this background flares the lightning-flash of the workers' and Ayamonn's hardening resolution–again that colour theme of contrasting darkness and brilliance. In the course of Act II the struggle gets into its stride and has, on the objective social plane, begun to transform the situation.

It is on this basis of private "preparatory work" and public mass action that Ayamonn is able to unite and activate the slum-dwellers. "Public" events have provided the ground on which his personal qualities can be mobilised and potential powers changed into actual. It would be wrong therefore to show Ayamonn's success on the bridge as being solely the product of his on-the-spot rhetoric. In fact he achieves it with relatively few words. He moves swiftly from the almost matter-of-fact tone of his initial challenge (see p. 225) to emotion-charged images of the "hidden splendour" steeped in the colours of myth and saga. Ayamonn succeeds also because he is able to connect with this heritage. Unlike Roory he succeeds in injecting new validity and vitality into it by showing the present struggle to be, at last, the real and practical possibility of realising the cherished ideals and aspirations enshrined in this heritage. We must, he says, "pull down th' banner from dusty bygones, an' fix it up in th' needs an' desires of today." (287) In so doing he relies on what is there in the people themselves. The slum women may have become cynical about the great race of Irish prophets, saying they have degenerated to forecasting winners on the horses. *But prophets still run in their minds.* They may complain that the glory of Brian Boru and the old music has dwindled to the harp on the Guinness-bottle, *but their own talk still shows gleams of the old poetry.* Ayamonn *prophesies*: "Our sthrike is yours. A step ahead for us today; another one for you tomorrow. We who have known, and know, the emptiness of life shall know its fullness." (287) At this moment a shaft of sunlight cuts through the gloom and lights up Ayamonn's head so that it looks like that of the old warrior-prophet Dunn-Bo.

Degeneration had begun to spread into the sensibilities of the people. The older women's coloured vision of Dublin's former splendour is marred, ironically, in the same way as the harp of Brian on the bottle, of which they complain. They associate this spendour with the gaudy uniforms worn by their British-soldier gallants of bygone days. But in young Finnoola, from the wild Cork valleys, the vision and the healthy native colour-scheme is still clear. The uniform for her is the patched coat and white face of the Irish rebel, for "their shabbiness was threaded with th' colours from the garments of Finn Mac Cool of th' golden hair." (281) It is on this that Ayamonn builds, showing how the militant transport workers are made of the same old heroic stuff: "Look! Th' vans an' lorries rattling down th' quays, turned to bronze an' purple by th' sun, look like chariots forging forward to th' battle-front." (288) On a wave of awakened emotion Finnoola cries out as she dances with Ayamonn—"The Sword of Light is shining!" (290)

We have already seen how Ayamonn's success on the

bridge depends on his possession of the "Mullcanny dimension" in combination with the Brennan idea. It is now clear that it depends equally on his being able to combine his militant class-consciousness with his "Roory dimension"—his attachment to the revolutionary traditions of Irish national culture.

Synthesising all these components, and in tune with the forces of nature, epitomised in the sunset, Ayamonn carries the people with him into an emotional climax in which they burst into dance and song in celebration of themselves and the city which they pledge to free. Ayamonn, like his creator, trusts and builds on the deep emotionality of the people.

Something approaching a catharsis is evoked both in the stage-world and in the audience. In the course of it the mask of inevitability and perpetuity is torn from the "every day," the "ordinary," so that it emerges as in fact surprising, extraordinary, in need of and capable of being changed —exactly what Brecht sought to achieve with his alienating-effect which was aimed against catharsis! Catharsis, then, can be used to the same ends as its "opposite," the A-effect. In a functional sense catharsis can *be* an A-effect!

The bridge-scene works on three levels. First, it brings forward the personal story-line (Ayamonn in his developing relations to the masses). Secondly, it is a kind of concentrated metaphor epitomising the action of the play as a whole (the revolutionising of the Dublin working people). As Pauli points out[10] it is the first of these parable-acts of O'Casey's in which a process is portrayed. At the third level it symbolises the strategic world-historical process of the revolutionising of the popular masses as such; i.e. it generalises on the specific action shown in the play and indicates that larger perspective which the action itself cannot portray directly.

In creating this kind of visionary scene displaying the victory over alienation O'Casey had a tradition in revolutionary literature in English behind him going from Thomas More through Shelley to William Morris and Walt Whitman. In many ways this scene is like a part of Shelley's

Prometheus Unbound brought down from the sphere of myth into the actual world in which "the loathsome mask has fallen." [11]

Ayamonn, then, is, like O'Killigain, the adequate hero, the missing link. It is his absence in the world of the earlier plays (dealing with the situation after the decline of the Larkinite movement) which leaves the people unmanned and ripe for disaster. Ayamonn is the synthesis of all the strands of that alternative possibility which go tragically a-begging in the "Dublin" plays. He is that other road, inherent in the situation, played through to its logical conclusion. He is the true marriage of Boyle's capacity for dreaming and Juno's sane realism. He is Jack Clitheroe sacrificing his "family happiness" and his life for the right cause. He is the Dreamer, no longer out in the cold, but given body and effectivity by being integrated into the actual working-class movement. Nevertheless, there is perhaps something in Pauli's criticism that "O'Casey gives the figure relatively limited scope for action to show, besides the magnitude of his decisions, the difficulties involved in the making of them." [12]

How does Ayamonn happen? If one fails to indicate the causality of this process then he must appear as a kind of lucky contingency, a sort of superman. Some of the dynamics of his making have already been indicated. There are three more points in this connection.

First: In the other working-class characters and their relations the basic prerequisite for a development towards universality is already there. O'Casey is careful not to present them simply, with each of them possessing one particular facet not possessed by the others, but in their complexity. Almost every one of them contains a constellation of at least two of the necessary positive qualities in combination. For instance, both Mullcanny and Roory are also loyal trade-unionists; Brennan has a similar warmth of humanity to Mrs Breydon, etc. Thus they are not closed and self-contained "systems" but open-ended and providing possibilities for further extensions in various directions.

In this sense each of them is already an Ayamonn in embryo.

Secondly, it is made clear that Ayamonn owes a decisive debt to his mother—"when it was dark, you always carried the sun in your hand for me; when you suffered me to starve rather than thrive towards death in an Institution, you gave me life to play with as a richer child is given a coloured ball." (232)

Thirdly, Ayamonn, as a rich and unique personality, also takes the initiative in making himself. The most important thing here is his preoccupation with the arts and the cultural heritage, especially Shakespeare. In his passionate devotion to Shakespeare he has no "precedent." Like O'Killigain, Ayamonn the worker-leader is the new Elizabethan, the all-round Renaissance man of the modern world. In his unity of thought and action, poetry and life he turns naturally to the greatest of the Elizabethans. Shakespeare, always there behind the scenes in *Purple Dust*, here steps openly into the centre of the stage that is life. Only the class-conscious worker can be fully heir to the living Shakespeare. He sees himself as Shakespeare's advocate among his fellow workers, for Shakespeare above all is the one who can help develop the dull patch of colour in each of them into the full-blown rose—"they're afraid of Shakespeare out of all that's been said of him. They think he's beyond them, while all the time he's part of the kingdom of heaven in the nature of everyman. Before I'm done, I'll have him drinking in th' pubs with them!" (229) Ayamonn twice quotes Shakespeare at some length. The first is from the scene where Richard Gloster kills King Henry in the last act of *Henry VI, Part Three* (Ayamonn's initial rehearsal with his mother). The second is from *Hamlet*: "But I am pigeon-livered, an' lack gall/To make oppression bitter; or, ere this,/I should have fatted all th' region kites/ With this slave's offal: Bloody, bawdy villain!" [13] These give us clues to the kind of qualities that Ayamonn found in Shakespeare and wished to propagate.

In the scene from *Henry VI* Ayamonn rehearses *king-kill-*

ing. His mother comments, "Th' killin' o' th' king be th' Duke o' Gloster should go down well." (228) In costume, both of them practise being *kingly*—a dress-rehearsal for the day when the spot of colour will have flourished into a rose more glorious than those of York or Lancaster. In both quotations there is a drive to fuse thought and action, will and execution in a total, poetic response to the demands of reality. There is the courage and the energy to act, on the one hand, and contempt for all "moderation" and shilly-shallying when faced with the need to act, on the other. There is endless immoderation and boundless presumption. As Mrs Breydon says—" Well, I better take this fancy robe from off me, lest it give me gorgeous notions." (233) The passionate this-worldliness of Shakespeare, coupled with his force of imagination, are qualities that Ayamonn is heir to. His exploit on the bridge has his experience with the great realist behind it. This force and scope of imagination which can "throw a whole world in colour" (251) on to a canvas or the stage is the cement which fuses all the various parts of him into one coherent and cohesive whole.

True, his preoccupation with Shakespeare and the arts is at first double-edged. Initially there is a hint of self-indulgence in him. He scolds his mother for sacrificing herself for others but is himself not above sending her out into the weather on an "errand of mercy" so that he can enjoy Sheila's company alone. His artistic doings seem to foster this. He is tempted to shut himself and his beloved Shakespeare off from the very people who, he declares, are most entitled to him. Explaining his pretence that he wasn't at home, he tells Sheila that he was doing his Shakespeare part and didn't want to be disturbed. At the outset he often betrays romantic and unrealistic attitudes, as if he were in a kind of self-intoxication of goodwill and facile optimism engendered through abandonment to the effects of art too little tempered by experience. The "romantic" element in his attitude to money has already been noted. Another example is his initial conviction that there will be no strike and that the men will win without a fight. Others know better. He underestimates not only the bosses but the forces of ignorance and prejudice when he says of Mullcanny that no harm will come to him because the people have enough sense to take what he says in good part. Others are more realistic. The very person (Sheila) who he thinks is his dearest friend is the only person from the people who has no part in his composition. He creates a Sheila through his romantic imagination who has little to do with the real Sheila. Answering his mother's objections to her he says, "Everything, it seems, is against her, save herself. I like herself, and not her faith; I want herself, and not her father." (231) Admirable Renaissance sentiment in the spirit of *Romeo and Juliet*, but dangerously naive in the actual situation. He sees, at times, not his real mother, but a figment of his own sentimental creation—"A well-tried leaf, bronzed with beauty, waiting for a far-off winter wind to shake it from the tree." (232–233) His mother (a sturdy woman of no more than fifty) promptly deflates him. Often that heightened rhetoric which so many critics have found fault with in Ayamonn is partly associated—in the earlier scenes—with his romantic illusions. He is still in the teething stages rhetorically, sometimes trying out his "bronzed" imagery on unsuitable objects. The frequent debunking or relativising retorts of the others act as a kind of alienating-effect here, as when his mother comments, "Ah, go on with you, Ayamonn, for a kingly fool." (232)

All this makes nonsense of Kosok's claim that "Ayamonn [. . .] shows no weaknesses."[14] In fact he goes through a marked development. When it comes to the crunch Ayamonn puts all these self-indulgences behind him, and, in the course of the struggle, it is these very qualities gained from the cultural heritage which stand him in such good stead. At the outset there was just a possibility that Ayamonn might succumb to the "Davoren-alternative." As Krause says, "Thematically, Ayamonn's situation is somewhat like Davoren's in *The Gunman*; however, when Ayamonn's poetic aspirations are threatened by the chaotic world around him he becomes the man Davoren might have become because he is able to relate his aspirations to that world." [15] In the situation created by the class struggle, art and life can come together through Ayamonn's entry into the centre of the arena.

In the society he lives in art and life have been the prince and princess of the German folk-song, who could never meet together because the water between was too deep. This and its overcoming is an underlying contradiction and theme of the play. Ayamonn and the Constable reproduction which he longs to have epitomise this split. They cannot come together as things are but only through winning the magic shilling in the struggle. There is a fear and distrust of art among the people. Ayamonn's song, dedicated to Sheila, disturbs and annoys her. The loungers on the bridge feel a disquieting challenge in Brennan's sensuous love-song and order him to get to hell out of it. The young singer, a man from the working people, when he comes to present "Red Roses for Me," is almost overcome with diffidence. He is loth to enter the room (life), and when he sings he turns sideways to his audience. To encourage him Brennan reminds him he's not in his working clothes now and is an entirely different man as a consequence. (245) Art and daily life seem mutually exclusive.

But at the high point of the revelation on the bridge, which is also the moment of entry of the slum-dwellers into the mass struggle, art and the masses, the prince and princess can come together at last. They break into dance and song. Ayamonn sings the first verses of his song himself, the rest take it up from the third verse—"We swear to release thee from hunger an' hardship,/From things that are ugly an' common an' mean;/Thy people together shall build a brave city,/Th' fairest an' finest that ever was seen!" [16] (290) The scene ends with voices, which, we are told, may be those at some distance, taking up this verse again. It spreads.

Shakespeare, then, is essential. But he is no foreign import. He is there already in their language, in their imaginative and passionate response to the world. The way Mrs Breydon, Brennan and the rest express themselves has, in

some ways, more of Shakespeare in it than there is in Ayamonn's often somewhat literary rhetoric. (O'Casey cut down
several passages of this type in his last revisions.) The job,
then, is to help the people recognise themselves in Shakespeare and Shakespeare in themselves.

In other ways too, the working people are the true heirs
to cultural tradition. Inspector Finglas, on the Liffey bridge,
reminisces prosaically about the great Dublin days of Dean
Swift as of something past and finished. He has no living
contact with this tradition—only a miserable hankering after the gaudy uniforms of those days. But the women, whom
he despises as ignorant dirt, are steeped in the living lore of
their city. They too, it is true, are in danger of having their
connection to it reduced to the Inspector's memories of military uniforms. Nevertheless, although they may never
have heard of Swift, his spirit moves in them still, in
their anger and irony against the degradation of their
city.

A few words to finish with on the general shape and proportions of the play.[17] The action of the first two acts is
confined, in typical O'Casey manner, to a slum flat. The
portrayal concentrates here on individual relations. The
"outside world" of social struggle moves in on this and
wins Ayamonn to its cause, away from those who would
keep him confined. The masses at first appear only spo-
radically and are scarcely individualised. In the form of
the slum-dwellers they appear as the passive playthings of
events and tend to avoid the centre of the stage. Act III
expands to encompass the city as a whole. The submerged
masses have come out on to the streets, and are on the
bridge leading to the distant shore across the deep water.
Ayamonn, the individual hero, and the mass now share the
centre of events and the stage. The mass now begins to
shed its monolithic anonymity and assume individual faces.
The process begins by which they cease to be the passive
objects on which "forces" work. They start to take their
fates into their own hands. In Act IV there is a certain narrowing and reconfinement, but they are not driven back to

their hovels to live worse than before, as in the similarly shaped *The Plough and the Stars*. No one is the same. The Rector is discovered composing a subversive hymn and his resolution to stand up for the right has hardened. Even the slavish verger seems to have gained confidence, and, as for the two vicious Orangemen Foster and Dowzard, there is an almost impressive "presumption" in them, albeit towards the wrong ends. Eeada may say she repents following "that mad fool, Breydon," (306) but Finnoola, who should have been Ayamonn's rightful partner rather than Sheila, has gone through the fire for him and liberty. The individual hero makes only one fleeting appearance in this act, otherwise the whole stage, foreground and background, is occupied by the people, now much more individualised and at the same time socialised. The stage directions tell us that they now hold themselves erect, and, though their faces are still pale, they are set in firm lines of resolution. Each of them is wearing a golden-rayed sun-badge in the bosom. The faded patch of colour has changed into this. The spirit of the strike and the sacrifice of Ayamonn win over his mother and Sheila at last.

This was a true and valid sacrifice at Easter. Not those who died at Easter 1916 represent–in O'Casey's opinion–the true analogy to Christ's sacrifice to redeem mankind, but the sacrifice of those proletarian fighters at Easter 1913. Inspector Finglas, in his final attempt to woo Sheila, cunningly says: "Sheila, Sheila, be sparing in your thought for death, and let life smile before you." (311) In a formal sense this is the very argument used by O'Casey himself to justify those who turn away from the senseless "deaths" of those volunteers who went to war in *The Silver Tassie*. But the correctness of attitudes is always relative to changing reality. Ayamonn's sacrifice has been real. His heroic life should be honoured and his death remembered. The death of this true hero is not a burden grinding down the survivors. Finglas' argument is opportunist here, the tactic of a veritable Richard Gloster–not Gloster the king-killer but Gloster the gangster. Unlike Lady Anne in *Richard III*, Sheila repulses him—"Oh, you dusky-minded killer of more worthy men!" (311)

The poet Yeats wrote of Easter 1916—"all changed, changed utterly: a terrible beauty is born."[18] O'Casey puts against this—born of 1913—not an utter change and a terrible beauty, but a subtle change and a tentative beauty—the possible beginning of a real change. In an effort to teach where the true tradition lies O'Casey works out the "optimum possibility" inherent in the 1913 situation, a possibility which, in his view, went a-begging at the time.

Notes

1. *Drums Under the Windows*, op. cit., p. 572
2. Letter to the *Irish Worker*, Feb. 21, 1914, in *Letters*, op. cit., p. 40
3. The words in square brackets differ from those in the published versions of the play. They represent O'Casey's own last revisions which he sent to his G.D.R. translator, Otto Brandstädter, a few years before his death. In my remarks I have indicated the more important modifications. Wherever my quotations refer to the modified version I have indicated the fact. The late revisions do not change the overall shape and statement of the play.
4. The Christian name given to Mullcanny in the last revisions.
5. This is part of the additional dialogue added by O'Casey in the late revisions sent to Brandstädter. It is part of a longer exchange inserted into the text as it appears on p. 274 of the Macmillan edition *Three More Plays by Sean O'Casey*.
6. Kosok, op. cit., p. 214
7. Ibid., p. 205
8. Katharine Worth, *Revolutions in Modern English Drama*, London, 1973, p. 113
9. I have used the English translation of the sentences from Nikolai Ostrovski's novel *How the Steel was Tempered* as quoted by David Lambert in his novel *He Must So Live*, London, 1956, p. 96
10. Pauli, op. cit., p. 87

11. Cp. *Prometheus Unbound*, Act III, Scene IV, the lines begin-
    ning, "and soon / Those ugly human shapes ..."
12. Pauli, op. cit., p. 72
13. *Hamlet*, II, 2
14. Kosok, op. cit., p. 217
15. Krause, op. cit., p. 223
16. In the late revisions sent to Brandstädter O'Casey arranged
    the verses of this song differently from the order as in the
    published English versions of the play. He missed out the
    second verse, sung by "The Rest" in the published text
    ("We vow to release thee from anger an' envy"). Verse
    three ("Fair city, I tell thee that children's white laughter")
    he placed at the beginning. Thus the revised version con-
    sists of three verses, the first two sung solo by Ayamonn,
    the third by "The Rest together."
17. My remarks here are partly indebted to Pauli's interesting
    passages on this question in his chapter on *Red Roses for
    Me*, op. cit.
18. W. B. Yeats, *Easter 1916*

PART FOUR THE REVOLUTION
POSTPONED

The bourgeois critics have reserved their severest savaging for Sean O'Casey's post-war plays. There is much talk of failing creative energy, loss of judgement and control, the flogging of dead horses, etc. These plays have rarely seen the stage in the English-speaking world, and where they have, the productions have often been so inept as to be an added disservice to the playwright's reputation.

O'Casey's post-war plays are, chronologically speaking, the plays of his old age. But far from displaying a falling-off of power they in fact represent a new kind of high point in the sophistication of his own particular type of dramatic model.

The reality which they model had changed. With the opening of the cold war against the forces of socialism and democracy after 1945 the prospect of revolution, opened up by the fight against fascism, receded in countries like Ireland and Britain. O'Casey shifts his emphasis accordingly. The models of revolution are not dropped, but they take a different form—that of lyrical-dramatic fantasies, a sort of revolutionary-romantic anticipation of the inevitable revolt and victory of the healthy forces of youth and joy *(The Drums of Father Ned, Figuro in the Night)*. In the centre of interest, however, is the question: what is hindering the mobilisation of these forces and preventing their victory under conditions as they are? What is threatening to pervert them? The general answer is—intellectual, spiritual and bodily subversion, inquisition and terror, the essence of the cold war in its crusade against man's humanity. Once again O'Casey goes unerringly to the heart of the matter at this particular stage, and, in doing so with his characteristic realist intensity, he creates artistic models whose vitality outlives the particular situation.

In plays like *Cock-a-doodle Dandy*, *The Bishop's Bonfire*, and *Behind the Green Curtains* O'Casey reveals where the real campaign to grind down the human spirit is being practised—not in the lands of socialism, but in the dear little Emerald Isle and the world of capital for which it is a metaphor. The return to medieval obscurantism commonly called the cold war was the chief threat to the soul of man and there was no better object on which to illustrate this truth than the state of "independent" Ireland. There, cold-war strategies, effected mainly through the hierarchy of the Catholic Church, merely aggravated a state of affairs already of long standing. There, a witch-hunt against all forms of spiritual, intellectual and bodily "sin" had been going on for so long already that it had had time to bring forth its fullest blossoms, its subtlest, most insidious ramifications.

The state of political awareness displayed by the mass of the characters in these plays is low. This and the lack of acknowledged and effective leadership leaves them vulnerable. Proletarian and socialist forces do appear and take action, but, as yet, they are too small and isolated to be able to put their stamp on the situation. This is a true representation of the relationship of forces in Ireland at that time when the trade-union leadership, on the whole, had more in common with a lackey than with Larkin. Nevertheless, the Communist who does appear directly (Beoman in *Behind the Green Curtains*) contributes an essential touch of enlivening red to the colour spectrum of the plays. Another handicap for the Irish was that they had not participated in the anti-fascist war as had, for instance, the British people, alongside the socialist Soviet Union. Thus their resistance to anti-socialist subversion was exceptionally low.

Be that as it may, in these plays, to an even greater extent than before, the presence of their own revolutionary traditions is made to shine through the superimposed mental degradation. One witnesses them spontaneously producing the basic "stuff of revolution" at the very moment when they seem most totally and finally cowed—the historical hallmark of the "indomitable Irishry!" If things do not shape themselves towards a revolutionary situation it is certainly no fault of the masses as such.

O'Casey intends this portrait as a sign and an inspiration to all peoples labouring under the same "mental manacles," and also as a counter-blow to the slanders on the human race issuing from the well paid poison-penmen of his world.

Four plays will be dealt with in this section–*Cock-a-doodle Dandy*, *The Bishop's Bonfire*, *Behind the Green Curtains*, *Figuro in the Night*.

IX COCK-A-DOODLE DANDY

Written 1947–9; published 1949; produced 1949 (People's Theatre, Newcastle-on-Tyne)

> "The cock that fights and runs away,
> will live to fight another day."
> Sean O'Casey

With *Cock-a-doodle Dandy* O'Casey opened his series of plays modelled on the contemporary situation in "independent" Eire. In its thoroughgoing synthesis of the historically specific and socially individualised dimension with symbolism and fantasy in the image-making it is perhaps the most complete expression of O'Casey's dramatic programme. O'Casey says, "It is my favourite play; I think it is my best play—a personal opinion."[1]

The play's three Scenes are set in the garden of Michael Marthraun's house in Nyadnanave, a rural district in Eire, run down and parched. The time the present. In Scene I Marthraun and Sailor Mahan meet in the garden to discuss business: Michael over sixty, grim and prim; Mahan fiftyish with still a touch of the old salt. Formerly a small farmer, Michael now owns a lucrative turf-bog. He has become Councillor and Justice of the Peace. Mahan owns the carting firm which transports the turf. The older man is disturbed: the house has been full of evil whisperings ever since lovely Loreleen, his daughter by a first marriage, came back from England to spend her holidays. (Michael got his new wife, young Lorna, and the bog for fifty pounds to be used to send Julia, Lorna's crippled sister, to the shrine at Lourdes.)

The two small capitalists haggle over the price of transporting the turf. Two Rough Fellows who work for them arrive with the threat of a strike for higher wages and better conditions. The workers flirt with Loreleen, but when they go to follow her they see her change, to their consternation, into a cock. Black magic is abroad, warns Shanaar, the local "ancient." A mysterious fowl gets into the house,

causing alarm and disorder. Prostrate with fear the capitalists send Marion, the servant-girl, to fetch Father Domineer,
the parish priest. Her lover, Robin Adair (the Messenger),
brings Marthraun a telegram which he is too agitated to
read. Robin enters the house and leads out a cock of more
than mortal attributes. It has destroyed Marthraun's new
top hat, bought to wear when he greets the President of
Eire, due on a visit. Shanaar preaches against materialism
and women and goes to alarm the Civic Guard. A crowd
gathers to give Julia a send-off to Lourdes. Father Domineer
arrives to take charge of the proceedings which include the
mayor and mace-bearer.

Scene II. Later. Marthraun and Mahan are now discuss-
ing, not business, but whether God would deign to notice
the prayers of a place like Nyadnanave. Mahan maintains
that only important people like Bing Crosby have heaven's
ear. More wonders—their chairs collapse simultaneously,
their whiskey is bewitched. They threaten the contemptuous
Robin with jail if he doesn't stop kissing Marion in public.
Marion says she'd like to make a wreath of roses to put
round the cock's neck.

A porter arrives with a top-hat replacement. *En route* a
hole has been shot through it by the Sergeant when it had
turned into a cock. Thunder and lightning. The hat changes
back into a cock before their eyes, then disappears. Mahan's
recurrent scepticism is being worn down. The terror-struck
men blame the "gallivantin'" women and the evil influence
of books. A Bellman, in fireman's garb, orders the people
into their houses, for "Th' Cock's comin'! In the shape of
a woman!" At Loreleen's call all the women come out of
the house dressed in carnival costume for the ball that
evening. They enchant the men, and drink to the cock from
the whiskey bottle, as do the men who are seized with a
delightful euphoria. The two employers vow to forsake personal gain and cooperate for the weal of the nation. The
men and women dance in couples.

Domineer enters to a clap of thunder. The cock crows.
All except Loreleen stop dancing and prostrate themselves

before the priest. He orders Mahan to get rid of Jack, his best driver, because he's "living in sin" with a woman. Mahan refuses. When Jack comes to inform his boss that the turf workers have gone on strike (this was the message in the unread telegram), Domineer orders Jack out of the district. Only if Mahan orders him to, Jack replies. Infuriated, the priest strikes him dead, and intimidates everyone, except Robin, into agreeing it was an accident.

Scene III. Towards dusk. A hue and cry to kill the cock. The cock waltzes through the garden. Domineer arrives with One-eyed Larry to purge the house of evil spirits. Loreleen runs in, pursued by a mob, whereupon Lorna and Marion sally out of the garden. Mahan, alone with Loreleen, offers her money to help her get back to England; she agrees to meet him clandestinely.

Ructions in the house, tottering towards collapse. Domineer and Marthraun come out battered but "victorious," and order the women back into the house. Loreleen denounces Domineer, grabs her books, which he's threatened to burn, and makes off. The cock appears as she disappears, dancing to the faint sound of an accordeon. Enter the Sergeant: shooting, darkness, chaos. When the scene clears, Domineer and the cock are gone.

The two capitalists pick up their haggling. They quarrel and Mahan leaves in high dudgeon. Lorna angrily dissociates herself from her husband's money-grubbing. People come and report that Father Domineer has been rescued from the cock by some kind of a duck—or goose. A mighty wind springs up, whipping Marthraun, the Bellman and One-eyed Larry around the garden, in imminent danger of losing their trousers—much to the amusement of Robin and the women, to whom it is only a gentle breeze.

Domineer comes to rally his forces, followed by a mob, including the two Rough Fellows, beating and tearing at Loreleen. She was caught in a car with a married man (Mahan). The latter has been pelted back to his own house. Domineer orders the tortured girl out of the district. Lorna, Marion and Robin opt to go with her into emigration. At this point Julia arrives back from Lourdes uncured. Left forlorn, Michael asks Robin what he should do. "Die. There is little else left useful for the likes of you to do," he answers, and goes off singing a love-song to Marion.

Here O'Casey's penchant for the "loose," "episodic" structure seems at first sight to have got the better of his dramatist's discipline. We are apparently faced with a jumble of rather repetitive, semi-nonsensical "happenings" arbitrarily strung together to fill out a couple of hours. Unlike other plays in a similar structural vein such as *The Plough and the Stars*, *Oak Leaves and Lavender*, or even *Purple Dust*, the foreground action in *Cock-a-doodle Dandy* is not "stiffened" by being related to a large social movement in the background (the Rising, the Second World War, the gathering storm). The only shaping and uniting principle seems to be the vague common reference to the general theme—the conflict between the forces of Joy-in-Life and Death-in-Life. Imagination and fantasy seem to have run amok and put an end to all line and logic and to the possibility of any productive artistic modelling of life.

A closer examination reveals the play to be an object-lesson for aptness and virtuosity in the means used to organise and shape the particular statement it is making. O'Casey never made the same statement twice and never twice used the same "procedure." Each play is a challenge, in form as well as in content, to our preconceived notions of what drama is—also to our preconceptions of what an O'Casey play ought to be like.

To have put the events taking place in Nyadnanave in the kind of dynamic general context used in the other plays mentioned would have run counter to the basic statement that the playwright is seeking to make. He sets out to portray a situation marked, as a whole, by isolation, stagnation, self-repetition, discontinuity and provincialism. An apparently interrupted succession of *seemingly* arbitrary, repetitive episodes is a method eminently suited to bring this atmosphere out. Form melts into content and vice versa.

But how episodic is the total structuring of this play? Can one, as has been suggested, interchange and leave out episodes at will? To decide these and related questions we must try to retell the course of the action on a level at once more analytical and more generalised.

Scene I. Two small capitalists are finding great difficulty in getting down to business, i.e. cheating each other and exploiting their workers, but also getting a useful industry going. They are continually being side-tracked by superstitious fears implanted in them by the "wise men" of the Establishment (the "Missioner," Shanaar, etc.). The forces of burgeoning life, which they have been persuaded to fear, are stirring, especially since the arrival of Loreleen from the outside world. The other women are beginning to show a lack of due reverence for their Lords and Masters, the respectable menfolk. No longer willing to hide in the house, they look out of the window, come out on to the porch, etc. This growing repudiation of the way things are takes other forms too: the workers are showing signs of combining (the two Rough Fellows enter almost together), and they are determined to take up the class struggle for a life more like what life should be. Significant too, is the way the two workers interweave their awakening militancy with a gallant wooing of the lovely Loreleen. Two sides of the same coin—the lust for life. Ominous, however, is how superimposed fears get the better of them. But the *new magic* is potent enough to have smitten even Sailor Mahan. This spirit takes the shape of a magical Cock. He boldly enters the house, and leaves it again for places far afield. The objects of his attacks are the holy insignia of church and state: the holy pictures and the top hat. The house itself is undamaged. Inspired by him, Marion, alone at this stage, makes an attempt on the "ferocious chastity" of the men and wooes them for a moment almost into a state of normality. Thus, from the opposite pole and for other reasons, another force threatens to divert them from business as usual. But their ingrained fears quickly get the better of them when they see the horns on Marion's head. A new magic is abroad, a magic hinting that settled reality may not be finally settled. Modest miracles occur indicating that things can change.

At first the forces against life rely for their hegemony on their everyday "peaceful" instruments—stoking up mental stupification through traditionally accepted channels (the Missioner, Shanaar). But these, though still partly successful begin to appear inadequate: Marion is enchanted by the Cock; Mahan fails to respond satisfactorily to the old magic. So bigger guns are mobilised in the background: Domineer and the Civic Guard (the military). Domineer, chief witch-doctor-cum-witch-hunter, arrives on the scene at this stage to lend his authority to the strong medicine of the Lourdes carnival—supported by the ritual and paraphernalia of the state: the Mayor in his robes of office, etc. This reverses the tentative move towards a true integration and community and a false "community" is established through peaceful psychological persuasion functioning at full stretch. The old magic seems to have scored a victory over the new.

Scene II. The Lourdes ballyhoo has diverted the two captains of industry completely away from their real subject into the realms of Hollywood fairyland (Bing Crosby). The revolt of the women grows. Lorna too, now sallies out of the house and joins Marion in championing the Cock. All three women join forces with Robin Adair and make a combined assault on the abnormality of the men, mobilising all the weapons of life at their disposal: charm, carnival dress, music, drink, song and dance. Exploiting the situation in which Mahan sings a swashbuckling sea-song awakening in him memories of his past, they bring about a second moment of integration and normality at a higher level. The two captains of industry vow to leave off profit-hunting and to work together for the good of the nation, i.e. they begin, as organisers of production, to overcome their bourgeois character. A taste of liberated living immediately implies potential revolution. Alarm.

The forces of anti-life become more aggressive in their counter-campaign. Mass hysteria is spread through the com-

munity at large against the Cock and women (by the Bellman, here the media). The armed forces (Sergeant) are
swung in alongside continued "peaceful" subversion, and
threats of state repression are issued (jail threat to Robin).
On the other hand the forces of life step up the magical confusion of their enemies through ever more unexpected *transformations*. Domineer must now enter the lists earlier and
more directly. His magic and that of the Cock confront each
other. Again he succeeds in blasting the dangerous moment
of community in the bud. But Loreleen now defies him to
his face. Mahan too, still under the influence of his euphoria
refuses to knuckle under to Domineer's interference in the
relations between him and his workers, while the bog-work-
ers themselves now go on strike. The strike might have
been avoided if Marthraun in his confusion hadn't forgotten to read the telegram. Faced with the new-type revolt of
the worker Jack, Domineer is driven to naked murderous
violence (kills Jack), an interference which completely distorts the development of normal relations between employer and employee. Physical terror has been given the
green light. The mood darkens.

Scene III. Dusk. Now church and state go hand in hand
in the total mobilisation of all the forces of reaction. Hysterical chaos everywhere. The two men of business break
off their negotiations and part enemies. The Cock effortlessly evades its adversaries. Mahan, still in open rebellion,
shows signs of combining with Loreleen. In the process he
makes an even more determined attempt to re-establish living contact with his more adventurous past—this time
through acrobatic feats. Taking its cue from Domineer, the
mob goes over to physical violence in its effort to tame
Loreleen. But there is a new decisiveness now in the other
women. They take the next step in their "geographical"
progression—out of the garden (together) to face their common persecutors. Backed by mob violence Domineer intervenes even earlier than in the previous scenes. He enters
the house (a typical composite O'Casey metaphor meaning
sometimes Ireland, sometimes tutelage, especially that of

the women). It has now been more or less abandoned by the women. His witch-hunting leaves it in a state of collapse. But the old magic, combined with terror, seems to be gaining the upper hand. At once the women are banished back into the house. Again they beat a partial retreat, but Lorna quickly raises her rebellion to a new level by taking decisive action: she breaks with her husband's way of life.

The magic forces on the side of Joy-in-Life and the Cock also step up their campaign, whipping up a storm and, for the first time, laying violent hands on Domineer (his abduction by the Cock). The forces of the inquisition are thrown into disarray. Domineer makes his last dramatic entrance to rally his demoralised cohorts. In his wake the mob initiates a second and more violent witch-hunt against Loreleen and Mahan. The Sailor is cowed, it seems, but not Loreleen. The mob hysteria has now gripped the two Rough Fellows. These one-time admirers of Loreleen are turned into her chief persecutors. The strike and the cause are forgotten. But nothing can hold the united women. From repudiating these men morally they repudiate them physically by taking the next decisive step in widening their radius—together with Robin they will step out of the country altogether. Thus all the human forces on life's side have come together to act in unity. So although they are forced physically to vacate the field, the play finishes with a rallying and a new solidarity among the pro-life forces. The escalated exertions of their enemies to cow them have produced the opposite effect. For those who are integrated into the system the process takes place the other way round: the collapse of community, isolation, the destruction of hope (Marthraun, Julia). The treacherous charlatanism of the system's magic, the impotence of its "medicine" to do what the Cock's magic can do—cure the crippling of the people and restore them to normality—is indicated in Julia's return from Lourdes, uncured.

What emerges from this analysis is a highly sophisticated and original *formal organisation*. The division into three scenes now makes sense. Each scene and episode within the scene has its specific place and role in the rising *spiral structure*. Each circuit of this spiral passes over *a similar pattern of events* at a higher, more universal and more intense level as the dramatic conflict between the two antagonistic forces gathers momentum. The effect is cumulative.

Tracing the specific formal structure of the play in this way has led us willy-nilly to a recognition of the specific "content"—what it says about the world and how it says it are inseparable. In the following pages let us examine in more detail some of the salient points which have already emerged.

The Bourgeoisie, the Working Class; their Relations to Society and to Each Other

O'Casey has two bourgeois types not only because it facilitates the development of the action but because he was not willing to write the bourgeoisie off entirely as a potential force for progress under conditions prevailing in Ireland. Because of the specific history of Ireland as an oppressed colony fighting for its national liberation the local bourgeoisie had a) never had the chance to develop normally but had remained, on the whole, petty and aborted, and b) played a centuries-long and not inglorious part alongside the common people in the struggle for national liberation. When the so-called Free State was set up in 1922 this was the class which took over political power, such as it was. However it was not their militant traditions that came to the fore but their bourgeois lack of character. Quickly they assumed the paraphernalia of "respectability" to convince others and themselves of their worthiness and solidity. They were, as a class, so weak and uncertain (and objectively still so much under the tutelage of their British Big Brother) that even after they took over formal political power they still remained incapable of rising above the level of petty undertakings and squabbling among themselves, still failed to take their historical destiny into their own hands. Instead, they tamely allowed themselves to be tied to the cassock-strings of the Catholic Church. The archconservative, medievalist hierarchy of this church became the real power in the land. It pursued its own interests which were not those of the nation or even of the development of trade and industry. As Father Domineer says in reprimanding Mahan, "We're above all nations. Nationality is mystical, maundering nonsense! It's a heresy! I'm the custodian of higher interests. *(Shouting)* Do as you're told– get rid of him!" (186)

Thus, as O'Casey sees it, the Irish bourgeoisie, or sections of it, and the working class, have still got certain interests in common as regards furthering the economic development of the country, i.e. the breaking of this theocracy's stranglehold on the economic, political and intellectual life of the community. The witch-hunt does not confine its victims to the "lower orders." The play shows how the local bourgeoisie fail to face their responsibility.[2]

But the old traditions are there, and O'Casey, who never ceases trying to unearth hidden potentials, is out to help revitalise the savable and useful element in the Irish bourgeoisie. Reality does not necessarily have to go the way it is going. The alternative potential is there for a different, better road. Hence the need for *two* characters from this class.

Marthraun is clearly the "classical case." His relationship to his past (the past of his class in its better days) is too withered ever to bear fruit. In the case of Sailor Mahan the contradiction is taken into the personality itself. This double way of viewing the same contradiction had to be used because no significant part of the bourgeoisie had yet begun to take the alternative course. Despite the justified ridicule heaped on Mahan, the point is that he almost makes the grade. His fund of natural sense is strong and resilient and the Establishment has to pull out all the stops to break him. Twice–in his singing the sea-shanty and in his acrobatic antics–we see him making a real effort to re-establish relations with his adventurous "youth." These "reminiscences" have a different meaning to those of Captain Boyle; Mahan really *was* a sailor. The report of his collapse at the end makes sense in view of what one has learnt about him, but it is only reported, and, in this play, it is advisable not always to take reported happenings for gospel. The thing to emphasise is that, given even slightly more favourable general circumstances, Mahan has the material in him to take not a leading but a useful place in the people's front. The difference between the two men seems indicated in their surnames. The word "man" is hidden in both, and in both it is split and mutilated—in the case of Marthraun almost beyond recognition. The two types of undertaking in which they are involved also brings out the difference. Marthraun, the stick-in-the-mud, owns a bog, while Mahan, the one perhaps capable of movement, owns a fleet of lorries. Taken together they are a logical projection of one possibility already inherent in Brennan o' the Moor.

Their practical self-subjugation to the church *diktat* hinders and diverts the two of them from getting down to the job of being capitalists and of developing trade and industry. Mahan expresses his awareness of this when he complains, on hearing that Domineer is leading Marthraun to purge the house of evil, "Oh, can't they do first things first?" (192) The hierarchy is a rogue elephant, an alien Third Force bringing the normal development of relations between the classes into disarray. Through this interference the class struggle is aggravated artificially and perhaps unnecessarily. Thus the relations are worsened between two class forces which might conceivably still have some productive grounds for temporary cooperation. There is evidence the strike might have been avoided through compromise if Marthraun had read the telegram when he received it. But as he says, "The tension here put it out of me mind!" (187)

In contrast to the majority of O'Casey's earlier plays *Cock-a-doodle Dandy* is no longer set among the workers and plebeian masses of the city but in a backwoods country district. This shift is characteristic of most of the later plays set in Ireland. It is not a retreat into a traditional setting on O'Casey's part but is his response to a retreat forced on society by those in power. Irish society had been pushed in the direction of provincialism, stagnation and obscurantism. This state of affairs could be best epitomised in the image of the backward village. At the same time the country milieu gave the dramatist the opportunity of working up a picture of the forces of nature as the embodiment of those vital energies and objective laws which he sets against the destroyers of life.

In this stagnant bog the same pressures and forces which confounded the bourgeoisie also hindered the working class from developing normally and playing the role it ought to play. The Soviet critic Sarukhanyan is right in pointing out that O'Casey was giving a balanced picture of the actual relations of class forces in introducing the workers and their struggle as an episode only.[3] Nevertheless, within these limits, the image of the workers in the world of Nyadnanave is important and complex.

They are portrayed at two levels: that of the two "rough fellows," and that of Mahan's lorry-driver, Jack.

The Rough Fellows represent the rank and file just emerging out of their peasant background (many of them are turf-diggers). Two potential avenues of development are indicated: the adjective "rough" should be understood to mean, initially, still to be worked out, unhewn as yet; later it means simply brutal. The first possibility indicated is the healthy, normal way, which, as part of the general upsurge of cockiness, they seem to be taking at the outset. There are the beginnings of class-consciousness, unity and self-respect. They have no illusions about the "fellas" who employ them. Like the capitalists (among themselves) they too, haggle with their opponents over a shilling. But to them, as to Ayamonn and the workers in *Red Roses for Me* the shilling is not just a mite added to dead cash-enrichment, but the key to the kingdom of life. Perhaps the most significant thing is the fusion of their militancy with this lust for the good things of life, whereby they do what Mahan wishes their "betters" would do—they put first things first: "*2nd Rough Fellow (to Loreleen)*. Wait, lass, till I'm done with these fellas, an' I'll go with you till youth's a shadow a long way left behind!" (130) They, more than any other figures in the play, have the same basic grasp of how things are, the same poetic relationship to reality and the same eloquence to express it as O'Killigain and O'Dempsey in *Purple Dust*.

Tragically, the potential beauty and strength of these men is marred and spoilt, for it is in the opposite, second possible direction that these two rough blocks are in fact hewn. The superstitious fear of women and sexual freedom instilled into them by the "Missioner" gets the better of them just as they are setting out to "ketch up on th' fine, fair lady." (131) Instead of bearing her by the hand they are soon reduced to bearing the crippled woman, Julia, on her litter (i.e. supporting the sick way-things-are). The horrible but logical conclusion is their "leading" role in the witch-hunting and physical injuring of that same fine, fair lady whom they had once pursued with soft words in the full flow of their militancy on the side of life. Thus they are led astray from the proper pursuance of the job in hand—their strike and their cause. Enterprises of great pith and moment are turned awry and lose the name of action. Ironically, the free time granted them by the strike to achieve some elbow-room for living is misused by them to constrict life, as they themselves have been misused. Being hitched to the band wagon of the witch-hunt has corrupted their best impulses: instead of their initial brave stand so as to gain money to live a more human life, they have been reduced to robbing Loreleen of the money given her by Mahan to make her escape.* The last we see of them they are still "united" in bearing up the dying body of Julia. Yet here again, given certain quite conceivable shifts in the total relations of forces in the play, these two could have taken the better road and themselves have helped to modify these

---

* The attitude to money and the use it is put to again constitutes one of the many hidden systems of contrasting parallels. Compare for instance Mahan's willingness to sacrifice part of his profits for the sake of Loreleen and life with Marthraun's "gift" of the £ 50 to send Julia to Lourdes and death.

relations so as to have created a more favourable general context for advance.

Jack, the lorry-driver, is much nearer the modern, mature proletarian. O'Casey describes him in his stage directions as a compact man with a sturdy, independent air about him. His face is weather-tanned and his clothing bears witness to a life of varied experience–khaki army trousers, an oil-stained cap, etc. He sports a well-trimmed moustache. Nothing rough about this fellow. The priest's moral *diktat* has no hold on this man. In openly "living in sin" with a married woman he is tugging at the central pillar holding up the whole edifice of moral taboos by which the oppressors seek to pinion society. In the same way Jack completely rejects the priest's usurped claim to authority in social and economic matters. In opposition to it, he makes a determined effort to clarify and preserve normal, uncluttered class relationships, in which neither priest nor questions of personal moral behaviour have any place: Domineer commands him either to leave the woman or the district. The lorry-driver ignores the ultimatum–"I come to speak with Mr. Mahan, Father." He goes on to explain to his employer in a precise and practical way how it came to the walk-out on the bog. Again Domineer interferes: "Never mind turf or tension now. Are you going to go from here?" To which Jack replies, "I'll go, if Mr. Mahan tells me to go." (all 187)

It is the realisation that here is something unprecedented and totally immune to his "magic," a threat against which his usual weapons are powerless, that makes the priest *lose control* and overreach himself. However, the fact that the priest can kill Jack and not really take the consequences also indicates Jack's isolation. Mahan stands passively by while his best worker is killed. And those others who should have been standing by him in his mission, the two Rough Fellows, are off on some wild-goose chase.

All through the depictions of the bourgeoisie and especially the working class runs the tragic implication of valuable energies misdirected and potentials wasted. These figures are, in their main tendency, individualised images of precisely placed social and national types. As a special component of the play's image-system one of their jobs is to provide the essential solid foundation, or point-of-reference to which the figures which function more on the symbolic-metaphorical plane can productively relate. The main member of this second category is of course the Cock, but Robin and the women, as far as they are personifications of the spirit of youth, rebellion, and the joy of life, tend to live with at least one foot in this allegorical dimension.

The Figure of the Cock

What is this Cock that struts through the action? Werner Hecht says in the notes to his *Cock* production at the Berliner Ensemble in 1971: "O'Casey uses a most effective means to comment on the superstitious hallucinations of the old-world people–he shows the things they conjure up in their minds actually happening on the stage. But they are only 'seen' by those who imagine them. Thus he remodels the idea of the emperor's new clothes, giving it a different critical function. By a process of *reductio ad absurdum* he delivers over the ideology of the church, which plays on the credulous fears of its believers, to the loud and liberating laughter of the audience [. . .] Our theatre can only stage the play in a way which will do O'Casey justice if we reject the idea that any objective marvels actually occur in it."[4]

With regard to the Cock, at least, this kind of interpretation does anything but justice to O'Casey's intention. It is simply not true that the more normal figures apprehend the Cock as an everyday piece of poultry. Marion and Lorna, both countrywomen for whom farmyard fowls hold no terrors, are frightened out of their wits by the Cock when it first invades the house. They cannot even agree on what sort of fowl it is. They come to terms with it when Robin, the Messenger, shows that it is "Just a gay bird, that's all. A bit unruly at times, but conthrollable be th' right persons." (144) It obeys Robin–crowing to the accompaniment of thunder and doing the Irish goose-step after him out of the garden. The women–not only the old men–apprehend all this. Marion follows, joyfully imitating the step of Robin and the Cock. Marion is enchanted by its cock-sureness: "Wasn't it a saucy bird! An' th' stately way he done th' goose-step! *(She playfully shakes Michael's shoulder)* Did you see it, sir?" (145) The Cock becomes their emblem, their ally and their champion. When the witch-hunters are out for the Cock's blood, Marion says that the place will lose its brightness if the Cock is killed. To reduce the Cock to a common-or-garden bird would mean ignoring or suppressing this whole celebratory side of the play.

O'Casey himself makes both the Cock's symbolic meaning and his function as a *dramatis persona* unmistakably clear: "The Cock in the play is, of course, the symbol of burgeoning life. We know this bird of old, for he's famous in poem and story, a mythological symbol. He is the symbol of life itself, of resurrection, courage, determination, of rising up, not lying down [. . .] in the play he is the scourge of all superstition and hypocritical palaver."[5]

In a way somewhat similar to Ayamonn in *Red Roses*, the Cock unites within himself qualities scattered in those around him—the quintessence of that cockiness existing in the women and in Robin, in the workers, and even to a certain extent in Mahan. This is the spirit which the obscurantists fear above all else and that is why the Cock must appear as monstrous to them.

Robin and Loreleen are most completely in tune with the Cock. It is quite possible that Loreleen changes into the Cock on occasion (but she has no monopoly of him). She and the Cock are never on stage at the same time. In her dress she comes nearest to his decorations. Her saucy bright-green hat is topped by a scarlet ornament reminiscent of a cock's comb. Robin, Marion and Lorna have similar, if less marked, cock signs about them. These people recognise their best selves in him and that is why they love him. He epitomises for them the synthesis of what they have in common and therefore the possibility and power of unity. He demonstrates this before their eyes, parading these qualities constantly before them. If one reduces the Cock to a farmyard fowl and to a figment of fevered imaginations, such a recognition and the resulting *activation* of the healthy figures would be unthinkable. For the Cock is the catalyst, "the crystallisation-point around which potential rebels against the superannuated state of affairs gather; in an apparently set and settled world he sparks off a process of polarisation."[6] He is, then, the detonator of the dramatic conflict, which he could hardly be if, as Pauli points out, he were "just another piece of poultry."[7]

For anyone acquainted with O'Casey's development there is nothing surprising or problematic in his use of fantastic figures and happenings. From the outset he had experimented with "non-naturalistic" images. The move from the symbolic to the outspokenly fantastic is easy and natural. It already takes place on a massive scale in the flood-image at the end of *Purple Dust*. What is new in *Cock-a-doodle Dandy* is that a fantastic image, now militantly independent of the prosaic laws of "everyday" life, steps right into the commanding centre of the action. The use of such figures by O'Casey is not a sign of the break-down of his realism but a proof of the truly popular roots of his realism. The art, literature and drama of the common folk is peopled with fantastic creatures, and what people and what tradition is more steeped in these things than the Irish. To a people brought up on sagas and legends in which the incredible and fantastic feats of giants and magicians are part and parcel of everyday life, the Cock will cause no consternation or embarrassment, even in his co-existing on one stage with apparently "ordinary" people bound by the customary laws of nature. Shakespeare, that other great rule-breaker and popular realist in English-speaking drama, has ghosts and spirits galore. The Cock clearly stands in one line with Ariel in *The Tempest* and Puck in *A Midsummer Night's Dream*. The Cock himself has a noble pedigree in the culture of the common people everywhere. O'Casey indicates some instances in the passage quoted above. The Cock became the symbol of the risen people in the French Revolution and their cap of liberty took on the form of his comb.

Everywhere he was the sign of reawakening life, rebellion, fighting spirit, fruitfulness and birth.

The Cock-figure enables O'Casey to deepen his realism because it allows him to uncover and highlight the hidden potentials for unity and liberation inherent in his community without forcing the socially concrete figures. These, as individuals, can remain true to the daily realities and yet at the same time be given a perspective and a poetic dimension beyond the limited concrete situation. O'Casey does not doctor or romanticise these figures in an effort to squeeze out his optimistic perspective from his material at "ground level." He refuses to manipulate the actual proportions and balance of forces in the sector and type of reality he is examining in order to win a hollow victory over this reality. The quality of the reality he is dealing with presents him with a problem. It cannot yield up its full revolutionary realist potential through the familiar historically concrete type of image imitative of the forms of everyday life–at least not through these alone. The raw material is too scattered, undeveloped and impure for this. The playwright must *add* something which will act as catalyser and focussing lense while leaving his uncompromising model of the real state of affairs intact, *un-added to*. This he does through inventing the fantastic figure of the Cock.

In creating this kind of image O'Casey is also making a virtue out of necessity. The type of under-developed and intransigent situation, of which Nyadnanave is an artistic model, calls for *heightened* means–symbolism and fantasy, to open it up, to "complete" it and place it in a wider context. It is a challenge to the creative imaginative fantasy of the revolutionary and realist artist.

The Cock has no complete equivalent among the individual human characters in the play. He is greater than each of them, than all of them, and at the same time he is less than they. He is greater because he embodies the unalloyed essence of their best selves. He is less because he is not wholly of this world but a fantasy-animal. This spirit finds no equivalent nerve-centre in the actual social world of Nyadnanave. O'Casey sets out to show that such a revolutionary point of mobilisation is necessary, possible, and, as an effectively functioning mass phenomenon, still lacking. The rising revolutionary urge is there, generated by the people, not out of promising premises, but out of the "desert." The fantasy-cock is an artistic brain-wave enabling him to do all these things. The relative "backwardness" of reality calls to life the fantasy-cock by force of necessity.

The Cock, in this form, is not enough. Despite his presence and undoubted effect, the people on the side of cockiness are physically defeated and forced to leave the field in the possession of their enemies. The implication is that to free themselves they must and can re-embody the spirit-cock in his human equivalent, re-integrate the "spirit" with the "flesh" in terms of real leadership and a mass movement. Thus for the Cock to be finally victorious he must be "abolished" in this sense.

In the shape in which we meet him in the play, that is as an unruly animal, the Cock also epitomises the as yet elemental and largely spontaneous level of the popular revolt. The anarchy of it in this form is also something which gets in the way of an ordered running and development of society. When no longer forced into this fantastic form these popular energies will flow in an ordered course from which even the capitalists might benefit. Thus the Cock indicates both the strengths and the weaknesses of the people.

The Natural and the Unnatural

There is another aspect to the Cock which still remains to be discussed. This is the Cock in his relationship to the forces of nature. He is simultaneously the embodiment of the human qualities we have discussed and of the dynamic, healthy qualities of nature as a whole. He marks the confluence and fusion of these two things. The Cock demonstrates that these qualities of the people are at one with nature. Thus a theme basic to *Purple Dust*, and present also in *Red Roses*, is picked up and developed.

The behaviour of the oppressors and those defeated by them is unnatural, an affront to nature. It is in this context that the sexual emphasis must be seen. O'Casey is not putting forward the thesis that sexual liberty is to be identified with liberty as such or that the female sex is necessarily the exclusive vehicle of the forces of joy and life. All this must be understood metaphorically. Sex and the battle round its inhibition or its natural expression—fear of it, or joy in it, is ideally suited to epitomise two diametrically opposed attitudes to what, in human beings, is pre-eminently natural, to nature.* Women become a metaphor for this natural dimension to humanity.

The obscurantists and their minions fill women, sex and nature with a thousand devils of their own making. Their fear of women is the expression of their fear of everything which is natural and self-assertive, not to be domesticated and cramped into the twisted moulds in which they hope to keep humanity imprisoned (see their unsuccessful attempts to confine the womenfolk to the house and thus cut nature off from nature). Once let sexual liberty and the emancipation of the women have their head and the flood-gates are opened. Let the natural and life-affirming win here and their whole anti-natural conspiracy against humanity begins to crumble. Thus the witch-hunting and exorcising in this play, purportedly measures taken in the interests of the security of the community, emerge, in being aimed first and foremost at the women as the source of all evil, as an attack on the very core of man's natural humanity. "McCarthyism" and the contemporary political inquisitions of the cold war are never actually mentioned but the implications can scarcely be overlooked. The nearest that one comes to an open tie-up is in the attack on reading and the burning of subversive books. But it is enough. The play provides a kind of middle ground where the identity between medieval witch-hunting and the persecutions of the cold war can be established.

* This will be discussed again in connection with *Figuro in the Night*.

In transforming nature into a hive of devils the anti-lifers are out to make the natural unnatural, turning it into a servant of their unnatural theory and practice, disregarding, distorting and vilifying its true nature and laws. In reply to this assault *nature itself becomes sentient*, begins to retaliate by taking an active hand in confounding and confusing the confounders. A general rising of the natural. This is surely a more positive and poetic understanding of the magical happenings in the play than to interpret them as mere hallucinations of the duped characters. To reduce them to the latter is to reduce the play's content to its critical-satirical aspect and to ignore entirely its celebratory quality. For O'Casey dramatic art is not only a critique but a celebration of life, and the metaphorical-fantastic dimension to the images is essential to this.

At first sight, however, there seems to be evidence to support the hallucination interpretation. Robin and the women maintain throughout (except with regard to the Cock of course) that they see nothing miraculous happening, and call those who witness these things "fools." But the fact that the miraculous Cock is there for all to see must give us pause.

There are two possible ways of interpreting things here. One: the women and Robin do not see these things as miraculous, not because they are not happening, but because nature has entered upon a private war with its enemies, in which the natural people are not directly involved. Their appreciation of what nature is capable of is so generous that even its most outrageous tricks seem normal to them. Two: they pretend not to see what is happening. In the stage-world of the Cock such a thing is perfectly feasible. It is significant, for instance, that when Marion grows the horns which so consternate the men, her "face has changed too, and now seems to wear a mocking, cynical look, fitting the aspect of her face to the horns," (150) of which she is supposed to be unaware. They are in cooperation with nature in this war. This interpretation makes a great deal of sense in the light of O'Casey's general concept of the relations between healthy humanity and nature (see also *Purple Dust*).

Nature, then, in league with its human representatives, begins to break its own accustomed laws, instead of having them broken by others. The world will not necessarily wag as it has "always" done. Nature and all those in tune with it have some unexpected novelties up their sleeve, in the form of *transformations*. So it comes to a battle of magics in the play, a battle well known in fairy-tale and folk-legend. In this competition of magics, that of the oppressors seems to win a victory, but it is a Pyrrhic victory whose ultimate hollowness is exposed in its failure to cure Julia. It is the natural magic of resurgent nature and humanity which is alone capable of healing (Lorna and Marion) and transforming.

Not all that apparently happens necessarily happens however. The play leaves room for real hallucinations too. A number of minor miracles are demonstrated to us. But an equal number are only heresay, for instance Loreleen's transforming herself into a Cock, and the whole business of Father Domineer's rescue by a bird of some kind. All this is merely reported, and decorated in the reporting. The argument about whether it was a white duck, a speckled duck or a barnacle goose casts strong doubts on the factuality of the occurrence, and at the same time gives scope for that strong Irish talent for legend-making. In Ireland the line between myth and reality has often been indistinct and mobile. The forces of stupification have all along tried to misuse this fertility of the imagination. In this case one has the impression that it is awakened nature which uses this faculty to confuse and unmask the confusers and the confused for the benefit of the living people in the play and in the play's public. Nature provides a few wonders as tinder to their inflamed imaginations. The rest they do themselves.

It is a kind of revenge taken by the power of the popular imagination, by fantasy, against its misusers. Fantasy, functioning in the interests of the people, emerges as a powerful instrument for change. This is not only illustrated *in* the play, but *by* the play as such, in its brilliant use of the fantastic to juggle with apparently fixed and inevitable relationships. It is the ultimate extension of that alternative possibility hidden away somewhere and betrayed in Captain Boyle's talent for "reconstructing" the world in his fertile imagination.

Domineer and his underlings do dirt on natural innocence. The green garden that should be a natural Eden, is parching into an arid yellow because of them. The image of the garden, with its associations with Arcadia, Eden, etc., has already been noted in *Within the Gates*. These associations with Arcadian pastoral in O'Casey's plays are discussed by Robert Hogan.[8] He draws attention to the silvan world of Robin Hood in the names of the young lovers, Robin and Marion. Michael Marthraun he identifies with a foolish satyr "who has cozened a young nymph into marrying him,"[9] etc. Certainly Loreleen, Robin, Marion and even Lorna have suggested connections with a golden age in which human beings and nature are in complete harmony. The poetic metaphor of an alternative and better society is embedded in this. It is from this "hinterland" that the forces of humanised nature draw their strength to resist and to attack. Hogan concludes however talking of *Cock-a-doodle Dandy*–"but finally the Pastoral figures go down to defeat. In this world the Pastoral is fighting a losing battle, for the world is already a Wasteland."[10]

This pessimistic interpretation leaves too much out of the reckoning. First, it separates man and nature in a way which runs counter to the whole spirit of the play. Yes, the human individuals might be locally defeated and driven from the scene for the time being. But nature as a whole cannot be defeated. The Cock is neither caught nor killed at the end despite the more and more massive mobilisation of church and state against him. He waltzes through the culminating scenes of chaos, leading them all a merry dance. Thus the forces of nature play with their adversaries instead of simply stamping them out. Their self-confidence seems boundless. It is there too, and rising, in nature's human representatives, in their growing contempt for their pastors and masters. It is as if they can no longer take these medievalists seriously. This is a sign both of weakness and strength. The play underlines that these oppressors have still to be taken very seriously. It is going to need more than making fools of them to defeat them finally. One function of our laughter at these goings-on is, as in the earlier plays, to make us ask ourselves upon reflection what on earth we were laughing at, to make it clear that these people cannot be laughed off the stage. This is the function of the combination of comedy and tragedy, for there is a dominant element of tragedy in the deadly results produced by apparently petty incidents. The discrepancy between the horrific results and their ridiculous beginnings acts as a shock or alienating-effect on us.

At the same time there is something tremendously encouraging in the playfulness, the sense of humour with which nature toys with its prey. It shows that these people and what they stand for are, like Stoke and Poges, historically superannuated, doomed. The Cock has his symbolic antagonist, the top hat, completely within his power. This is an important aspect of the play's implied perspective. Our laughter is therefore also our realisation of this. Self-assured nature, in the broad metaphorical sense, has this relaxed confidence because it has the flood from *Purple Dust* up its sleeve.

The victory in *Purple Dust* was, however, only gained by man and nature in total integration. Here the human side is compelled to leave the scene. It has been made clear in the course of the action that the anti-lifers cannot be defeated *by the spontaneous action of non-human nature alone*. So the local defeat of its human representatives means a temporary but real set-back for nature as a whole: in O'Casey's world men and women in aimed and organised action are nature's executive, and only through their practical revolutionary action can nature come fully into its own.

Does this mean that the human forces are banished for

ever from what might have been Eden? They go to "a place where life resembles life more than it does here." (221) The ending of *Cock-a-doodle Dandy,* like so many of the endings of the later plays, reflects the actual facts of life in Ireland, a country from which the youth emigrated *en masse,* leaving the old to stagnate. Is not all perspective destroyed by this?

First, one has to take into account the metaphorical implication of the ending. The play implies something not confined to Ireland, but valid for dying societies in general. The ending can be understood thus: life (youth, gaiety and beauty) turns its back on a social order ruled by Domineer (himself a metaphor for spiritual and bodily terror), refuses to go along with this form of society any longer. They take with them the seeds of a new and better world, which they will build in spite of all the difficulties and set-backs.

Secondly: for those who know their Ireland, the ending, even when interpreted on the more specific level of the Irish Republic, is not so pessimistic as might appear. Emigration has not always meant an unmitigated loss for the Emerald Isle. Those who leave take Ireland with them, and all through history great impulses for radical change have come back home from abroad: pride and self-confidence in the ability to beat the "invincible" oppressor from the exploits of men like Sarsfield and his "wild geese" against the English armies on the continent; the heart and brain of the rising of the United Irishmen, coming home with Wolfe Tone from his exile in revolutionary France; the spirit of the 1913 strike with Jim Larkin, returning from Liverpool; scientific socialism coming with James Connolly, the son of Irish immigrants, from Scotland; the experience brought back from fighting, as O'Killigain did, with the International Brigades in Spain; these savage plays themselves, launched by O'Casey from his English base. In the play, Loreleen is a returned *emigré* (on holiday) and it is she who brings with her the tinder which kindles the unrest. Ireland and the world have not heard the last of her and her friends.

Notes

1. Sean O'Casey, "Cockadoodle Doo," in *Blasts and Benedictions*, op. cit., p. 142; first published under title "O'Casey's Credo," in *The New York Times*, Nov. 9, 1958

2. Kosok interprets the Marthraun figure as a lesson to those who "grant" freedom to colonies before they are "ready" for it!—"O'Casey diagnoses in Marthraun a danger which has manifested itself in many countries: the rise to power of a social stratum which is not prepared for it and, as a result, believes every charlatan and follows every demagogue." (Kosok, op. cit., p. 273) This is surely the height of critical irresponsibility!

3. Sarukhanyan, op. cit., p. 90

4. Werner Hecht, "Über den Zauber," in Notate des Berliner Ensembles zu *Kikeriki*, dated Oct. 14, 1970; quoted in Pauli, op. cit., p. 159

5. From an original contribution by O'Casey to the printed programme of the Wuppertal Theatre's production of *Cock-a-doodle Dandy* (1960–61); English original not traceable; retranslated from the German by the present author.

6. Pauli, op. cit., p. 160

7. Ibid.

8. Robert Hogan, "In Sean O'Casey's Golden Days," in *Modern Judgements*, op. cit., *passim*

9. Ibid., p. 167

10. Ibid., p. 168

X THE BISHOP'S BONFIRE

Written 1954; published 1955; produced 1955 (Gaiety Theatre, Dublin)

> "Thy tree hath lost its blossoms, and the rind,
> Chopp'd by the axe, looks rough and little worth,
> But the sap lasts, and still the seed we find
> Sown deep, even in the bosom of the North;
> So shall a better spring less bitter fruit bring forth."
>
> Byron

Ballyoonagh, a small town somewhere in the Republic of Ireland, is on the verge of an official visit from Bishop Bill Mullarkey, one-time local boy. Canon Burren, the authoritarian parish priest, and Councillor Reiligan (who owns the whole district including its Member of the Dáil) direct the preparations. A bonfire of "bad books" is to be the centrepiece of the celebrations.

The action is set on an autumn evening, in the garden and drawing-room of Reiligan's pretentious house. Two masons, Richard Rankin and Dick Carranaun (known as Prodical) are building a wall round the Councillor's property. Rankin is a prayer-mumbling, sin-ridden, woman-scared tame Catholic working man. Prodical has more spunk but is given to the bottle and an unpredictable sense of sin. Their labourer, Dan Clooncoohy, and Keelin, Reiligan's younger daughter, are clandestinely in love. They too, are weighed down with feelings of guilt. Reiligan forces the vivacious Keelin to do household drudgery, while reserving Foorawn, the elder daughter, for prayer. Manus Moanroe, Foorawn's former lover, had begun to study for the priesthood, but had run away to serve as a fighter-pilot in the British air force during the war. Now returned, he works as Reiligan's steward, embittered at the state of Ireland and by Foorawn, who has taken a vow of perpetual chastity. Young Father Boheroe braves the wrath of Canon Burren, his superior, to encourage young lovers, as does old Codger Sleehaun, castigator of the status quo and Reiligan's gardener and general handyman.

Once again there is no strongly developed individual "plot." O'Casey sets out to display a whole society in its significant interrelations, where the course of events is not a straight, inevitable line from A to B but the result of a myriad of influenceable forces produced by the interplay of things as a whole, and can therefore appear as local discontinuity, as a series of seemingly non-organically related incidents. This dictates the "episodic," "discontinuous" structuring.

Act I. The Canon and the Councillor are hard taskmasters but as soon as their backs are turned things get sidetracked. The workers bicker among themselves about the possession of bricks or whether their "stattus" allows them to do a labourer's job. A keg of spirits draws some of them off behind the laurels; Keelin makes playful assaults on the "ferocious chastity" of Rankin, who has stayed behind; the Codger bursts a bag of cement on the new carpet. Lovers pursue each other instead of their "duty." Manus makes a desperate attempt to force Foorawn to confess her suppressed love for him. The contents of the keg inspire Prodical, Dan and the Codger to proclaim their dreams and demands for a better and happier world.

Act II. Dusk. The drawing-room is being prepared to receive the Bishop. The Codger and Prodical dump paint and a plucked duck on the polished table. Reiligan's son, Lieutenant Mick of the Irish army, tells them his patent plan to frustrate a Russian take-over of Ireland—every able-bodied manjack in U.S. jeeps with walkie-talkies. A distraught porter arrives from the station to deliver a statue of St. Tremolo, the Bishop's personal saint, but on the way the effigy had goaded him into hysteria by trumpeting into his ear whenever any thoughts of enjoying himself had entered his head. Rankin brings the effigy. Foorawn and the Codger do a secret dance till St. Tremolo withers them with a loud honking. Encouraged by Father Boheroe, Daniel and Keelin swear to fight for their love. The entry of the Canon, now a Monsignor, and Reiligan, now a Papal Count, blasts the moment in the bud. The "heroic" Dan caves in, but Keelin stays defiant.

Act III. The drawing-room is ready. Dark outside. Prodical and Daniel, both dressed in ill-fitting waiter's garb, do a take-off on the Bishop. Canon Burren bursts in, indignant at the goings-on in his absence. He announces their plan to marry Keelin off to the Bishop's brother, a "young active lad" a bit over fifty. Keelin demands her Dan. Reiligan orders his underlings to do menial jobs in the kitchen in preparation of the Bishop's dinner. Mutiny becomes general and there is a rising tendency to "carelessness" with the Councillor's goods. The Codger is sacked out of hand. Manus now reappears and announces that he is leaving the country. Most make for the bonfire. When they've gone Manus sneaks in and steals the money Foorawn has collected for the church missions. Surprised by Foorawn, he denounces her and priest-ridden, Reiligan-owned Ireland. As she attempts to phone the police Manus shoots her. Dying, she scrawls a note giving the impression that it was suicide and confesses her unaltered love for Manus. Manus slinks away as the flames of the bonfire rise higher. Codger and Prodical celebrate with whiskey in a corner of the darkened garden.

There are obvious similarities of theme and material here to *Cock-a-doodle Dandy*. A blazing centre-piece like the Cock-figure is absent however. The tone is more sober, even sombre on occasion, and the tragic implications are more fully worked out: A sad play within the tune of a polka, as the sub-title says. The role of the fantastic is reduced to the incidental interference of the trumpeting statue. Any massive intervention of fantastic powers here would run counter to O'Casey's aim of compelling us to make a sober appraisal of the difficulties facing the forces of life—which is now the aspect of the situation that he wishes to emphasise. We are again dealing with a microcosm-model, in the form of an allegory or extended metaphor, of a whole social system. This implies a high degree of symbolism in the figures and actions, and, in fact, *The Bishop's Bonfire*, the child of his old age, is one of O'Casey's most subtle and balanced syntheses of the heightened or symbolic dimension and the individual and everyday.

What is O'Casey's particular concern in *The Bishop's Bonfire?* This is the way he once put it himself: "Take *The Bishop's Bonfire*, for instance. It deals with [...] the great war between State and Church—they've always been antagonistic. The one has always tried to conquer the other."[1] Is O'Casey being purposely obtuse here? Surely the thing illustrated in this play is that church and state go hand in glove in their offensive against the people?

That depends on the definition of church. In a society like Ireland the clergy have never been seen as "the church" over against the laity. Rather the whole community of the people has been conceived of as the church:

> One point of Catholic doctrine brought out as a result of such examination is the almost forgotten, and sedulously suppressed one, that the Catholic Church is theoretically a community in which the clergy are but the officers serving the laity in a common worship and service of God [...]
>
> It seems to be unavoidable, but it is entirely regrettable, that clergymen consecrated to the worship of God, and supposed to be patterned after a Redeemer who was the embodiment of service and humility, should in their relation to the laity insist upon service and humility being rendered to them instead of by them [...] They have often insisted that the Church is greater than the secular authority, and acted therefore in flat defiance of the secular powers, but they have forgotten or ignored the fact that *the laity are a part of the Church*, and that, therefore, the right of rebellion against injustice so freely claimed by the Papacy and the hierarchy is also the inalienable right of the laity. And history proves that in al-

most every case in which the political or social aspirations of the laity came into opposition to the will of the clergy the laity represented the best interests of the Church as a whole and of mankind in general.

Whenever the clergy succeeded in conquering political power in any country the result has been disastrous to the interests of religion and inimical to the progress of humanity. From whence we arrive at the conclusion that he serves religion best who insists upon the clergy of the Catholic Church taking their proper position as servants of the laity, and abandoning their attempt to dominate the public, as they have long dominated the private life of their fellow Catholics.[2]

Thus James Connolly, Irishman, Catholic, and Marxist. *The Bishop's Bonfire* is a dramatic expansion of the truths contained in his words. This is one fruitful explanation of O'Casey's apparent paradox quoted above.

In *The Bishop's Bonfire* the lay community of the church is forced to serve the higher clergy (the Canon and the Bishop) as menials. The rebellion is of this lay community, the true heart of the church against the usurpation of all power by the mere servants within the church. This is the dramatic conflict basic to the play.

To understand fully the identification of the church proper with the community of the people one must recall the special history of Ireland. This was a history in which the persecution of the working people and of the Catholic Church were two sides of the same coin, so that the people came to identify themselves with *their* Catholic Church—the emblem of their humiliation and their cultural resurgence—to a peculiarly intense and universal degree. The church and the community as such became coextensive—a kind of extended family which embodied some of the kinship concepts of the old clans at a higher social level. The people's outlook on life received an indelible Catholic-Christian stamp. In turn *their* aspirations become, therefore, the only true and legitimate expression of the church. The hierarchy have, as Connolly shows in the same place, all through history betrayed the church in betraying the aspirations of the common people. This has not on the whole, however, estranged the people from the *institution* of the Roman Catholic Church, but, by slow degrees, from this hierarchy. The institution of the church remains the only tangible and objective mode of existence of the church as such, also in its wider sense of the people's community. To this, therefore, they remain loyal.

This deeply rooted conception of the church as the people and of a people's church was clearly something which preoccupied O'Casey. It explains the setting of the last act of the revolution play, *Red Roses for Me*, at a church with a clergyman in attendance. In time of crisis the church is turned to as the natural point of sanctuary and mobilisation. It is an ironical comment on the state of affairs within the institution of the Catholic Church that the church and the clergyman who, in *Red Roses for Me*, demonstrate something approaching *truly* catholic (all-embracing) qualities are in fact "Protestant"—an exception within an exception! And even this "ideal" example of a traditional Christian church and churchman is crippled in its present form (see p. 218). Their universality is circumscribed in comparison to that other church-like centre—Ayamonn and his flat. On the other hand, the Ayamonn centre cannot fully supersede the traditional church centre. The true people's church which will realise the potentials inherent in the existing church, can only come into being through a mutual penetration of all that is best in the traditional church community and the new revolutionary and socialist institutions of community (the Party, etc.).

In the world of *The Bishop's Bonfire* the usurpers within the church put *their* stamp on the course of events. Witch-hunt and inquisition, bodily and spiritual degradation, on the whole, define the scene. Ballyoonagh, according to Manus Moanroe, is a place "where the rust of hell is on everything that's done there." (10) Is Manus giving the

whole story? Is the Canon's characterisation of the underdogs just?–"Can't you understand that their dim eyes are
able only for a little light? Damn it, man, can't you see
Clooncoohy can never be other than he is?" (79–80) If so,
then the world of Ballyoonagh isn't topsy-turvy but the
right way up, and the position of the working people as
hewers of wood and drawers of water for the holy men is
just because it accords with their God-given baseness. The
series of defeats and capitulations in the play, including
that of Dan, would seem at first sight to bear this out.

Near the start, Rankin, himself one of the underdogs,
says, "He is what he is; you are what you are; I am what
I am." (15) Nothing can be changed. Things go according
to their preordained and immutable nature. This is a statement of that fatalistic and static view of man which had
often determined the older drama, especially what was
called tragedy. It was a view which Brecht set out to banish
from the theatre. In his new theatre the character "is conceivable not only as he is, but also otherwise, as he might
be, and the social relations too, are conceivable as being
different from what they are." [3] He emphasises that the
actors should act "so that one sees the alternative clearly,
so that his playing allows us to guess at the other possibilities and presents only one of the possible variants." [4]

Rankin and the Canon, or Bertolt Brecht? O'Casey's
loosely jointed, discontinuous, open-ended method of construction which has much in common with Brecht's "epic
plot," strongly suggests *by its very nature* that the course
things take is only one of several possibilities.

What sort of characters does O'Casey build into the context thus created?

Rankin, the mason, would seem to bear out his own view
of man. Yet even this more or less broken victim still shows
glimpses on occasion of another person in him, now almost
obliterated. The advances of Keelin conjure up a contradictory response which is partly an attempt to distract himself
and partly the stirring of the sense of a freer life. As she
nears him he blurts out something about having seen a

young swallow that morning carousing close to heaven. Keelin advises him to do his carousing closer to earth for there's a far prettier bird standing right beside him. Rankin, bending his head down, "I didn't look at you, I don't look at you. The swalla musta been a young one; alone there, up so high, dancin' like in a wide, wide space of blue light." (22)

Two men coexist in the breast of Daniel Clooncoohy, builder's labourer. The one puts its tail between its legs when authority appears. The other, in wooing, has much of the Elizabethan eloquence of the men in *Purple Dust*: "What's it matter whether a man's born under turrets or under a thatch? It's the man with the gay heart that rides the waters an' the winds; who shakes life be the hand when life looks fair, an' shakes her be the shoulder when she shows a frown." (71)

The one Dan never "contaminates" the other. There is no internal conflict between them. Full of brandy-bred bravado, he vows to let work go hang, he'll go listen to the lark in the clear, clean air. His dream and Rankin's vision are expressed in an almost identical image of untrammelled soaring (the opposite to kneeling in prayer). Their alternative selves meet on common ground. Each is not only "what he is."

In the elder Reiligan daughter, Foorawn, there is a bitter suppressed struggle between two "persons" within her. Clothes play an important symbolic role in this play. Keelin says of her sister that if she knows anything there's silk knickers and nylon stockings under Foorawn's so sober skirt. A passionate young woman is hidden within the devotee of chastity and death. This passionate youthfulness bursts out willy-nilly in a distorted, alienated form—in the "inappropriate" vehemence of her language in denouncing Manus, and in her ambivalent dance with the Codger, in which the healthy urge to jig for joy at the prospect of festivities (the Bishop's visit) is sublimated into a "dance of death." Her deep attachment to the Codger in itself "allows us to guess at the other possibilities" hidden within her, waiting to be freed. The character of Foorawn's dramatic partner, Manus Moanroe, will be analysed later.

In Prodical Carranaun it is the lusty sociable man who makes demands on life that is on the offensive. His negative possibility (the whimpering, sin-ridden repentant) is, in this case, the one "coming from behind." As a working mason Prodical is, in the long or the short of it, more susceptible to the hard facts of life than to angel-policemen. Rankin implores him, for the good of his soul, to act as if the keg of spirits wasn't there. Prodical's reply is: "The keg's here now, an' can't be avoided, can it? We'll have to suffer it, like it, or dislike it." (18) Prodical's inner struggle, though put in comic terms, and in no way inhibited, is as real and deep as Foorawn's, despite the fact that it centres round his vow to give up the drink.

He is not sure of himself in either role. The one Prodical is frightened of the other, but especially the conforming pledge-taking Prodical of the rebel drinking Prodical. The former only has a chance so long as the facts of life are hidden—"must shove it outa sight, outa me mind. I'm lost if I don't," he says as he hands over his bottle of whiskey to the Canon for "safe keeping" (88). The victory of the better, Dionysian Prodical distinguishes him from Foorawn to whom he (and not Rankin, as has sometimes been suggested[5]) is the nearest equivalent on the comic plane. The fact that he is a worker and has true comrades (the Codger) is a source of his inner strength, whereas Foorawn, set aside by the division of labour from the world of work with its solidarity and its hot line to reality, is deprived of these weapons and can only follow Prodical's example and break her joy-denying vow when it is too late. This division of labour is one of the sources of her tragedy.

Her sister Keelin, on the other hand, has been designated, in this division, to be one of the workers of the world. In her case, as in Prodical's, this provides a solid foundation in reality on which to stand her ground. It is the common denominator of work which explains the possibility of the love-relationship between her and the labourer, Dan. For the figure of Keelin functions, like so much else, on two levels. On the first or socially specified level she is the daughter of a "ruling" bourgeois family; on the second, metaphorical level she is Martha, the working woman within society as symbolised by Reiligan's family. Keelin's better possibility is to the fore from the start. In her somewhat perfunctory doubts in face of Dan's wooing it becomes clear that her negative possibility (caste snobbishness) has no real conviction left in it–because she is aware of its nature. Unlike Prodical, Keelin quickly finds her way to an uncompromising position of rejection and confrontation. She is "ready to defy them all." (85)

At first, however, she falls into the customary role of "the weaker sex," depending on Dan's assurances that he will take the lead in their challenge to the Establishment. When her prop lets her down she cries, "Dan has forsaken me, forsaken me! I will never marry. I will die as I am." (80) But she is able to muster up the strength to take over the role abandoned by her "hero" and her last word, when others are giving way, is–"I hope yous'll all be settled spiced in hell, soon . . . !" (104) There is a fight within Keelin, and the victory she achieves is really on the plane of her self-emancipation as a woman.

As a personality, old Codger Sleehaun is, unlike the other figures from the people, what he is, all of a piece. As such he is the personified quintessence of the better selves, the optimal personalities of those in whose midst he is so firmly rooted. He demonstrates the unity of their possibilities and the possibility of their unity. In so doing his function in the play's structure has certain similarities to Ayamonn's in *Red Roses for Me*. In his living he demonstrates the true "religion" (church) which Father Boheroe defines when he says that merriment may be a way of worship. In this chief representative of the true church there is no room for a servant-master relationship between him and his God, no room, then, for praying on one's knees–that epitome of subservience. The Gardener and God are partners, in partnership with nature:

Codger (holding the geranium forth). Here's the geranium for your urn. A handsome plant. Lovelier than the Count in all his glory [. . .] God's work, gentlemen an' lady.

Father Boheroe. Helped by man, my friend; it's a cultivated plant. God and man together.

Codger. Helped be man, right enough. Man has to finish what God begins. (100–101)

But it would be a mistake to present the Codger as a purely spontaneous "liver" in contrast to the "thinkers." This old peasant, in his eighty-odd years, has observed and analysed his society with a thoroughness which none of the others can match. He is not content to describe the *misère*, he explains its source (to Reiligan): "You own them all. You own the land, own the tavern, own the shirt factory, own the dance hall, own the store, an' God help us, you own the people too. You're a menace to the world, Reiligan." (37)

When the Canon intervenes, he adds, "Oh! the Canon's voice. The Church an' State's gettin' together." (37) At this point one feels strongly the allegorical nature of the Ballyoonagh world as standing for important aspects of state monopoly capitalism. The Codger is the only person with a suggestion of how to change the situation, and, for all its anarchic naivety, it is revolutionary. The decent thing to do, he says, would be to make one great bonfire of Ballyoonagh, Bishop and all. (29)

For the people the old man is a kind of mascot. He is a rallying point, an inspiration, a source of moral strength. He is the voice of their healthy conscience externalised. This is dramatised in his "wrestling" with Prodical to stop him delivering up the whiskey-bottle. He is the antagonist, as it were, of that other warning voice, the trumpeting St. Tremolo.

The Codger wages perpetual war on the forces of oppression, using every method in the traditional Irish armoury, from blunt frontal attack to withering irony and sabotage disguised as peasant clownishness. In his human wholeness he is, by his very presence, a denial of that image of the people propagated by Burren and a demonstrative danger to their hegemony.

Gardener-Codger is the keeper and presiding spirit of that magic land of laurels and kegs whose gateway is a symbolic ash-tree at the house-corner. This land is their hide-out and the base from which they draw their strength and vision—and launch their rebellions. Their best proclamations are made while in more or less physical contact with the ash-tree. The associations with Arcadia, with a golden age, with the old Garden (and the new), which we noted in Robin, Marion and Loreleen in *Cock-a-doodle Dandy*, are made much more concrete in the Codger. Mostly he appears carrying things which associate him with the old gods of the fruitful earth—a keg of spirits, a trident-like hay-fork, a scythe, flowers. The echoes of Bacchus, Dionysus, Silenus, Saturn, Neptune, and even the avenging Old Father Time, are unmistakable. He carries the image of the Golden Days (the burden of his nostalgic songs) like a lamp into the Dark Age: "Ah, them were the days when th' sickles were keen,/Th' barley bright yellow, the grass a rich green," etc. (16) He and his songs set up a poetic alternative, the vision of an intact world, and his own very being, together with the potentials in the others, relativises his nostalgia. His sallies into the world of the drawing-room (the whole play is a savage comment on those fashionable "drawing-room comedies" which O'Casey so hated) usually take the form of raids launched from his base in the natural world of the Garden beyond the French windows.

Clearly, then, the metaphorical-symbolic dimension is very marked in the Codger. As an embodied spirit he takes on something of the function of the mythical Cock, and is, on this plane of his being, as unbanishable. Reiligan, in one of his better moments, says that no one but God can remove the crafty Codger from Ballyoonagh. (97) But in his role as Man of Property he soon presumes to usurp the role of God and banish the old Adam from the Garden: "Outa the garden; outa any property of mine." (101) He has the presumption, but not the power. The Codger continues to lurk in the shrubbery—Prodical's "ubique," a genie with a lamp who can be conjured up by his friend's whistle—"I'm here, me son; waitin'." (115)

But unlike the Cock he also functions as a mortal, socially determined individual. And it is the tension between these two planes of existence that creates that peculiar inner contradictoriness which makes him come alive. Thus we see that the Codger too, is, after all, not simply "what he is"— though the contradiction is of a radically different nature to that in the others.

He is not devoid of weaknesses. He loves his bottle. He too, is a little apprehensive of the "bookaneeno" (St. Tremolo). His sympathetic susceptibility to the people around him can lead to his getting temporarily "carried away"—as when Foorawn almost wooes him into "reforming himself." (67–69) He has the typical foibles of an old man—nostalgia and a touch of vanity on the score of his physical prowess. These are the "weaknesses" of his community and go to make up that rounded and universal image of themselves which the people take to their hearts.

Thus Codger Sleehaun is, paradoxically, both a metaphorical assertion of the immortality of the spirit of youth, and an urgent warning that time is running out: "Wife dead (rest her soul), two daughters an' three sons away, away in America, leavin' me the one lone, mohican Sleehaun left standin' in Ballyoonagh." (26–27)

What of the potential "second person" and alternative possibility in the case of the oppressors?

Councillor Reiligan is typical of the contradictory portraits of the aborted bourgeoisie in O'Casey's late plays. He is a man whose worst characteristics are aggravated by his acceptance of the role of second fiddle or senior menial to the clerical usurpers (they also usurp his position). Nevertheless he emerges as possessing, in spite of everything, certain potentials and interests in common with the working people whom he exploits. Of course he is the typical bourgeois in many ways. He is the domineering philistine whose only gauge of the worth of a thing is the fact that

"I own them all." (37) He is responsible for splitting the "family" through a crippling division of labour. He himself labours under the illusion that his unequal partnership with the theocracy is in his own interests, and at first sight this may seem to be so, for the Canon tells Rankin that when he is working for Councillor Reiligan, however menial the work, he is serving God. In the long run, however, it becomes clear that they are working solely for the profit of the church Establishment. Reiligan is browbeaten into lavishing vast amounts of money, sorely needed for constructive enterprises on the church tower and the unproductive Bishop's visit, which merely aggravates waste, slavishness, idling and rebellion and is anything but conducive to the aggrandisement of his private property. Reiligan's capitulation forces him to condone and contribute to the atmosphere which drives off good workers like Daniel and Manus, his own right hand. He is even pushed into dismissing that irreplaceable fixture, the Codger, against the dictates of his own good sense.

When the clerical Big Brother is absent (he normally takes good care to be with Reiligan), the Councillor at once begins to show a kind of realism which could, in a better context, be a productive force. Formal prayer, that menial relationship to "God," to which he is forced to devote part of the potential work-force, is swept aside as a nuisance. He calls Rankin a "prayer-gasper" who would do better if he prayed less and saw more. And when things hot up he orders Foorawn to get out of the way, for "prayers are no use here now." (35) At times another Reiligan peeps forth quite clearly. Right at the start he reveals an unexpected hankering after roses, but even this falls under the ban of the Canon's disapproval, and he caves in at once. Even at the end he can still be moved personally by Manus' desertion: "Your goin' would leave the stars over Ballyoonagh lonely." (107) Manus replies that, bar the Codger, Reiligan is the only man who ever told him there were stars over Ballyoonagh.

The implication is that the road taken by Reiligan is not

inevitable; he could be something other and better than "what he is," if he could only find the backbone to be himself.

Canon Burren says that Dan can never be other than he is. This is true only of Burren himself. It would be wrong, however, to present the Canon as a flat caricature. In fact this usurper shows himself to be a formidable adversary, flexible and intelligent. The persuasiveness and "reasonableness" with which he argues the monstrous case why Keelin should marry the Bishop's brother proves this. And the point is that he can *seem* to become a different person:

Canon (almost putting an arm round the Prodical). My dear Protestant friend, this is a rare occasion; only this once; you will, won't you?
Prodical (yielding). Maybe this once, then. (104)

Like Jonathan Wild, the Canon has the demagogue's knack of appearing to have the generous humanity of those he wishes to dupe, i.e. he exploits that better nature whose existence in the common people he denies. He misuses their conception of the church as their extended family, telling them they must be united for the coming great event. When Keelin's defiance endangers even this he adds the Mother Ireland touch—"A united family, Irish too," and makes sure by getting them to join him in singing the popular evergreen, "When Irish Eyes are Smiling." (104) There is a typical hidden contrast here with the way in which the Codger and Co. endow a similar well loved sentimental ballad, "My Bonnie's Gone Over the Ocean," with a new and surprising emotional truth by using it as a comment on the emigration of loved ones.

This is why the Codger must go. He is Burren's most threatening rival for the hearts of the people. "Be off," he says to the Codger, "you mischievous poacher on men's desire to do good deeds!" (91)–which is exactly what he is himself. Burren is what he is. It is folly to look for potentials in him. Burren is barren.

What we have here, then, is a model of a dynamic *system* of alternative possibilities. They are portrayed at various stages in the process of developing and disintegrating, whereby the mobile relationships between the actual and the potential are played through in manifold variations. Taken in their totality, all these alternative selves and relationships strongly suggest the inherent possibility of an alternative and better community (society) within the womb of the existing one.

The people are being forced into roles which are not natural to them (as indicated in the ill-fitting clothes which most of them wear). They can only be held to their alienated parts through constant supervision. When this supervision is absent they begin to veer back to their natural and healthy selves, so that each time the Powers that Be return they are faced with some new "impertinence"—"What's this, aw, what's all this?" (Reiligan, 58) This is the form which the basic conflict takes, and it determines the general rhythm of the play. The people, however, have also an "invisible" policeman to contend with, when the oppressors are not actually present—the built-in fears and inhibitions inculcated into their consciences since their earliest days. This invisible inquisitor is made dramatically visible in the form of the trumpeting "bookaneeno" figure. The fact that their consciences are alienated from them is epitomised in a *dramatis persona*, someone *outside* themselves, a hollow pseudo-being possessed by the usurpers. This explains why the figure's trumpeting is sometimes heard only by some of the characters and sometimes by all.

Nevertheless, in the course of the action the "usual" checks make less and less impression, and after each check the characters bounce back again more defiant and united than before. This is because it is not a self-repeating process but a rising spiral (cp. *Cock*). We tune into this process at a point of dramatic collision and qualitative leap.

In connection with the preparations for the Bishop's visit the pressure on the people is becoming intolerable. In this sense the visit and the preparation of the bonfire are the detonator of the dramatic collision. The reason for the people's violent reaction lies, on the one hand, in the stepping up of the campaign to subjugate the true church (the working community) to joyless servitude to its supposed servants, and, on the other hand, in the fact that the Bishop's welcome takes the form of a festive event—a bonfire. These two mutually exclusive propositions between them act as a forcing-house on the people's alternative, revolutionary selves.

The true church which is being denied and humiliated as never before under the pretext of the Bishop's festive visit is clearly defined by Father Boheroe, reprimanding Rankin for thinking the church itself is the only sacred place: "All places are sacred, man; the church we pray in, the homes sheltering us, the shops where we get the things we need to go on living, the halls we dance in; yes the very place we walk on is holy ground . . ." (25)

Things have reached flash-point. This is dramatised in the "transformation" of an episodic character, the Porter. He is introduced as a middle-aged man with a pair of spectacles eking out weak eyes. He looks worn down and his face bears an ingrained expression of fear. But his cup is full and overflows:

Porter (suddenly coming to alert life, and standing full front before the crowd, waving his hands excitedly, moving a step forward, a step back, a step forward again). Listen, you blatherers! A question for yous, a question! Does a prayer lift you up or get you down? Are these prayin' people right an' proper in a world like this at all? How'd you like one of them to start on you, an' you sittin', glass in hand, listenin' to some gazebo singin' a shut-eyed song? Or one of them with a hand on your shoulder, freezin' a body, an' you trying to shout victory to your county football team? Would you feel at ayse to shout? I'm a wild man when I think of these things. I'm askin' yous something, Is prayer good for you? I don't mean the odd nod of the head most of us give to God, but the prayer that's the real McCoy—does it lift a man up, or does it cast a man down? *(They stand, as they have stood for some time, in a semicircle around him, gaping, stiff and still, only moving back a step or two when he has come closer, waving his hands.)* There's no answer; *(in a wail)* there's no answer! We don't feel comfortable with them here, we won't feel comfortable with them there. What are we doin' but weavin' a way through life, content with an odd prayer to propel us towards where none of us wants to go! How'r we to know if we're comin' up upstream, or goin' down downstream? *(He catches sight of the big duck on the dish on the table.)* Jasus! Who owns the massive duck? (62–63)

O'Casey gives this important speech to a minor figure in an episodic scene in order to bring out the sharp, deep-going and all-embracing nature of the crisis: even this man, this man above all–obscure, long-suffering, "beaten," is *transformed* by it before our eyes. The obscure and lowly (a mere porter) are coming to the end of their tether and undreamt-of energies are being released.

He swiftly gets down to challenging basic assumptions of the society he lives in. What finally sparks him off is Foorawn's advice that he go pray. This touches the nerve of his resentment and turns him into a "wild man." The prayer-mongers he feels as a deadly danger to the community of the true church in that they inhibit the "congregation" from worshipping in their own genuine way–through the festive celebration of all the senses (eyes, ears, taste, etc.).

The transfigured Porter exudes such a forceful sense of purpose that the others, including his persecutors, stand hypnotised and helpless before him. He has got himself moving, he begins to outgrow himself. But then he falters in mid-flight and falls back into the labyrinth. The spell is finally broken by his self-alienating switch of attention to the ownership of the duck. It is his directly raising the question of private property, and bringing people "down to earth" in this way that snaps Reiligan out of the spell, and he sends the man about his business. Certainly, all is not as

you were with the Porter, but, isolated and without guidance, he retreats, and a moment supercharged with possibilities goes a-begging.

This scene is, in many of its salient features, a kind of
miniature of the play as a whole–a metaphorical summary
or key, standing in relation to the whole somewhat like the
Liffey-bridge scene does to *Red Roses for Me*.

A festivity lies at the centre of this play, as in the case of
most of these later plays. The people spontaneously exploit
all opportunities to celebrate the festival of life. A struggle
begins for control of the festival. The urge to celebrate it
clashes with the drive to turn it into a festival of death.
How is this theme developed here? This emerges best if we
retell the story in a different way.

Act I. Irritation at the idea of being minions or servants
to other "unqualified" people lies behind the quarrel about
labourers (fetchers-and-carriers). There is also incipient repudiation of "keeping one's position" in Keelin's attempt
on Rankin's virtue–as yet, however, practised only against
a petty minion of the usurpers. Other points of rebellious
departure are suggested: Manus Moanroe pours bitter irony
on the state of the nation, Codger bursts a bag of cement
on the drawing-room carpet (no respect here for that hallowed precinct of the "well-made play" – the drawing-
room!). At this stage however the rebellious flash-points are
scattered and isolated, and the first punitive raid by the oppressors soon has the situation apparently in hand.

At the same time a sort of mini-festival of the popular
forces is celebrated around the keg of spirits behind the
laurels. Sallying forth from this Arcadian base the participants, somewhat alcoholised, proclaim their demands and
dreams: "*Prodical (to the world and to Father Boheroe).*
Prodical Carranaun demands a wider world, Father Boheroe; a world where a man can roar his real opinions out;
where night becomes a generous part of a day, where rough
seas tumble in on a lonely shore . . ." (44) Thus the demand
for liberty and the urge to revelry and festival (night as a

generous part of day, etc.) are fused at an early point in the play. At this stage a marked community of standpoint and mood is already achieved, but the moment of synthesis is relativised in two ways: first, it is artificially stimulated, through alcohol (alcohol is important in the pattern of the play as a key to festivity under existing conditions); secondly, Codger tempers their euphoria by giving lyrical expression to that which is preventing the coming together of two lovers for their festival: the sundering of bodies and hearts by the wide waters of fear and persecution, the already familiar theme of the two kings' children, the severed couple: "My Bonnie's gone over the ocean."

Act II. The Codger—the embodiment of Festival—moves more to the fore. He gives the cues in the rising tendency to "accidents." In the scene of the mocking of Lieutenant Reiligan and his plan for Russian-proofing Ireland, the Codger and Prodical begin to function as a pair, their target still being, however, a junior specimen of the Establishment. Then comes the inburst of the Porter, that messenger "from outside," bringing a new and sharper tone into the maturing situation. He is isolated and burns out, yet a flame, it would seem, has been ignited. This and Rankin's enthusiastic description of the decorations in the town centre send Foorawn into her *conspirative dance* with the Codger. Again a promising pair-up, but one torn by inner contradiction. This dance is, in its way, symbolic of the struggle for *hegemony over festival,* with Foorawn trying to twist it into a dance of death—"To th' tomb!" (68)—and Codger simply dancing for the fun of it. But of course the conflict runs through Foorawn herself—as if she is trying to convince herself that this human feeling of joy which she experiences in anticipating a festive event is really the ecstasy of the flesh-rejecting spirit. Once again, but this time without alcohol, the moment of synthesis is marked by a fusion of festivity (dance and song) with the idea of revolution—the tune they dance to is the "Marseillaise," lilted by the Codger.

The next and higher moment of synthesis involves the pair Keelin and Dan who pledge themselves to defy the inquisitors and stay loyal to their dream. This time a third person, Boheroe, is pulled into its orbit. Their insurrection at its highest point moves once more into musical rhythm. Harmony is dominant now, rather than inner contradiction. The name of the song that Father Boheroe plays for them to dance to–"Blue Bonnets over the Border"–is declaimed by them as a slogan symbolising their determination to transgress set boundaries. Revolt and festivity go hand in hand. Boheroe cleverly uses the moment of ecstasy to suggest a strategy for liberation. You have freed yourselves from the domination of the big house with the lion and the unicorn above the door, he tells them; don't go and allow yourselves to be bowed down beneath the meaner yoke of the big shop with the cross and shamrock on its gable-end. (77) But again the partnership is unable to withstand the punitive incursion of the oppressors. The advances apparently made in the "drunken" moment of catharsis evaporate as swiftly as the fumes of alcohol, it seems, in the cold wind of adversity. *Catharsis cannot change the world.* Yet there is an important residue: Keelin, although deprived of her partner, now refuses to submit, as does Father Boheroe, in his own way.

Act III opens with a new pairing-up. Prodical and Dan combine to play a satirical skit on the Bishop and his servant. There is a new level of rejection and revolt here and again there is the link-up between festival (play-acting) and rebellion. In playing their persecutors and the topsy-turvy master-servant relationship they demonstrate a degree of mastery over them in which the servants become the served. For a moment a true bishop of the true church (Prodical) is on the throne and gives his orders–a rehearsal of the world stood on its feet which is similar to the Shakespeare rehearsal at the start of *Red Roses*.

Deserted by Daniel, Keelin enters into the most deeply lyrical "alliance" portrayed so far–with the Codger. That is, she is driven into the arms of an "old man." There is complex irony in this as a comment on the attempt of the Canon to drive her officially, as "lawful spouse," into the ageing arms of the Bishop's brother. But at this ploy to transform *the festival of her life* (the marriage-feast) into a marriage-hearse, Keelin turns at bay–"I want me Danny!" The woman has emancipated herself from her conception of her subservient role and begins to give a lead.

The pressure to reduce the true church to menials reaches a climax as the Bishop's arrival approaches. Now revolt begins to congeal into a general and social phenomenon, culminating in an incipient *general strike:* "The Bishop can peel his own spuds!" "The Bishop can pluck his own plover!" (102) This is their reaction to the part allocated to them in the approaching festival of the community. They, who should by right and regal inclination be decked in festive robes and sit at the head of the table, are expected to don the clowns' suits of lackeys and wait upon the feast-usurper. Within the festive tendency of their living as suggested in the first two acts lies the deeper source and explanation of their insurrection.

The Codger is more and more the presiding genius in all this, urging things cunningly along in the background and openly in the foreground. Their tone of voice towards their "betters" becomes the brusque tone of masters to superfluous and interfering dependents–"Oh, shut it, will yous, for a minute?" (the Codger to Reiligan and the Canon, 90). The new spirit even touches poor Rankin. In reaction to this the usurper (Canon) is forced to drop the arrogant tone of master to servant: *"Canon (smoothly).* Not ordering, no, not ordering; just appealing to your generosity, Prodical." (103) For this gambit to succeed it is essential to try to banish their rival in this, the Codger, the genius of the counter-festival. This drives Foorawn to the point of joining the rebels. On the other hand it does succeed in dissipating this most promising constellation of insurrectionary potentials. What remains? Keelin in revolt; Foorawn stays away from the bonfire; so do Boheroe, the Codger and Prodical. The bonfire takes place, and what might have been the people's festival of autumn remains *the Bishop's* bonfire. The logical and natural culmination of their whole festive trend is alienated from them. The people go to it, contributing their little votive lights to its bale-fire, and, as Prodical says, "A lot of the glamour's goin' into gloom." (115)

But at the same time a nucleus of the true church survives in the bosom-friends Prodical and the Codger. In the depths of the Garden, their domain, the true festival is simultaneously celebrated, a secret cell of the immortal golden age glowing in a corner of the blacked-out world.

But things might well have taken a different course. The play has revealed that in this apparently cowed and terrorised world of the witch-hunt, so potently suggestive of the state of affairs created in the whole capitalist world by the cold war, the suppressed and discontented "church" of the common people endlessly and universally produces the raw material of revolution. Even at this *lowest ebb*, the *Flood* is building up. A word in season to all those discouraged perhaps by the apparent success of reaction in brainwashing the masses. No human material was better suited to bring out O'Casey's point than the Irish people with their long history of rising again after each "final solution" inflicted on them.

The Porter tells Reiligan, "What's the matter with you an' me is a world's question." (61) The matter, in the course of events played through in this particular case, is that adequate leadership is wanting. It is for lack of this that the people allow the festival of life to be alienated from them and turned into the festival of barrenness and death (epitomised in Foorawn's fate).

There are several possible centres of mobilisation and points of leadership indicated.

Reiligan, that bourgeois *manqué*, might have been such a point, at least in a subordinate capacity, if he had not tied himself to the cassock-strings of the hierarchy.

We have seen how the lowly Codger does function, in his way, as a mobilising centre for the scattered elements of "cockiness." But his kind of "partisan" lead, important as it is, is too archaic and on too low a level of conscious organisation to be adequate to the pressing strategic demands of the situation. On his metaphorical plane, on which he is more legendary spirit than mortal man, he clearly cannot be put forward as a practical proposition to lead "real" men and women any more than the Cock could in *Cock-a-doodle Dandy*. On his individual-concrete plane he is an old man with the weaknesses of an old man. But he is more than just this. He also embodies the old revolutionary and democratic tradition of the Irish peasantry. It is out of this heritage that he is able to conjure up his vision of a golden age. But its great weakness is that it provides only a backward perspective into a nostalgically idealised past. In the figure of the Codger O'Casey pays tribute to the last of a mighty race. The time has come for him to hand over his torch to a new generation, a new type of revolutionary who will no longer fight a hit-and-run guerilla war but will combine the Codger's qualities and vision of the full life with the necessary modern intellectual equipment and practical perspective of struggle. Where are the young people who will be this social spearhead? Is the Codger to leave the world a solitary? Time is running out. As he says, "Odd, how the old leaves drop so early an' the young ones come so late." (17)

One possible young leaf is Reiligan's son Mick, a young army officer. He bursts upon the scene, as an episodic character, from the "wider world" of contemporary national politics. He has put provincial obscurantism behind him and has a free and easy attitude to the old "saints." There is a natural democracy about him. His being a lieutenant has not affected his friendship with the labourer Dan. He thinks on a national and even international scale and is genuinely concerned for the future of Ireland. Unfortunately his ideas are the mad ideas of a supposed "Russian threat" to Ireland. Unlike all the others this inventive young man has a concrete perspective for his countrymen: "Every ablebodied man in Ireland in a jeep here an' a jeep there ..." (55) The unfortunate young victim has fallen out of the frying-pan into the fire–the old regimentation and waste in a new form! Given his lunatic starting-off point, Mick argues with "logic" and "realism"–"You see, men, Ireland's so important, geographically, that, in a war, the Russians would need to take her over within an hour." (54–55)

This man has a potentially effective alternative self but he is betraying it by allowing himself to be duped by the new form of the old thing from which he thought he had emancipated himself–in the shape of the cold-warriors. Thus a potential young new broom is turned into a clown who deserves and gets the rich ridicule of the people:

Codger. . . . If Russia be anything like what the clergy make it out to be, any Russians flutterin' down from the Irish skies on to our emerald sod will be poor divils seekin' an asylum.

Prodical. An asylum? It's a lunatic asylum you must be meanin'? (56)

This young leaf is withered before its prime. The figure of Lieutenant Reiligan forms the concrete link between what is going on in Ballyoonagh and the general cold war. The episode is, therefore, not just inserted as a foreign body into the play because the anecdote happened to have taken O'Casey's fancy, as some critics have suggested.[6]

The most promising and the most tragic potential leader portrayed is Manus Moanroe. At thirty he is at the height of his powers. He is a man of formidable physical courage (an ex-fighter-pilot), implacable of purpose and completely self-assured. As Reiligan's chief steward he displays qualifications which the people lack and need so much–precision and organising efficiency. He has broken totally with the ideological-administrative church Establishment. He sees contemporary Irish society clearly as a conspiracy against the people: "The fraud of clericals forbidding drink in the dance halls, though here, in Ballyoonagh, drinkers from Reiligan's tavern go to the dance hall to dance, and dancers from Reiligan's dance hall go to Reiligan's tavern to drink; the fraud of Reiligan's town stores where there's nothing in spirit or manner to show that life's more than meat, and the body than raiment; the fraud of his mean meadows where his bunchy cattle low their woe to God for want of grass; the fraud of his shirt factory where girls work but to earn enough to leave the land, and where there's more melody in the heart of a machine than in the heart of its minder." (117)

He has a deep appreciation of the sensual pleasures of life and encourages–at least initially–their celebration. It is he who drums up the keg. To Keelin, showing a leg, he calls out enthusiastic encouragement. And Manus can set hearts a-flutter thinking of glorious things gone by, for he combines his practical qualities with an ability to conjure up the living heroic past in a way similar to O'Killigain: "The ash, Codger, gave the wood for the shafts for the spears of the ancient Greeks, and for the pikes we used our-selves to free Ireland through the sad year of Ninety-eight." (17)

But there is another Manus–the embittered cynic, defeat-ist, egoist and misanthropist who makes no attempt to inspire the people of his generation with belief in themselves as the heirs to this tradition. Life and power for Manus clearly lie in combating this second Manus through cultivating his common ground with the people. He is capable of respect and friendship with simple people. When he is standing in the vicinity of *their* ash-tree he is at his strongest and most integrated. Divorced from them he is doomed. The tragedy is that Manus Moanroe fails to become the leader he seems predestined to be. The negative alternative in him comes more and more to define him as he retreats ever further in-to isolation. His qualities are turned against the community of the people instead of being at their service.

The course taken by the characters and action offers him enough opportunities to make the kind of fruitful connec-tions which would have taken him in a different direction, but he consistently fails to exploit them. The reason lies in his special relationship to the church.

Through abandoning his study for the priesthood Manus

has, willy-nilly, put himself outside the church and into head-on confrontation with it. But we have already explained how, due to the special historical conditions in Ireland, the church and the community of the people became coextensive. T. A. Jackson says, "English trade-unionists who know how firmly the tradition of trade-unionism was laid in England when the unions were banned as 'seditious conspiracies' by law, can understand why adherence to the Catholic Church came to be a point of honour with the common people of Ireland."[7] Thus to excommunicate oneself from the church in the narrow sense so drastically and negatively as Manus does is to run the risk of excommunicating yourself from the community at large. James Connolly, the founder of the first revolutionary socialist party in Ireland, knew this, and remained a member of the Catholic Church–as did Jim Larkin. These examples stand behind the figure of Ayamonn Breydon, revolutionary and "pillar" of the church community (albeit the Protestant Church). They all knew that revolutionary advance could never be achieved through head-on confrontation with the Catholic Church but only with it (in our broad sense) and through it.

Manus, unlike these, casts himself into suicidal limbo. This is well symbolised in his becoming a lone flier, a fighter-pilot, not as Drishogue does in *Oak Leaves and Lavender*, to fight the monster, but to seek physical annihilation. Ironically, Drishogue dies, while Manus lives on, and yet remains in danger of death though physically unscathed.

In initially dedicating himself to the priesthood, Manus was dedicating himself to serve the community. But the church in the narrow sense betrayed him by turning Foorawn, the flesh-and-blood person he most loved on earth, into a life-denying "nun" of no use to him or anyone else. Thus his dedication to things outside himself has been turned against him. This was what he got, it seemed, for seeking to be a true servant and priest to his people. He identifies the institutions of the church in the narrow sense with the church in the true catholic sense. Failing to see the inner contradiction between the two aspects of the church he vents his spleen on them both. They are all to blame.

This is the experience that drives him to be the isolated and self-centred thing he becomes. Ironically, the church oppressors have notched up a victory over this implacable negator. That anti-human view of man as venal dust which is expounded in reactionary church ideology *becomes absolutised in him.* He epitomises the very thing he reacts against. His humanism is made a caricature of itself, by being reduced to loyalty to himself alone. All humanity is drained from the community into this one vessel whose job it becomes to revenge and assert humanity against the human community. Knowing itself to monopolise the "middle ground" as it does, the church has nothing to fear from those who fly from its bosom in this way. They degenerate into impotence and self-contempt. Manus has already started on this road when he first enters–"He looks slovenly now, with a beard of a week's growth" (9) and his unkempt appearance shocks many of those who knew him before.

The career of Manus Moanroe is the playing through of one possible variant facing the rebel in Irish society–the tragic possibility of the man who, failing to find a firm basis in the working-class movement from which to renew his relationship to the church and thus to renew the church, finds himself in the desert. Given the balance of class forces in Ireland this must still be a danger facing many. Implied indirectly throughout is the need to develop the revolutionary political movement so that people like Manus (and Codger!) do not go to waste.

Cut off and estranged from the people's church community, Manus is cut off from the rich well-springs of humanity. They dry up in himself and he is less and less able to recognise, let alone encourage, these rich potentials continuously bubbling up around him. His personal divorcement from physical labour aggravates this.

We meet him at a moment of qualitative worsening in this process of decline. Most of his fine characteristics are strongly expressed only in the first act. It seems that the failure of his bludgeoning appeal to Foorawn in this act finally puts the seal on his defeat. He fails to rally the people at the various promising junctures indicated. If he is present at all his contribution is mainly sarcasm and invective—"you wizened wisps of dust" etc. But usually he is *conspicuous by his absence*. This is especially glaring in the last act when the revolt begins to assume mass proportions. When on stage he remains a commentator from the sidelines, occupying the centre only after the others have relinquished it. Not only does he deprive the people of his help when most needed; by his efficient work for the usurpers he actually strengthens the latters' hand.

He fails to develop a possible alliance with the Codger and purposely avoids a potentially very fruitful one with the man who tries to help him—Father Boheroe:

Manus. You are a kind, good man, Father. *(He pauses.)* Would you do me a great favour?
Father Boheroe (eagerly). Of course I would. You've but to tell me what it is, Manus.
Manus (tonelessly). Just leave me alone. (43–44)

He fails to provide the people, at a higher level, with that spiritual uplift which the keg provides fleetingly at the lower level. In omitting to cultivate their generous emotional qualities he delivers these over to be "cultivated" by the enemy. He could perhaps have rescued his beloved Foorawn. As has been shown, Foorawn's healthy self gains the upper hand at times, especially in connection with the more or less spontaneous rising of the community in the last act. He could have used these communal moments to integrate Foorawn into the people's community and lead her to liberation via the collective. But he cannot use the "family" as Burren misuses the sense of family. The method he does employ on Foorawn is a kind of individual spiritual castigation—"puritanical bitch," (117) "you mournful, empty shell of womanhood!" (118) By acknowledging defeat too soon, by rubbing her face in her own misery instead of lifting up her head gently, by showering contempt on what she holds most holy he drives her further down the road to destruction. Manus' shooting of Foorawn at the end is the logical culmination of his "killing" of her in this sense in the course of the play. Those critics who complain about the supposed melodrama of this shooting[8] have not grasped the ironic symbolism involved. Doubtlessly, here as elsewhere O'Casey refashions elements from the Boucicault tradition in melodrama which he had so much enjoyed as a boy.

Heinz Kosok has got quite the wrong end of the stick when he contends that Foorawn is responsible both for her own death and Manus' desperation.[9] In the furious exchanges between them at the end it is Foorawn who emerges as of greater stature. There is more truth in her fierce assaults on him—"you gaspin' throw-away from the Church eternal," (117) "you spoiled priest"(119)—than there is in his upon her. There is dreadful *unmeant* irony in his claim that she "wants me to be barren as herself." (116)

In faking suicide she reveals a selfless lack of barrenness which is at the opposite pole to Manus. She who apparently only had eyes for the spiritual life to come, commits, for the sake of her earthly love, a double sin—the sin of lying and that of shielding a homicide. For the sake of this life, at the very moment when she is leaving it, she risks her place in heaven without a thought. As for her place on earth—to save this other person whom she loves, she that is a paragon of saintliness and purity is willing to heap upon her memory the special odium reserved for those who commit that most heinous of sins, self-murder. This was a woman for whom, unlike the bourgeois philistines in the play, life was something more than mere "stattus!"

In breaking her vow for the sake of this world, she most truly keeps her vow, in its essential spirit, and attains a true purity at last—a saint in the service of the true church of life. Thus her taking the blame on herself is as little a convention of sentimental melodrama as her shooting by Manus. It is the poetic vindication of that alternative self which Manus fails to recognise or cultivate. And now it is too late. There is something of Minnie Powell's sacrifice for

Davoren here, but on an immensely higher level of poetic complexity.

Just before his first fateful meeting with Foorawn in Act I, Manus says to the Codger, who has invited him to pay a second visit to the keg, "I'll join you in a few minutes, old friend." (40) The irony is that those few minutes become eternity, for he never joins them again. He has no part in their final celebration of the counter-festival in the garden. In stealing the church mission money he is taking back something purloined from the people (in his terms, from him). It will be used "For Manus and his doxies now." (116) That is, to celebrate–but an anti-social, hole-in-corner celebration. In contrast, the Codger and Prodical–who also take back something wheedled out of them (the whiskey-bottle from under the St. Tremolo figure where it had been put by the Canon)–use their "booty" to celebrate the true festival of fellowship. It is the poorer for Manus' absence.

At the end, when he hears the Codger's voice from the dark garden, Manus, who has a lighted lamp with him, conceals himself, "holding the lantern so that its light cannot be seen by anyone outside." (120) Codger exclaims pointedly that the lantern has disappeared from the top of the bricks. That is, Manus hides his light "under a bushel" so that his potential comrades cannot find it, leaving them to fumble in the dark with only the Bishop's bonfire to light things. When he finally exits he puts the lantern back on the wall. It will have to be picked up by someone else.

Thus Manus Moanroe is indeed the "dead priest" whom he drinks to in himself. (108) He declares: "I'm glad I escaped from the honour and glory of the priesthood!" (108) The tragic irony is that it is that other "priesthood" of that better church dedicated to the service and liberation of the people, which should have been his power and glory. Ayamonn Breydon was that kind of priest to his people. And only a "priest" can fill the bill. It was Manus' rightful destiny. Father Boheroe cannot be that priest because he is a Priest. But Manus lets his light go out.

The figures of Manus and Father Boheroe are complementary. They have, initially, much in common. Boheroe is what Manus might have become had he stayed with the priesthood. Boheroe takes on, as well as he can, his true priestly duty–he is always there when needed, standing to his ideals and his people: the ideal of selfless service, fanning the budding moments of festive insurrection as best he can, even though he endanger his own "stattus" thereby. The message he propagates is in open contradiction to the tenets and behaviour of the official church. He challenges Manus to be true to the other, better self within him: "Come, let yourself fall in love with life, and be another man." (43)

But he fails, for all his eloquence, and there is truth in Foorawn's accusation that he has given no concrete leadership. His rather lame answer that "I did my best," and that she shouldn't be too hard on a poor priest unable to work wonders, clearly indicates his objective limits. So long as he remains a priest within the church Establishment he is hindered from taking the action necessary to back up his words. Also, the fact of his being a priest creates an image in people's minds which conditions their responses to his "unpriestlike" agitation: "What kind of a priest are you, sayin' such things! Muddlin' a young girl's mind..." (Foorawn, 112) Logically he ought to leave the priesthood, but there begins the "Manus variation" – perhaps.[10]

The basic situation portrayed in this play has something important in common with the "Dublin" plays and *Within the Gates*: it is a period of confusion and partial retreat by the people. In the earlier plays it was the aftermath of the aborted revolution and the economic slump. Here it is a parable-model of the state of affairs created by the cold war. The difference lies in the greater universality and clarity with which the potentially world-changing qualities and energies of the common people are worked out in this later play. The portrait of the people has therefore won tremendously in poetry and beauty. Under these conditions of "setback" they display *more* of the qualities necessary for revolution than in the immediate *pre-revolutionary* situation depicted in *The Plough and the Stars*. Thus the period of the apparent triumph of the forces of reaction emerges as *a potentially pre-revolutionary period*, in spite of everything. For, as has been indicated, the "storm-in-a-teacup" of Ballyoonagh is symbolic of a whole society. In *The Plough and the Stars* the main source of their discontent is physical want; here it is mental-spiritual oppression and the alienation of their basic human rights. Both plays reveal the possibilities of human intervention to change the course of events—the hallmark of the truly popular and revolutionary realist in the spirit of Brecht.

In both cases there is a crisis of the masses only in so far as it is a crisis of leadership. In *The Plough and the Stars* the leaders are not the right leaders and therefore fail the people; in *The Bishop's Bonfire* certain potential leaders fail to become leaders. This play follows up various negative possibilities of the relationship between the potential leadership and the masses. The historical necessity of building the revolutionary and democratic movement emerges by implication. If people like Manus are not to go to waste then the movement must be strong enough to "catch" them.

Notes

1. *The Sting and the Twinkle, Conversations with Sean O'Casey*, ed. E. M. Mikhail and John O'Riordan, London, 1974, p. 119

2. James Connolly, *Labour, Nationality and Religion*, first published 1910, reprinted in *James Connolly, Selected Writings*, ed. P. Berresford Ellis, London, 1973, pp. 58–59 (italics, JM)

3. Bertolt Brecht, *Über Realismus*, Leipzig, 1968, p. 209 (translation, JM)

4. Bertolt Brecht, *Werke in fünf Bänden*, Band 5, Berlin, 1973, p. 289 (translation, JM)

5. Kosok, op. cit., p. 292

6. Cp. Pauli, op. cit., and Kosok, op. cit.
7. T. A. Jackson, *Ireland Her Own*, London, 1971, p. 86
8. Kosok, op. cit., pp. 287 and 295
9. Ibid., p. 288
10. For an interesting study of the position, possibilities and problems of a defrocked priest in Ireland see the figure of Keegan in Shaw's *John Bull's Other Island*.

XI BEHIND THE GREEN CURTAINS

Written 1959–61; published 1961; produced 1962 (University Theatre of the University of Rochester, New York)

> "It is my duty to place before you certain facts about the present position in Europe. From Stettin on the Baltic to Trieste on the Adriatic an iron curtain has descended across the continent."
>
> Winston Churchill, Fulton, Missouri,
> March 4, 1946

Scene I. Place: a street adjacent to a Protestant church and graveyard, in a provincial town in the Irish Republic. Time: the present. A sultry summer's day. Angela and Lizzie, two ageing one-time street hawkers, idle in the street. The notes of the "Dead March" in *Saul* issuing from the church distract Lizzie from basking in the sun. Angela muses on the picture of a bearded face displayed in a window; which saint could it be? She is scornfully informed by Beoman, foreman engineer at Senator Dennis Chatastray's factory, that it is the face of Parnell, their national hero. The two women fall to mutual recriminations, accusing each other of secret drinking and thus breaking the vow they have taken to touch no alcohol till the protest march for Cardinal "Minteyzenty" (Mindszenty) is over. Having modified their vow Angela and Lizzie make for the pub. Whereupon a group of writers, actors, etc., enter. They have come to pay their last respects to Lionel Robartes, Protestant patron of artists, whose memorial service is about to be held in the church. All Catholics, they shilly-shally, however, inventing reasons for not entering upon infidel territory. There is also the question whether they should march on the protest demonstration for the "persecuted" Hungarian cardinal. Beoman, a Communist, belabours them with ridicule from the side-lines.

Chatastray, Beoman's employer, himself a patron of artists and the acknowledged leader of this group, impatiently presses them for a decision. On the verge of risking at least an entry into the graveyard they are stopped by the arrival

301

of the feared "Catholic activist" Kornavaun of the *Catholic Buzzer* newspaper: the Bishop has forbidden participation in the funeral service. Reena, a young nurse, member of the Legion of Mary youth organisation and a literary enthusiast, enters the church. Beoman follows. Kornavaun orders the group to pull themselves together and get ready for the protest march. Angela and Lizzie return drunk and incapable, having taken one or two over their vow. They collapse in front of the intellectuals.

Scene II. Chatastray's sitting-room. Green curtains. Books in Gaelic. The intellectuals—McGeera (playwright), Hoorawn (poet), Bunny (actor), McGeelish (gossip columnist)—are waiting for Chatastray. Preening and backbiting. McGeelish roots out what he calls dirty postcards in a drawer. Chatastray arrives late—trouble at the factory over a Protestant worker marrying a Catholic worker. Kornavaun bursts in with a questionnaire from the *Buzzer* for Chatastray to fill up with comments in favour of the Mindszenty march. But the group has taken evasive action. Confronted only with Chatastray's maid, Noneen, Kornavaun makes a pass at her, is repulsed, and retires breathing vengeance. The others re-emerge full of resolve to stand their ground. They will not carry the banner, "Free Thought in a Free World," neither will they march.

Beoman comes and reports that the factory-girls are threatening to strike on the marriage question. A deputation is on its way. Chatastray gives Beoman the postcards, which are in fact reproductions of famous paintings. Reena arrives, sent by Kornavaun to make sure there's no backsliding on the march issue. She is starry-eyed with admiration for the great men and great thoughts alive behind the green curtains and is staggered by the fact that Beoman, an Irishman, can be a Communist.

Noneen ushers in the deputation, plus Kornavaun. Chatastray warns the girls that a strike would lose orders. Kornavaun demands obedience to the church command on marriage. Chatastray stands his ground. The strike will take place. Immediately, armed thugs burst in and kidnap

Noneen. They are going to teach her a lesson for being alone in the same house with an unmarried man. Chatastray protests, Beoman acts. But none, not even his friend Chatastray, lifts a finger to help—except Reena. The masked men take Chatastray away as well as Noneen.

Scene III. Chatastray in dejection. He has been beaten up. Reena brings news of Noneen. Legion of Mary lasses had tied the latter half-naked to a telegraph-pole and left her there all night. Noneen is bitter against religion and Ireland but is bearing up. Reena has thrown off her illusions, including those concerning the intellectuals. But she works to win Chatastray; Beoman's way is right. Outside, the demonstration gathers, to the music of the "Marseillaise." Reena draws back the green curtains and challenges Chatastray to face life. Kornavaun leads in the intellectuals, all clad in the sackcloth jacket of repentance which they have been persuaded to wear. Noneen and Beoman come to say good-bye. They are off to England. Chatastray is ordered to don the sackcloth jacket. Reena's courage and counsel inspire him to make a stand. Beoman and Noneen leave. Alone, Chatastray and Reena move close. While Reena watches the demonstration pass, Chatastray sneaks out, minus the jacket, and joins it. Beoman returns and, declaring his love, invites the disconcerted Reena to go to England with him and Noneen. They pull the green curtains over the sorry scene and Beoman carries her off through the door.

This play is far from popular with a certain school of critics. "It is O'Casey's weakest play,"[1] announces Kosok, and talks of "ebbing creative energy."[2] The play embarrasses perhaps because the old man, far from being mellow, now metes out his rough treatment to his "own kind," the artists and intellectuals. More embarrassing still, this play gives no chance of avoiding the contemporary political implications. It talks explicitly about what its predecessors had dealt with more or less at one remove: it exposes the anti-Communist crusade of the cold war as the new, deadly, global form of the age-old spiritual inquisition of the oppressors against the oppressed. In the process it unmasks the real motives behind the Western "dissident" ballyhoo. It indicates where the real "iron curtain" is to be found, and it portrays a Communist worker as the best of men. In judging it the critic must take a stand on dangerous ground. In fact O'Casey puts the critic in exactly the same position of choice as the intellectuals within the play. And it is all, it seems, just a little too near the bone. The general tendency to dismiss the play as irrelevant is especially marked in some West-German critics. Kosok hopefully announces that "the situation depicted [. . .] has no meaning beyond its particular time and place."[3] A remarkable assertion from that quarter considering that West Germany is one of the homes of intellectual intimidation ("Berufsverbot").[4]

The first scene of the play and its relation to the following two scenes seems to have puzzled some critics as much as the function of the "cryptic" first scene in Brecht's *The Caucasian Chalk Circle*. Klaus Völker complains that the scene with Angela and Lizzie contributes only "local colour,"[5] and finds it impermissible that the two women never appear again in the play.

Let us begin by taking a closer look at this first scene.

For O'Casey the masses are always the starting-point, and this is no less the case in this play about intellectuals. He starts to talk about the latter by talking about the masses, represented here mainly by the two women.

Undeniably, the scene with Angela and Lizzie has no direct mechanical "plot" relationship with the scenes following. Yet it is not only relevant, but essential to a proper understanding of the play as a whole.

The state of these women is approaching tragedy. We are introduced to them almost at the bottom of a downward process. The national economy has not been able to integrate them. Previously street hawkers they are now semi-beggars living on charity. They are thus being forced to exist as outcasts on the verges of the human community; barely middle-aged, they are regarded as old women. This enforced idleness and isolation is the element (or rather the vacuum) in which their ties with their cultural environment and traditions grow more and more tenuous. Even that traditionally central part of their cultural community, the Catholic Church with its rituals and institutions, is fast becoming a foreign country to them. A bishop's mitre is "them comic consthructions they wear on their heads when they're processin' some particular church doin's." (Lizzie, 4) The helmet of a Mars-man! They can no longer quite remember things they once knew, things like the name of that old Irish Saint who used to let birds nest in his beard.

But the *non-terrestial* Catholic dignitaries, the Saints and Blesseds, are still very real to them, especially Angela. In fact they have delegated all responsibility for their life and well-being to these, which reflects their growing poverty of real concrete social relations. This drives them further into themselves and passivity. These insubstantial ghosts have become more real to the two women than real flesh-and-blood fighters (one reason perhaps being that there are so few of the latter around?). Thus they can no longer recognise the historic face of Parnell, who was once their uncrowned king, but take him, that intellectual and sensitive man who was martyred in their cause, for some obscure saint. Only a hazy memory flickers: *"Angela (in deep reflection). Where, now, did I see that sterun face before?"* (5) Their twilight is not Celtic but cultural.

In this way the content of their lives is being reduced to the enjoyment of pure sensation. The lucky chance of a bit of sun, the next couple of glasses of stout are happiness to them. Their life-programme is reduced to this: "Yis; ordher o' th' day–sip be sip, be sip." (25) Even a simple vow is a thing with too much perspective and self-discipline in it for them to keep. The pursuit of a sensation of bodily and spiritual well-being on this level leads to bodily and intellectual befuddlement, and finally to collapse of all the human faculties–prostration on the ground.

All that these women seem left with in the way of moral-intellectual landmarks are vague feelings of guilt and a sense of sin—inculcated into them by the clergy—at satisfying the only needs they recognise in the only way they know. So they have to hide themselves from themselves, in order to indulge their natural urges.

Thus, for all their drifting out of the ken of church institutions the power of the church's "moral instruction" is still the sole power strong enough to enter into and occupy the intellectual vacuum within them. In fact their spiritual darkness makes them ideal material for the oppressor's purpose. They are effortlessly tied to the cart-tails of the anti-Communist band wagon—in support of a foreign cardinal who to them is more a saintly personage from "the world beyond" than a flesh-and-blood churchman. In support of this rich and reactionary prelate, these poor women, who have so little left, are persuaded to take a vow depriving themselves of that little (drink) till the protest demonstration has taken place.

This then is the situation of huge sections of the "free" Irish people in a Free World, people who are expected to be ready to die rather than to sacrifice their freedom of thought to Communism! Mental darkness behind the green curtain in the "quiet" land of Erin. This process of lumpen-proletarianisation, of curtaining off the masses from the cultural community is reaching a crucial juncture. What is necessary to save the situation is clear: an economic set-up which would give them a basis at least for a life-function within the community and thus stop the moral and cultural rot; intellectual and cultural enlightenment, encouragement and leadership. This is a life-and-death matter.

O'Casey's portrait of these women is more complex than appears at first sight. Contained within their weaknesses are the possibilities for the negation and abolition of their weaknesses. Unexpected potentials emerge which could provide the basis for their regeneration.

For all their tendency to lose contact with the social community they remain close to the realities and needs of concrete living. Even within their idiotic preoccupation with saints and blesseds their practical, hard-headed, humanising urge is at work.

Angela. ... a Blessed buzzes down, all ears, minute he hears his name mentioned. What I say is that th' Saints get kinda stuck-up, y'know, an' th' one chance a body has is with th' Blesseds.

Lizzie. Don't I know it! Th' Blesseds has to keep on their toes to get notice, if they wants to be hoisted up into higher places. (12–13)

No awe here before the heavenly hosts! The difference between heaven and earth is abolished and the great ones of heavenly earth are cut down to size. The hierarchy appears moved by mere human motives and are clearly conceived of as servants of the people.

Angela and Lizzie have a healthy bias against denying themselves the material and spiritual good things of life, as they understand them. Despite all doubts and shilly-shallying their decision to go to the pub is crisply taken and promptly put into effect. Their vow against it? These people will break any vow sooner or later that gets between them and their interests. Thus, although they are, on the whole, the passive playthings or pawns of social forces, they do demonstrate an inherent capacity to decide on and carry out actions on their own initiative.

Their almost pagan hedonism, their susceptibility to sensuous-emotional appeal, their capacity for simple, full-blooded enjoyment—all this makes them potentially responsive material for the influences of art to work on. This hedonism is more marked in Lizzie than in her friend, who is more influenced by the remains of religion. For all their surface similarity there is a great deal of differentiation in their characters.

The loosening of their bonds to heaven's terrestial representatives (church and clergy) is not only an aspect of their drifting away from the traditional community and culture; it is at the same time a potential liberation. The clergy and its doings represent another, alien world for which they have contempt rather than fear—"or maybe, you've taken up with them lay apostles th' clergy are always blatherin' about at th' missions?" (7) asks Lizzie sarcastically. This withdrawal leaves a cultural and intellectual clear field in which other, more healthy things can be planted without fear of weeds. In this context their solicitude for Cardinal Mindszenty (still further off than their own clergy) is clearly seen as something injected into them from outside and quite foreign to their character.

Above all, there is in them an unextinguished curiosity about and susceptibility to the productions of art. Angela's dogged interest in the portrait in the window annoys Lizzie, but Angela can't let it rest—"All th' same, I like siftin' out things." (6) Lizzie herself responds more emotionally: the "Dead March" disturbs and depresses her. Angela informs her that it is a "dirge" and can pick out the drum-beat in it. But Lizzie has demands to make on art: "It's something to get us up we want, Angela, an' not nothin' to get us down!" (7) On the other hand, when the verger comes out and sings, "Oh, what a beautiful morning!" and proclaims that "Everything's going my way!" (12) she reacts with a snort of contempt for this type of facile uplift.

There is real conflict within these women. They are not so close to their misery that they have become unaware of it. They realise that their plight is getting worse. Their struggle is between this vaguely recognised drift to demoralisation and the conviction that they should do something against it. When they reach the end of their tether and collapse at the feet of the intellectuals there is real urgency in Lizzie's appeal, "For Jasus' sake, Angela, thry to pull yourself together." (25) But they cannot "get themselves up" by their own efforts alone.

Clearly a mine of potentials is here for the practitioners of culture to latch on to. And the necessity to do so has become acute. It is the social responsibility of the intellectuals and artists to stretch out a helping hand to the prostrate people in their effort to rise. This is especially true in a situation where one of the main forms taken by oppression is cultural deprivation and enslavement. In such a case the intelligentsia have also particularly favourable conditions for intervention to help guide things into a better course.

A scene sketching in the salient features of the petty-bourgeois intellectuals and artists is inserted into the Lizzie-Angela story. A field of tension is set up for the audience between the two groups, veering between the poles of similarity and difference, comparison and contrast.

The first thing we learn about the intellectuals is that they want to avoid any contact with the common people (represented by the two women). The snooping gossip writer McGeelish arrives first, alone, sees the women, and sneaks off again. No doubt he reports back that the women reacted with suspicion when he stole up to the church (which they did). At any rate the "brains" only arrive on the scene when the women have vacated it. They are afraid the common herd might see them a) enter a place of Protestant worship, or b) being too scared to enter it. They are afraid of the people.

They too, like the women, have made a vow. Theirs is—"come what would, to attend th' funeral" (17) of the man who had stretched out his hand to them, Protestant though he was. Like the women they are incapable of keeping their pledge. But these men do not break their vow in the interests of their "natural urges," but in betrayal of their better impulses. The women boldly enter the place that is supposedly anathema to them (the pub); but the intellectuals do not enter the Protestant church.

Unlike the women they are equipped with the necessary knowledge, insight and culture to guide them along the right road. But they betray this knowledge and themselves. In the women there is a minor victory over fear and inhibition; in the case of the intellectuals the victory is of fear over them: fear of the church's reprisals, which could damage their "chances," their reputations and their positions. The actual Church Almighty is as massively present to them as the heavenly hosts are to the women, but the boot is on the other foot. They grovel before those "powers" whom the two women naturally regard as their ordained servants. The innate practicality of the women drives them to take action; the "practical sense" and "realism" of these men (fear and watching out for Number One) consists in *not* putting their theoretical decision into practice. Thus the shilly-shallying, which as such is common to both parties, has, in each case, an entirely different source and function.

At the end of the scene the intellectuals have collapsed as completely as the women, but with far less justification. The physical falling down of the women also contains a symbolic cross-reference to them. The women make efforts to rise and there is urgency in Lizzie's call to Angela to pull herself together. Three times the same call, in almost the same words, goes out to the intellectuals: from Chatastray, Reena, and Kornavaun; that is, not from within the core of the group but from three relative outsiders. The only call they take seriously is the one in the church's sense issued by Kornavaun. There seems, then, to be very little of that vaunted "inner struggle" of the *Hamlet*-intellectual in these people. In *Hamlet* the bourgeois intellectual as hero makes his magnificent entry on to the world stage, and his quandary—to act or not to act—is of truly tragic calibre. This play shows to what a sorry spectacle this has dwindled now. Hamlet has become a bunch of third-rate Poloniuses. When Angela and Lizzie re-enter drunk, they are supporting each other, arms linked. (25) Now, although the intellectuals lack the richness of individuality of the two women and act as a group-personality, there is, nevertheless, none of this mutual support among them, only back-stabbing, distrust, potential betrayal.

These "intellectuals," then, do not inspire confidence that they can meet the demands of the crisis by latching on to the needs and rich potentials of the people. It is made clear that they need the people at least as much as the people need them. Their divorcement is having tragic results for both sides.

It certainly cannot be said that they are unaware of the people's plight. The latter force themselves into their unwilling ken by collapsing at their feet. But they don't react. The breaking-off of the scene at this point underlines the blankness caused by their self-preoccupation.

In this first scene the Communist worker, Beoman, functions as O'Casey's "chorus." In treating both groups with identical biting sarcasm, Beoman, their common point of reference, brings out what they have in common (which is not the whole story, as has been pointed out). To modify a sentence of Engels' somewhat, the rulers of this world seem intent on creating not only a lumpen-proletariat, but a lumpen-intelligentsia as well.[6]

Is the "Funeral March" issuing from the church the fitting accompaniment to the situation portrayed?

The whole scene is a devastating alienating-effect on the men of art and letters. And yet, even in their case, modest potentials for a more adequate course are hinted at. They did, after all, take the decision to come to Robartes' funeral. They know what they ought to be doing. There are slight gradations in the degree of spinelessness. Whereas McGeelish, the gossip writer, seems completely demoralised, the others show signs that they might, under resolute leadership, muster up enough courage to take a stand. There is, for instance, the playwright McGeera's call to ignore the brutish Basawn (admittedly a very minor Kornavaun minion) and open the gate to the churchyard. (24) The others take up the call and seem set on going through. But Kornavaun himself proves too much for their resolution.

Senator Dennis Chatastray, industrialist and patron of artists, gives strong indications that he perhaps has it in him, if not to be a Yeats (often a fearless champion of artistic integrity in the face of threats), at least to pick up the tradition handed down by the man they have come to pay their last respects to as an encourager of artists—Lionel Robartes. (Under the latter name O'Casey may be hinting at Yeats' younger colleague at the Abbey Theatre, Lennox Robinson, 1886–1958. O'Casey had no very high opinion of

the younger man but he thought him a cut above the pyg-
mies of latter-day Irish intellectual life.)

Chatastray is impatient at the irresoluteness of his set.
Even Kornavaun seems to hold few fears for him. Kornavaun can go to hell, he says—let us all go in together. You
can lead a horse to the water but you cannot make him
drink. Chatastray, however, only *seems* to lead his horses to
the water; in fact he tends to drift with the tide. (He has a
playbill for the Abbey play, *The Drifting Tide*, hung up in
his sitting-room.) He arrives late on the scene, with a plausible excuse to be sure, but since he does the same thing
again at the start of Scene II one is driven to wonder if it is
not partly a way of ensuring that, by the time he arrives,
the decisions have already been taken—"Thought yous
have been all in th' church be now." (17) Significant also
is his unwillingness to develop his promising friendship
with Martin Beoman: "Now, now, Martin, don't be inter-
ferin'. *(To the others—apologetically)* Beoman, my foreman
factory engineer." (18) Nevertheless, a possible bridge
across the gap separating the intellectuals and the working
people is hinted at here.

This first scene is "independent" of the rest of the play
only in so far as each important episode in the theatre of
"epic" tendency has an importance in its own right and
not simply as a link in an inseparable and single chain. The
first scene of *Behind the Green Curtains* is a signal example
of that tendency in the newer drama for important aspects
of the whole to be inherent in the parts. In a sense Scene I
is the whole play in miniature, the model of a model. One
does not know this however at the start of Scene II. Scenes
II and III give insight into the mechanics of the tragedy (of
the Irish scene as a whole) which one witnesses in Scene I,
explaining how and why such a situation could have come
about. In this sense they are really a kind of flashback leading up to Scene I—a kind of film or novel technique rare in
the traditional drama but quite in tune with the practice of
the "epic" drama with its emphasis on cool analysis rather
than "suspense." But they are not only this. They also give

the intellectuals and artists a "second chance." That is, they also move forwards from Scene I. The latter contains enough contradictory implications to indicate that this kind of story does not necessarily have to take the course shown: things were, after all, on the razor's edge at the final confrontation with Kornavaun. Scene II plays through the situation again at a higher level where there is much more at stake. Is there hope for these propagators of culture and enlightenment in that they learn from their humiliation at the church? Chatastray is clearly a key figure in this replay. Lastly, Scene I serves as a distancing-effect on what follows. Having it at the back of our minds we can never become so absorbed in the narrower close-up analysis of the men of letters that we can forget the wider social context of which it is a function.

Scene II expands the portrait of the intellectuals, including Chatastray. Reena, before her change, declares: "Yes sir; as Dr. Farren, Bishop of Derry, said, it is filthy literature that corrupts Irishmen and makes them ripe for Communism." (46) The work of these men disproves the good bishop. Indeed, they do produce, in point of quality, "filthy" literature. This we gather from their comments on each other's work, for when it's not a matter of themselves each of them is capable of withering insights. It is because it is filthy that there is no hope of their work ever influencing the people towards anything positive, let alone Communism. They have no intention that it should, preferring to pose and backbite behind the green curtains of Chatastray's drawing-room. Ironically, the bishop (like Reena) has more respect for the potential power of art to change people than these practitioners do. His misgivings seem superfluous in their case.

Yet he has, in general, some precedent for his worry, and for his "respect" for the influence of writing and drama. Artists and men of culture had made an exceptional contribution to the awakening of the Irish people in the past—Swift, Thomas Davis of the *Nation*, Parnell, Yeats and

Shaw, to mention but a few. Because of this, the most active spirits among the common people in the play, such as the nurse Reena, have great expectations of this generation too. The artist's potential "partner" within the people is exceptionally willing. Reena, when she first enters Chatastray's drawing-room, exclaims, "What great thought and high ideas go floatin' round here behind these lovely green curtains! [...] This is a proper place, sir, where th' writers come together; always brave, but will be braver from the grace given through the sacred Demonstration." (44–45) Even in its watered-down form of Lionel Robartes the great tradition is still potent enough to inspire her to run the risk of her church's censure (she is a loyal Legion of Mary girl at first) and enter the Protestant church to do her hero reverence. Thus art's power to inspire can rub out the barriers between Catholic and Protestant, can make people new and *create a basis on which to renew the traditional community*. Reena has taken up writing stories, a fact that underlines her concrete need for help and encouragement.

Reena's involvement with things cultural has made her a potential rebel. The two other brave fighters in the play, both workers, Noneen and Beoman, are also people in whom a need for culture has been awakened. This was Chatastray's work. With the patience of a father he has introduced them to treasures of the international and national cultural heritage. In so doing he is helping to turn them into enemies of the narrow-minded philistinism which marks life behind the emerald-green curtains screening the "Island of Saints and Scholars."

There are, then, all around this group, golden opportunities for rooting themselves in the people at dynamic points. Their leader, Chatastray, who is not only a man of culture but a man who in his daily business comes continually into contact with the masses, demonstrates before their eyes the modest beginnings of a model of what is possible.

But the great tradition is in danger of being snuffed out in this generation. In their feelings of inadequacy they wish, "If only we had Yeats with us now!" (Bunny, 18) Horawn retorts, "Oh, Yeats again! We have to live an' fight without him." (18) Right and wrong. Right in so far as they have to learn to stand on their own feet. Wrong in that to live as artists without Yeats' spirit is a betrayal of Yeats' fight. Horawn, the would-be poet, is clearly irritated at being reminded of the national poet. A glance at Horawn's contradictory artistic philosophy shows that, while it still retains something of the Yeatsian stand against the degradation of art in capitalism, it is the weak side of the great poet's position which gains the upper hand in him: "Our place is in no rabblement, no crowd, senses blurred be blarin' bands, even when it's led be a smaller rabble of mitred bishops [. . .] Th' writer's place is th' cool contentment of quiet, in a corner where no voice comes." (41–42) Yeats' heritage, because it has no adequate champions, has dwindled down to a fragmented formality which is appropriated and caricatured by the enemy. When Kornavaun enters in Scene II he is dressed, we are told, in an exaggerated arty get-up including a flowing tie, wider and longer than those worn by Yeats in his teens. The need for a proper relationship to the cultural heritage emerges, not as a desirable decoration, but as a necessity in the process of liberation.

But these intellectuals lack confidence in themselves, their art and the working people. The underlying lesson of Scene I (that the victory of the enemy's channels of intellectual and spiritual manipulation of the people is not total) is lost on them. Their isolation leads to a sense of impotence and this feeling leads them further into isolation. They have given up attempting to create for the people an alternative and better basis for community within the real community. They attempt instead to set up a pure "community of like souls" alongside existing society, screened from all its dangers and potentials, from enemy and prospective ally alike, behind the magic bourne of the green curtains. Is this proposal for an alternative, purer community the answer to the people's need–an example or model perhaps? In fact, as a magic frontier, it has none of the potency of the ash-tree bourne in *The Bishop's Bonfire*.

True, in the "land" behind it, as Chatastray says in his defence, "We're not afraid to have our independent thoughts. Many a time, straight things have been said in this very room." (62) And, indeed, many rebellious things are said behind the hangings. Does freedom and true community lie, therefore, in withdrawal?

The impression of a sanctuary where they "draw th' green curtains, an' blind some of th' squinting eyes," (35) is an illusion. They import the quick contagion of the "world" each time they enter. The sanctuary is poisoned from the start by their own corrupt presence. Even those much vaunted, but in themselves dilettante freedoms of thought and speech are severely relativised, for their best thoughts are too puny to live long in the presence of their mighty fears and their worldly interest. The world is too much with them—ambition, self-interest, snobbery and envy define human relations within this precious community of like souls. They remain remarkably "realistic," these seekers after a hermitage; their main interest is in securing their positions in the vulgar world outside. They don't really believe in it themselves.

And with justification, for the crazy edifice is like a leaky boat that lets the world in at all points without allowing anything worth-while to come out. A convenient arrangement for the powers that be. Perhaps a curtained cage is a better simile. A cage in which the human animals can indulge freely in their freedoms of thought and word in a vacuum, a circumscribed world where these freedoms can appear as freedom as such, i.e. freedom to translate ideas of liberation into action, for within the bounds of this *ersatz* world freedom of speech is the only kind of action possible. The ruling powers need have little fear that the impulses from these "freedoms" might spill over and lead to social action. Their exponents are too hamstrung in the ways indicated above. So let them amuse themselves. It keeps potentially catching things capsuled off from the general stream of life and makes them barren.

Nevertheless, just to check up and see that the animals

are behaving themselves, the keepers, or their tamers, burst into the sanctuary, or rather cage-drawing-room from time to time and crack the whip: Kornavaun's entry is swift and aggressive; two thugs burst in unceremoniously, with sticks in their hands, and shut the door with a bang, etc.

The claustrophobic setting of Scenes II and III in a *drawing-room*, which is really a cage at the mercy and whim of the outside world, is a development of the parodying and exposure of those endless contemporary "drawing-room" dramas, which O'Casey so detested, begun in *The Bishop's Bonfire*. The perpetrators of these "well-made plays" presumed to reduce the whole variegated world to the dimensions of the middle-class drawing-room. O'Casey reveals the real relationship between these unequal entities, and the disastrousness of confusing one with the other.

O'Casey is pointing out that these intellectuals and artists have not learned the lessons of history. The history of their own country gives them enough lessons showing that to bow to the pressure towards complete obedience to the inquisitorial church authority is to open the door to further suppression of intellectual life. They see that the "new" attack on "Reds" is but a stepping-up of the traditional crusade against all liberty, especially freedom of artistic expression. Under the mantle of combating Communism the throttle-hold is being tightened (questionnaire, etc.). As Horawn says, "Everything a man, anyway prominent, says if he dares to have a thought of his own, is given a slant by this *Catholic Buzzer* to make it appear to be sympathetic to th' Reds or giving hope and courage to anti-clerical feeling." (36) That it is on their consciences is seen in the fact that they again go so far as to take a vow to boycott the demonstration—which they again break. They knuckle under in the hope of softening the blow. The result is the same as with the Nazis.

In Chatastray's case there is an added reason why giving way to these forces is suicidal: "Catholic Action" and what stands behind it are destroying him as a "captain of industry." Its agents subvert his workers so that they stop production for a reactionary and unworthy cause. He loses important foreign orders as a result and has to sell out to a man from the North. The same forces make it necessary for Beoman, his right-hand man, to leave the country, and so on. The irony is that because Chatastray has neglected to resist systematically and strengthen his basis among the people, the one time he does stand firm—when he rejects the strikers' ultimatum on the Catholic marrying the Protestant— comes too late and acts against him, making it appear that to stand firm leads to ruin. The inability of industrial capitalists like Chatastray to assert themselves as such is certainly one of the reasons for the economic *misère* of the country and therefore for the dereliction of Lizzie and Angela.

The Communist Beoman repudiates the discredited tactics of appeasement. Those who complain of the "too-too noble Communist"[7] Beoman would do well to recall that it was above all the Communists in all the countries of Europe who refused to bow to the fascist yoke. Beoman embodies this, and he wins grudging respect from this new generation of semi-fascist thugs. The circumstance, however, that the latter make no real attempt on him is also due to the fact that their whole campaign is not really directed against the small number of Communists but against the basic human and democratic rights of all. They have quite a relaxed attitude to this real Red—"go, friend, an' leave us to deal with our own kind." (52)

That the "home" of these bourgeois intellectuals is anything but their castle is also seen in the fact that not only the oppressors but also the activists from the people walk in and out through their green curtain with hardly as much as a by-your-leave, bringing the inconvenient problems of the world with them. But the group refuse to take an example from these people. They cannot be kept out, but they are to be seen and not heard. When Beoman presumes to express an opinion he is told to shut up—what does a man like him know about the needs of creative minds? A curtain is drawn across at this point too.

Yet without the aid of the people they are unable to keep up even the pretence of their independent, better world. When the enemy is at the gate their only line of defence is to send forward Noneen to hold the gap of danger. She deals with Kornavaun while they seek refuge in the inner sanctum of Chatastray's office. When Kornavaun comes to have revenge on Noneen he takes the precaution of summoning reinforcements (three thugs). Her daily work is a life-experience which gives Noneen practice in standing up to the enemy. So when the time comes for her to show her mettle—as she has to when she is kidnapped and misused—she can come back fighting. The intellectuals, it seems, have no mettle to show. They behave as they are accustomed to behave—they leave her to her own devices. So they do rely on the people, but at the wrong point and in the wrong way, while denying them their support where they need it.

Thus the intellectuals' attempt at going into "inner emigration" is a fiasco. This can be no basis for a renewal of the community. As a variation on the theme of emigration it is far less valid than the way taken by those who physically emigrate at the end. It is a *false kind of distancing* from the community as it is. As a form of self-distancing it is no more hopeful and scarcely less pernicious than that involuntarily undergone by Angela and Lizzie. Their ivory tower is no Round Tower, no equivalent to that traditional strong point of the old Irish clan which stood, lighthouse-like, amid the tide of the barbarian onslaught and provided the whole community with a refuge and a basis from which to strike back.

We have discussed the writers all along as a group phenomenon. It is O'Casey's most sophisticated composite image of this type and is certainly not a sign of waning powers of individualisation. At one level it has a positive implication in so far as it shows these various kinds of word-purveyor to have a common relationship to the needs of reality and a common responsibility. This enhances our appreciation of the possibility of collective intervention on their part. It also works against the mystification of the pure "artist" in demonstrating that these (poets, playwrights) are made of the same common clay as "mere" actors and even gossip columnists. They are all in the same boat. Seen critically the gossip writer emerges as but a slightly aggravated form of what they all are. Apart from this the low-profile individualisation indicates their lack of character.

As in *The Bishop's Bonfire* the ruling powers use a combination of the iron fist and the velvet glove to keep their underlings in order. The velvet glove is used to soften the blow already dealt by the fist and give the intellectuals the chance of pretending to themselves that they have in fact been *persuaded*. Thus the group believe that it was the "cozy talk" they had over tea with the bishop which really won them for the march. There is something else, however, working within these people, something by no means bad in itself, which the oppressors recognise and exploit.

It is something deeply embedded in the consciousness of the Irish—their profound, historically conditioned *sense of belonging*, of loyalty to and identification with the community. It is something going back to Irish clan society, a feeling that their community as it is, whatever its rights and wrongs, is the world. This attitude, taken over from clan society, was hammered into a valuable psychological mechanism under the blows aimed at the national community as a whole by the foreign conqueror. Unfortunately, under present conditions this community has been usurped, monopolised and alienated by a set of "native" conquerors. This has not been immediately clear to the masses who habitually think in terms of the "family," and their new conquerors exploit this fact. They construct what is, in form, a communal event—the protest march for Cardinal Mindszenty, and offer it as a kind of ultimatum to the people, relying on the feeling that not to participate is to set oneself outside the bounds of the family. This problem was thrown up in *The Bishop's Bonfire* where Manus Moanroe is broken because he cannot solve it. Here it becomes the underlying point of thematic focus and organisation of the play as a whole. The people (Lizzie and Angela) are in danger of losing all contact with the cultural community of the nation, of becoming "wanderers" divorced from the clan. The petty-bourgeois intellectuals, as we have seen, have a very sorry thing to offer as an alternative conception of community—although they have a particular responsibility to do just that.

The oppressors cleverly organise their march as a kind of pageant, with the different sections of the community bearing their historical insignia. And *all* sections of public life are to have their place. In this way it appeals to deeply held historical associations and loyalties and also to the healthy underlying urge to communal *festival* (cp.) *The Bishop's Bonfire*, etc.). There is something inspiring in this march, leaving aside for the moment that they are "an army with banners marching in th' wrong direction." (Reena, 63) It *is* the army of the people, united behind one "cause," all sectarian religious divisions overcome for the moment. It is this that sweeps basically healthy souls like Reena off their feet initially and makes them into champions of their enemies' "cause": "All Ireland'll be there; first th' Bishops an' clergy, secular an' ordhers, then the Ministhers of th' State, then the Law. Youse will folley th' Legion of Mary marchin' in front of your banner, a blazin' torch over the motto, Free Thought in a Free World, headed be the band of th' Boys' Brigade." (46) Even Noneen is a little carried away by the pageantry: the judges in their wigs and gowns, the scholars in their robes, the dignitaries of the Irish Academy of Letters, etc. (37)

In allowing themselves to be integrated into the community on these terms, as part of the demonstration of the "rightness" of the way society is ordered at present, the writers are willingly conniving at their own public humiliation. They are to take their prescribed place in the rigidly hierarchical feudal train, and this place is well down the line. They are to dress in a kind of court-jester outfit and follow in the intellectual and cultural wake of the Legion of Mary and the band of the Boys' Brigade. If the intellectuals were to keep their vow they could break the universality of this solid phalanx and so dispute reaction's claim to be the community as such. But they do not recognise their own potential strength and influence and fail to do this.

The results of this failure are seen in Reena. Because she, initially, has been provided with no other conception of the meaning of the community than that imposed by the oppressors, she casts out into limbo anyone who seems to deny its basic tenets. Since it has been drummed into her that Communists do this she places Beoman (at first) beyond the Pale (the rulers of the Irish Republic also have their Pale!).

Unlike Manus, however, Beoman does not degenerate into a far wanderer from the tents of men. As a revolutionary socialist and part of a world movement that has established *his* kind of community in several countries, he has a firm alternative beneath his feet. In it the clergy must follow *behind* the people and their secular legality in the "march." "You see, young lady, they must submit to the laws of the land they live in; where they move an' have their being. They must be subject to the State, without any cod benefit or privilege of priesthood." (47) This basis gives him that relaxed, patient and positive relationship to those around him which was lacking in Manus. He gently turns Reena's guns against her, urging her to remember her motto: Free Thought in a Free World, and then says, "Well, thanks, pretty lady, for taking my fierce opinions so softly." (48) Here he begins to win her and woo her. It doesn't need much to set her on the right road. She has in common with Beoman a fierce loyalty to the true brotherhood of man. She is ready to love a brave man who fights for this. Towards the end she believes Chatastray might be such a man. When he fails her she turns naturally to Beoman's arms. So much for the "unmotivated" and "abrupt" falling-in-love of these two at the last moment.

This theme of the relationship of the individual to the community is most fully worked out in the portrait of Dennis Chatastray.

Enough has already been said to indicate the promising, and threatening contradictoriness of his character. Despite all his advantages he lets his followers down already in Scene I. All through this play the group of writers are never quite written off. Given certain modifications in the circumstances the chance is left open at least up to the end of Scene II that they might be led into an alternative, better course. Their chief "circumstance" is Chatastray. He is equipped to do it, but instead of practising success he practises failure—in front of the church at Robartes' funeral, and no doubt in a hundred and one similar "minor" instances. Practice makes perfect. What the play really says is that Chatastray's failure at the end of Scene II (during the confrontation with the kidnappers)—i.e. on a higher circuit of the spiral—is as much the result of habit, learned in his everyday evasions, as of fear or anything else. One must start with the "insignificant details." It is never too early to begin.

Chatastray's failure to aid Reena and Noneen at the end of this scene is fatal. It is the crucial point of decision in the play. What follows in Scene III is really more an epilogue than a dramatic climax, despite appearances. This was the last point where Chatastray, through decisive action, could have a) mobilised the intellectuals, and b) brought them together with those representatives of the militant people, Beoman, Noneen and Reena. In doing so he would have "realised" his potential nature. Only he, in this context, has the prerequisites to bring about this united popular front. He alone has the universality to do it. In previous plays O'Casey showed us the triumph of the universal man; here he shows us a case where universality is not exploited, partly because it is not universal enough, and the dire consequences this has for the struggle. Chatastray is both a man of real cultural and intellectual weight and a man in the mainstream of social practice—as a capitalist and manager of production. He has standing and influence in both "camps." In letting this opportunity slip he sets things on the course that leads to the final subjugation of the men of culture and the emigration of the best working-class forces. So the die is really cast at the end of Scene II.

At the start of Scene III Chatastray is in fact a hulk, a ship without the water to float it. He has by his own omission destroyed the potential alternative community from within which he could have acted with effect. His failure in relationship to his specific "community" parallels and epitomises the failure of the intellectuals towards the masses at large. He is "disillusioned" and even in a position to recognise his own failures, but his insight comes too late, and is never complete. He puts the blame on his community in the specific sense (the intellectuals) and upon the world at large. He washes his hands of them all and wants to shut the green curtains on the whole sorry scene—"don't want even to touch with my foot th' pavement in the street outside th' door!" (63) By introducing Tom Moore's song, "I Saw from the Beach," towards the end O'Casey symbolises Chatastray's position. Chatastray had taught Noneen to love this song and she, with unwitting irony, makes him a parting gift of a record of it. This song describes a ship which at morning sailed forward, with the sea, its natural element, supporting it, but as "I came when the sun from that beach was declining,/The bark was still there, but the waters were gone." (82)

This song is *his* epitaph when played at the close; it does not express the mood or position of those leaving the country.

What predetermines Chatastray's course in Scene III is his feeling of loneliness, of isolation from the community he knows. Reena makes a splendid all-out effort to educate and win him: "We're all frightened—those in th' North as well as us in th' South; th' men who took Noneen an' you away with them were frightened of faith, and of anyone setting himself apart from th' others an' themselves ..." (59)

She tells him he got what he got through his own cowardice and that of his "friends." Now, when she looks back, she realises that many a thing was done that should never have been done, but neither Chatastray nor his associates ever did or said anything against them: "You never tried to tell us how to think, what to do, where to go [. . .] Youse yourselves helped to form th' crowd that cry out against youse." (61) True and incisive words which summarise the lessons of the action. Yet, at this stage, words are not enough to win Chatastray. Ironically it is Reena's passionate championship of the necessity of keeping contact with the community of the people which helps to push him psychologically into the waiting arms of the community-as-status-quo: "No one and nothing can be left alone in this world. As long as you're alive, you'll have to bear being touched by th' world you live in." (60) There is one point where Reena's words can be misconstrued as an appeal to take part in the actual march—will he blend the patter of his feet with that of the marchers, she asks (64), or sit at home sullen, undecided, and afraid? What she means is that he should be with the people in the march of life.

The one thing that almost seems to save him still is the demand that he wear the sackcloth coat of the Brothers Repentant. This mockery of festival, the insolent attempt to transform it into its opposite, goes too far. But the fear that if he does not participate in this communal event, even on the terms offered by the enemy, he will end in a Manus-like limbo, is overpowering: "I don't want to [march]; I don't think I should; but it isn't a question of either; it is a question of I must. If I refused I'd be an exile from everything." (67) Reena warns that unless he *distances himself* from this alienated shadow of community he will never be able to take a step which is not in chime with its tune.

Those whom he failed and who, as a result, have been "integrated," return near the end with persuasive threats and appeals to him to take up with the old clan. His sins of omission come home to roost. Kornavaun and McGeera are vicious on the theme of driving forth all atheists and Communists. Horawn is more persuasive: "We cast them out! [. . .] Dennis, come with us. [. . .] Come and walk with your old friends whom you helped so often." (75) Chatastray successfully resists, but as soon as his old friends go and he is left "alone" with his new friend, Reena, the pull of the old thing reasserts itself–"all th' same, Reena, I'm thirty-five years old, an' this sash is a symbol of all I believe an' all th' customs I'm used to throughout them years." (78)

Reena's final bid is to offer him herself and the prospect of another life with her in another place, or, if he cannot bring himself to emigrate, then in this place. But it is too late for Chatastray to be able to make the jump to the tentative yet, for him, frightening beginnings of the daring and novel sort of community suggested by Reena.

In scuttling to catch up with the body of the marchers Chatastray is abolishing *all distance* between himself and the community-as-it-is. In *The Bishop's Bonfire* O'Casey brought out the need to keep plugged in to the people's community, even, or above all, in its present alienated form; in *Behind the Green Curtains* he is pointing out the simultaneous necessity of creating a "distance" between the progressive forces (the nucleus of a renewal of community) and the reaction-monopolised present community in order to be able to transform the latter.

These two plays really take the "Brechtian" emphasis on the alienating-effect out of the sphere of theatre *technique* as such, and discuss it as an essential form of relationship *to reality*.

One must have the courage to set oneself apart if insight and progress are to be achieved. The demoralised thugs are frightened "of anyone setting himself apart from th' others an' themselves." (59) Chatastray's last act shows that the final difference between himself and the dregs in this respect is nil.

Up to now we have seen two main forms of distancing from the body social and cultural, both leading into the wilderness–the involuntary drift of Angela and Lizzie, and that of the group of writers. At the end of the play a third form or variety of distancing is proposed.

In the mutual relations into which they enter towards the close, the three workers, Noneen, Beoman and Reena, suggest the nucleus of a new type of social living in which the new, the human and the communal are emphasised. Partly because of Chatastray's failure of responsibility in Scenes I and II, this nucleus is forced to emigrate. The physical emigration of this revolutionary community-nucleus is a rather bitter form of distancing, but it might under certain circumstances be one of the few viable alternatives left open. I have already had occasion to mention the fruitful returns from this enforced distancing in Irish history. One might add here the obvious parallel of the emigration of anti-fascists out of Hitler Germany, and their return, bearing the seeds of the commune.

In fact this "going abroad" in the context of this play also assumes the proportions of a symbol-metaphor for the necessity of creative distancing from the old community in our sense.

Chatastray will not be going with the three people with whom he had begun to establish a "family relationship." His loss is great–a "daughter" in Noneen, a "son" in Beoman, a wife in Reena. But their new community too, will, at first, be the poorer for his absence. There is a new "clan" a-forming, but the man who might have been one of its first *flaith* (a "father" of the clan) has added his weight and standing to the old and dying clan.

It was at the end of Scene II, then, that Chatastray allowed this chance finally to slip through his fingers. This means that the third scene is somewhat unusual in O'Casey's work in that the course it takes is largely *predetermined* before it begins: an epilogue on Chatastray. Its lesson: it is often too late to mend. The chances for social mobilisation and change must be taken on the wing, or they are lost. And this is tragedy. Thus the struggle in and around Chatastray in Scene III is really decided before it begins. The true dramatic irony and tension in the scene is generated by the fact that neither of the characters involved realises this. The illusion which Reena harbours on the score of a "new" Chatastray is revealed in a remark to him about his past: "You hadn't it in you to do more then."

(66) The irony is that "then" he did have it in him, but now he no longer has. Reena's almost vicious reaction to Beoman's attempts to comfort her after Chatastray's defection is not really caused by the desertion of "the man she loved," but by dismay at her seemingly inexplicable defeat after pulling out all the stops in an effort to woo a human being back to life.

There is nothing more that Reena and Beoman can do except draw the green curtains on Chatastray's drawing-room tomb, with Moore's mournful lament for the passing of life's chances as his fitting epitaph.

Notes

1. Kosok, op. cit., p. 317
   In similar vein:
   "... the scripts [of these late plays] are really a dead loss: tired, rambling inchoate things that may most charitably be thought of as unpromising drafts or garrulous sketches." (*Irish Press*, Aug. 15, 1975)
   "... an abominably bad and boring play." (*Irish Times*, July 23, 1975)
   " 'Behind the Green Curtains' is really an embarrassing piece of work, and did [it] not bear the O'Casey tag, no one in his right senses would consider putting it on the stage." (*Irish Independent*, July 23, 1975)
2. Kosok, op. cit., p. 318
3. Ibid., p. 312
4. "Berufsverbot"–the legalised practice in the Federal Republic of Germany of the sacking of persons in the civil service, teaching professions, etc. who are suspected of assisting or of being members of the D.K.P. (German Communist Party).
5. Klaus Völker, *Irisches Theater II: Sean O'Casey*, in the series Friedrichs Dramatiker des Welttheaters, Velber, 1968, p. 83 (translation, JM)
6. Cp. Engels' letter to Karl Marx, Oct. 7, 1858: "... this most bourgeois of all nations is apparently aiming ultimately at the possession of a bourgeois aristocracy and a bourgeois proletariat *as well* as a bourgeoisie."
7. Klaus Völker, op. cit., p. 83 (translation, JM)

XII FIGURO IN THE NIGHT
Written around 1960; published 1961

> "The road of excess leads to the palace
> of wisdom."
> William Blake, *Proverbs of Hell*

Scene I. A street in a new district on the outskirts of Dublin. At one end stands an obelisk to the young Irishmen killed while serving in the British army in the First World War. At the other end—a Keltic cross to commemorate those who died for Ireland. The street between looks lonely and forsaken. Every now and then during the scene a Young Girl pops her head out of her house. She sings in anticipation of her Johnny coming home with blue ribbons for her from the fair. She is smitten with a strange excitement. A drab old crone totters in and picks up the girl's theme-song of "Johnny's so Long at the Fair." She once had a Jimmy but he never did come home from the fair to claim her with blue ribbons. An equally decrepit old man enters from the opposite end (possibly her one-time Jimmy). He's taking a risk, he mumbles, being out on a night like this, for there's "some strange stir about." The two lonely old wrecks get into conversation. Both are intent on finding out what is afoot in the city centre. They vie with each other in painting their lordly origins and youth in glowing colours and enumerating their "chances" of marriage, which they were able, thank God, to evade. "Look to yourself when you begin to enjoy a thing," says the Old Man. The latter declares that the only salvation lies in a return to the idiot innocence of Eden, under God and the church's tutelage. All our troubles started when Adam tied a blue ribbon in Eve's hair. The Old Woman contradicts him and her pronouncements become more and more "outrageous" as she warms to her theme. She takes fright however when the Old Man suggests that they go together to see what's what.

Scene II. Later. The night has burst into bloom. Leaves and glowing fruits. Birds sing, cattle low, a cock crows. The hubbub from the city centre rises and falls, a symphony shot through with warning flashes. The two monuments are decked with flowers. Enter two decrepit, terrified and somewhat damaged old men. They have just "escaped" from a "riotous assembly" in the centre of the town. The Fair has been changed into a general hilarious uprising by the appearance of a figure reminiscent of the famous statue of the naked Pissing Boy at Brussels. Egged on by the Figuro's phallic feats the women and girls have all gone daft, chasing and embracing anything in trousers—including the Civic Guard, many of whom waver in their duty and show less than due outrage at being the chased for a change. Enter a Young Man who has barely escaped with his virtue, followed by two nattily dressed individuals, both newspaper reporters. The one is deaf, the other blind. They are linked back to back and move by revolving round each other. They badger the others for eye-witness and ear-witness accounts, which the two Old Men eagerly supply. The young people have proclaimed that "The Beginning Is Here!" The Old Men proclaim that the End has come. A Birdlike Lad enters, with the characteristics of O'Casey as the Green Crow. He announces that a similar revolution is springing up in every town and hamlet in the island. A concourse of young girls and boys enters, all brilliantly clad. Music. They begin a processional, festive dance. The young couple come out of the house and join them. All dance round the two old fellows who crouch clinging to the monuments. The Deaf Man and the Blind Man have been banished from the scene.

There are three monuments in this play. Two of them celebrate war and the dead (the obelisk and the cross). These are situated in a new district—a broad hint at the Irish Republic, and were erected at about the time the latter was founded. The war and "death" they really celebrate is the war against healthy, natural sensuality, and the apparent killing of this, the core of liberty, in Ireland. The obelisk is a phallus—a fossilised erection over dead manhood. The Keltic cross (thus: ⊕) is a kind of distorted petrification of the female sign ♀. Set in stone and alienated from the flesh these too, represent one of those sundered pairs which O'Casey so often indicates. Placed each at the opposite end of the new street, the rigid length of it holds them—it seems—for ever apart, like the deep water in the song. Man is man and maid stays maid, and never the twain shall meet. At the same time these symbols of alienated sensual joy, turned into a grim warning of mortality, seem to hold the street between them in a vice-like grip.

This pincer-like dead hand is, however, shattered "overnight" by the intervention of a third monument—the animated statue of the Pissing Boy. This is a monument with several special features. It celebrates, not something which has (apparently) been killed, but the resurgence and revolt of that same thing—joy in the functions of the human body and the senses. Its most prominent feature is, as with the obelisk, a phallus, but a far from fossilised one. In this, two things that belong together are brought together: the celebration of the natural urges and the revolutionary repudiation of the existing set-up as a whole—for the Boy pisses on the town.

Thus the healthy natural urges of the mass of the people can achieve magical *transformations*: they can animate a monument, transform art into a living thing. In this process art—when it is realist, as this figure certainly is—"comes alive" and intervenes actively on the side of the popular forces, mobilising them to transform the situation. Under its inspiration, in one miraculous Walpurgis-night, the massed forces of youth and total living sweep away the old enslavement and establish the dawn of the age of lusty liberty.

But is this socialist realism? How can such a fantasy help people to revolutionise reality? Does it not side-step all the very real problems facing revolutionaries and replace them with facile enthusiasm?

In fact it lays bare the core of O'Casey's revolutionary realism. We have seen that O'Casey was never one to use his art to illustrate the actual mechanics of making a revolution. In his revolution plays he always went for the human meaning of the revolution in terms of the liberation and reintegration of the whole man and woman alive. As a realist O'Casey realised that, in this period of the cold-war offensive of reaction, what the people needed was a sign, a blazing emblem, an inspiration to keep going against all the odds. This revolutionary-romantic and realist *anticipation* of the glorious Victory Night of human liberation functions in three directions simultaneously.

The first and definitive direction is in relation to the general "state" of the society O'Casey lived in. Never had this world seemed so cowed and corrupted, such a fen of standing water. It was all too easy to lose heart and think that no road led from there to glory. *Figuro in the Night* is the eighty-year-old O'Casey's great final denial and defiance of such a view. He re-establishes revolution as the *strategic* perspective: enslavement will fall because its nature runs counter to nature in general and to the human nature of the ordinary people in particular. Come what may, the Commune must come. The world spits enslavement out as something indigestible that has been lying in its stomach.

The play zooms in on this dramatic process just at the moment of spitting out, which explains both the terrific energies released and also the almost playful ease with which it is accomplished. Playful is a word to be conjured with, for the revolution, as O'Casey models it for us, is above all *fun to make*. Its association with sex and sexual pleasure underlines metaphorically the exquisite joy to be derived from the paramount act of love between man and his world. 'Tis a consummation ardently to be wrought for through all the futility, frustration and set-backs met with in traversing the valley-floor. In making this play like this O'Casey is encouraging us to do what the revolutionaries do in *Purple Dust*—"lift up their eyes unto the hills."

All this also indicates the second direction in which the play functions—as a polemic against the slandering of revolution propagated by such literary champions of the status quo and militant mankind-haters as Aldous Huxley and the detested George Orwell. The latter in particular had aroused O'Casey's contemptuous anger[1] by suggesting in *Animal Farm, Nineteen Eighty-Four* and elsewhere that the revolution was the arch-enemy of all jollity and sensuality. *Figuro* is O'Casey's counter-blast in which the revolution is identified with the opening of the Carnival of Life.

The play's third direction of reference is towards certain of the O'Casey plays which preceded it. In these he had shown how, even in the time of darkest night, the working people bear within themselves the ability and the will to transform life. And he had shown, further, how this was thwarted by the unsolved problem of leadership. Now, when he is about to take his leave, he puts these soberly assessed frustrations into perspective. *Figuro in the Night* is a romantic-realist anticipation of the great day on which these thwarted potentials will prevail.

In so doing O'Casey takes his place in a particular tradition which runs from Blake's prophetic books through Shelley's *Prometheus Unbound* to the Communist utopias of William Morris and Walt Whitman's hymns to the human body. To this vision O'Casey brings the raciness and humour of the popular-utopian folk tradition, of Cockayne, the Land of Milk and Honey, and the medieval festivals of fools with their rumbustious topsy-turvydom. These latter were dramatic performances, and O'Casey is the first major author to bring their spirit on to the modern stage.

Figuro in the Night, like other works in this tradition, is a vision, an anticipation, and can only express itself through "visionary" artistic means. Further, it is the poetic anticipation of a moment of *qualitative transformation*, the point in the social process when developments become vastly speeded up and telescoped. In fact, the revolution, as a moment of this kind, is the epitome of lightning and total transformation in which the "normal" and "eternal" laws governing the relations between things seem to go by the board, when things are suddenly pulled together in a way which reveals surprising, new, unheard-of connections, where the ordinary becomes fantastic and the fantastic everyday—the common element in which things move and collide. The revolution is itself the victory and realised embodiment of the creative fantasy of the masses, of their most daring dreams.

All this favours an artistic technique which gives the writer a free hand to juggle with and transform the elements taken from reality, to combine, foreshorten, omit, short-circuit, highlight and generalise—in a word, the free use of fantasy and the fantastic. And O'Casey uses these with a freedom and universality here surpassing anything in his previous work. The stage-reality of *Figuro in the Night* is *all* fantasy, and this is right and fitting, for the reasons given above. In a sense the play is a companion piece to *Cock-a-doodle Dandy*, the fulfilment of its hinted perspective. The Figuro is a reincarnation of the fantastic Cock. But here his isolation and tendency to abstraction are overcome. He and the people now become re-integrated with one another through the act of revolution. The Cock becomes a material force; it is his victory and homecoming.

This may be all very well, but where, one might justifiably ask, is that inner tension, that dramatic conflict without which a play may be many things, but not a play?

The inner tension that makes *Figuro in the Night* live is not between any groups of people, classes or individuals, though such contradictions do pop up, for instance between the Old Woman and the Old Man in Scene I, or between the Young Man and the others in Scene II. The contradiction that matters is the conflict between the humanised senses and a dehumanising false consciousness with its resulting inhibitions. This struggle of the senses *versus* an inhibiting "ideology" takes place *within* individuals and becomes through them a general social phenomenon. On the whole it takes the form of the irresistible *subverting* and erosion of the inhibiting attitudes from within, often from the "subconscious," whereby this subconscious is seen not as the storehouse of the irrational and the animal "instincts," but of the healthy and stable human core beneath the surface slick of superimposed inhibitions and fears.

It is the revolt of the humanised senses, which is the revolt of human sense, its liberation from folly. The bed-rock of this natural human sense are the sensual emotions of the masses, the inalienable heritage which they have amassed in the course of man becoming human. O'Casey's point is that this sensual-emotionality in which man is at his most human, will not and cannot be subdued indefinitely by any inappropriate, constricting and deforming moral strait-jacket. This being the thing he wants to put across it is right and natural that he embodies his theme in images of sexuality, of sexual emotions. As Marx says,[2] the sexual sense is the measure of man's achieved humanity. In it one can measure in how far man's human nature has become natural to him, in how far he has humanised nature. In it the natural and the human are wedded. O'Casey is not proposing that sexual liberation as such is the be-all and end-all of social revolution. He is using it as a potent symbol for the deep-going, thorough liberation of humanity, which is at the same time the liberation of nature.

In the first scene O'Casey sketches in his satire on the actual miserable state of affairs in a few deft strokes. What really interests him and us is the process of the subversion of this from within. The important point which emerges is how little it needs to set things into movement: the slightest sign of a loosening, radiating out from the centre. It is as if a high-octane fuel has been building up in reservoir, needing only a spark to set it alight.

The rising at the centre is being instigated by the young women. It is therefore natural that it should be the girl in the house in the "quiet" district who should find herself its main mouthpiece. It is also natural that she expresses herself almost entirely in the most intense and lyrical form of speech, in song. At those points where the new spell is broken for a moment and astonishment and horror overwhelm her at her own presumption ("Saints above, what am I thinkin', what am I sayin'!" 90) the song seems to burst out of her almost against her will, and sweep her over the danger zone of relapse. It is made clear that the younger generation, represented by this girl are not now going to repeat the tragic course of their elders (who in their day *had* followed meekly in their elders' footsteps). The Old Man and Old Woman, in their time, had stayed behind their windows. The Old Man had girls "knocking at me door, even tapping at me window, but I kept to me prayers." (94) Once, however, sitting by a window, the Old Woman thought she heard a blackbird sing. The new spirit has gone into the house and taken possession of the young girl within, so that she will no longer be confined: every now and then the door or window flies open and the bird inside pops out.

The faint hints in the air and the personification of the new feeling in the restless girl do not, in this outlying district, amount to a great deal. Yet it is enough to penetrate into the most solidified substrata and bring them into movement. In the case of the enfeebled and superannuated old people it seems almost literally to wake them from the threshold of death. But the victory of the sensual life resurgent can never be complete in them. They remain caught in their contradictions and backslide inevitably. In their fate lies the tragedy of wasted generations, who had the stuff in them, given different circumstances, to liberate themselves and celebrate life, but whose potential has been wasted. This is the real sombre tint in the variegated colour spectrum of the play. But what is indicative of endless hope and the irresistible power of the forces of sensual life is *their partial victory even within these two*–apparently the most intransigent of all possible "subjects."

Of the two it is clearly the Old Woman who is most thoroughly activated. She is smitten at once by the girl's song, and picks up its theme. This is just and proper in the terms of the play, where the initial impulses at the epicentre emanate mainly from the women. In fact the whole play brings the revolution as such and the self-emancipation of women into inseparable conjunction. We experience the

Old Woman abandoning her "time-honoured" position as underdog to the sovereign male. When the Old Man begins to pontificate complacently about the solidity of the old order, with the husband still king of the family and the mother the queen, she, the mere echo of the male, suddenly contradicts him to his face, telling him that they're now no more than a couple of cracked china "figaries" (not figuros!) on the mantlepiece of memory.

She begins to take the lead, to question, to criticise, to negate. From scratch, it seems, and in total contradiction to their general acceptance of the way things have gone as being normal and inevitable, she develops a revolutionary view of man's historical "mission" (her interpretation of the Garden of Eden and the Fall): "The farther we get away from the garden, the better. It was outside of it that the mind grew and the hands got their cunning." (102) The Old Man is unable to rise to such insight and rejection. His ideological position (his inhibitions and prejudices) remains basically intact. Yet his customary behaviour patterns too, are disturbed. He does risk coming out. He too, is drawn as by a magnet towards the city centre and the thing they supposedly fear. Decrepit as he is, he, like the Old Woman, suddenly finds himself, out of the blue, reliving the days of his youth and his glory in glowing words that belie his surface attitude towards the things of the senses: "Same as me, Cis. Good-looking ones, peace on their lips, fresh in the dew of younger years, came knocking at me door [. . .] many a maid of a sweet brown knowe, many a rose of Tralee, many a lovely Kate of Liskehaun, many a cailin deas crúite na mbó." (94 and 95) He it is too, who makes the daring suggestion that they actually go together, at night, to see the fun. At this point the Old Woman is incapable of following him.

In the apparent inexplicableness and lack of motivation of their talk and behaviour lies the secret. It is not a sign of O'Casey's decrepitude as an artist but a sign that his artistic cunning had outsoared that of many critics.[3] The two old people, even more so than the girl, are in the grip of forces from without and within which they do not recognise, which seem alien to them—"My God, what was I sayin' a minute ago!" (Old Woman, 103)

It is the rising force from within, in tune with the impulses from without, and answering to them, which must be emphasised. These two people are no empty vessels, neutral to what is being poured into them. Their suppressed feelings and sensual attitudes are in subtle and universal insurrection, so that a process of spontaneous subversion "from below" is continuously undermining the foundations of the superimposed enemy ideology.

The most subtle and poetic expression of this revolt is seen in their speech. This is permeated with rhythms and phrases from popular and folk poem and song, especially love-ballads. The entire second section of the Old Man's account of his youthful temptations as quoted above is made up of the names of heroines of love-songs, just as the Old Woman in her companion speech preceding it expresses herself through the names of young heroes of legendary song such as the Minstrel Boy, Brennan o' the Moor, etc. Thus their "detestation" of the evils of the flesh is mocked and denied in and through the very act of expressing it. The speech of the people is interwoven with references to or quotations from popular songs and folk-songs. One signal example from the climax of the relationship between the two old people in Scene I:

Old Man. We risk our souls' salvation talking. Let us go to where the stir in Dublin is.
Old Woman. I go the high road.[4]
Old Man. And I go with you.[5]
Old Woman. At this time o' night? No, John, no.[6] (103)

Song in this play is the distilled expression of the resurgent forces of the full human being coming into their own. Much of the talk of these two and others is already on the threshold of song. From the point of view of their puritanical, inhibited ideology their own language is in revolt. Language seems to take on a life of its own—sensuous, rebellious and creative. This is what lies behind the "absurd" wrangle between the two, beginning:

Old Man. . . . A garden is a lovesome thing, God wot,[7] and that was God's own garden, woman.
Old Woman. God's wot what?
Old Man. What God's what's what?
Old Woman. I'm asking you what's God's whot?
Old Man. How can I tell what's God's whot's wot? It's what's not your what's whot or my wot's what. Only God wots what His own wot is. (99)

And so on. This is language doing what the people in the centre of the city are doing—running riot.

All this indicates that life is ripe for revolution; ready and waiting, like the Codger in the garden; brimming with a quantitative accumulation below the surface.

For this reason one can scarcely agree with Manfred Pauli (one of the few critics who have given serious consideration to the play) when he says that, "The two parts are, in their diametrically opposed moods, placed in contrast to each other. The gloomy first part displays human destruction and deformity without a glimmer of hope."[8] In like manner Robert Hogan is simplifying the structure and message of the play in maintaining that it "depicts a triumphant transformation of the dead world into the Golden Age."[9] It does nothing of the kind. Dead worlds are dead and no amount of agitation can transform them. The point being made in the first scene is that the world, for all its degeneration and alienation, is not dead, and therefore capable of transformation.

The Figuro brings this quantitative build-up to a head. He is both the instrument of the inevitable change in quality, and also a personification and symbol of this change. It is this transition from quantity to quality which explains the explosive nature of the change, why such a relatively "minor" event is enough to touch off such a cataclysm. Pent-up energies are let loose, as accumulated water pours through a dam-burst.

339

That it occurs during a popular festival is natural, and also characteristic of O'Casey. We have noted how community festivals tend more and more to become the focal point of the struggle for control in O'Casey's later plays. In most cases this struggle was won by the forces of anti-life and the people deprived of their apotheosis in festival. Here at last it is they who, through the revolution, take over control of the festival and turn it into the Carnival of Life. Many of the previous festivals were compromised from the start by being formal events run by church or state. It is significant that this festival is an entirely secular and popular one–the Fair (carnival), descended from a purely *pagan* holiday. It is in the nature of things that the simmering rebellious energies of the sensual man and woman should bubble over just at this point. The revolutionary Figuro is both the embodiment and product of the Fair. The Fair of Life and the revolution are two names for the same thing.

In the second scene this revolution is in its flood-tide. The desolate suburb is transformed into a blooming garden in which nature and man in harmony rejoice. There is an allusion in this to the argument about Eden between the two old people in Scene I. We now see that both were right in their way, for every resolute step away from the original Garden of tutelage is in fact a step towards the Garden again. Now mankind repossesses Eden. Having gone through the fire of experience they return to a second innocence, but this time they are masters of themselves and the Garden. It is a new, volatile and lusty Eden which they create. This is O'Casey's crowning word on the theme of the Garden, its alienation and the possibilities of its repossession, which he first took up in *Within the Gates*. In its working out here he reveals how close his vision is to that of William Blake in *Songs of Innocence and Experience* and the Proverbs.

The second scene brings together those who have been pulled into the epicentre of the rising and return with their impressions to the periphery. Now a strategic similarity in general shape and movement between this play and *The*

Plough and the Stars begins to emerge. Here, as in the earlier play, a revolutionary cataclysm takes place "off stage" in the centre of Dublin. But the difference is the thing. The "revolution" in *The Plough and the Stars,* as a *revolution,* never comes "on stage." Certainly, there is, as in *Figuro,* a two-way commerce between the epicentre and the periphery (i.e. the everyday lives of the people) but it is of a very different nature. In the *Plough* the people go into the heat of it, *without* taking part, and haul back the material things which they need but which the revolution is not providing–things which at best can only provide a slight and ephemeral improvement. That "revolution" too, radiates outwards into the farthermost and innermost nooks and recesses of their lives–but as a *foreign* force (the English!) bringing only death and destruction. In this later play the people are drawn in and participate, willy-nilly, and also, willy-nilly, they carry back into the quiet streets of their everyday lives, not loot, which will change nothing (they could have done this but didn't!), but the spirit of that real revolution in human relations which will change all things utterly. This lava-flow, this irresistible and universal radiation is the burden of Scene II.

The two Old Men in the second scene bring out an important aspect of the conflict already hinted at in the old people in Scene I. Their diseased ideology and its inhibitions have gone deep enough to have created a sort of false sense-perception. They tend to apprehend certain things in a way which runs contrary to the actual evidence of their senses. The Old Man talks of his two fit hands and sees himself as a fair young fellow still. The Old Woman is slightly more realistic–her tiny hand is just a wee bit wrinkled now, she admits. In the case of the Old Men in Scene II this inability to apprehend things as they are means that to them the transformation is in the opposite direction to what is actually happening before their eyes. They see the new blooming and rejoicing of nature as a withering and disintegration, with the leaves dropping from the trees, the birds falling dumb and the sea-cliffs crumbling into the water.

(105) They seem in a certain sense to be blind and deaf. What the youth proclaim as the Beginning, they proclaim to be the End.

But they, unlike the Blind Man and the Deaf Man, do have physical senses, and these, stoked up and invigorated by their direct participation in the events, march in the opposite direction, negating the false evidence of their corrupted "sensibility." Where there is "sense" there is hope. They cannot keep the revolution out of themselves. It pours in through the opened doors of their senses, creating a subversive enthusiasm in them which they cannot help transmitting. They are, to their alarm, the "possessed" disseminators of the evil which they purport to abhor. They are incapable of responding to the Blind Man's demand—or their own for that matter—that they should take action to restore the status quo. Instead the 2nd Old Man finds himself eagerly relating how "I seen Kathleen Mavoorneen [another heroine of love-song, JM] sailing straight for a gossoon of a Civic Guard, and he standing gaping at her condescendin' bodice slipping, slipping down lower and lower, his innocent mouth open, eyes a-poppin', helpless; waiting to be coddled be the sin ablaze in her; then she whipt him into her arms, and then I saw them gone, leaving only two red flames twisting round one another!" (113–114) The others are all agog. The Old Man covers his face with his hands, the very telling of it frightens him, he says. The Young Man avers that he doesn't believe a word of their fantasising:

1st Old Man. Jimmy, what're you saying? You can't deny the proof given here, this very minute, of a young lad lost be a look at a handsome hussy's bodice slipping away from her bonnie breasts.

2nd Old Man. What are you saying, Michael Murphy? Realise, man, that you are provokin' dangerous thoughts in a young and heedless head! [This old man was actually the instigator of these reminiscences, JM]

Young Man. It's not the first time they were mentioned. I

know a Gaelic song that sings of the delight of the snowy
breasts of a true love. How could he ha' known they
were white as snow, if she hadn't shown them to him?
2nd Old Man. See, Mr. Murphy? Your careless blather is
doing great harm.
Young Man. I'll sing the song to show yous I'm right, so I
will.
Blind Man. We want no song o' that kind sung here, boy.
(115)

Fully in tune with the role of song and music in this play
the Young Man feels urged to justify what is happening
through the precedent provided by folk-song. Notice that it
is not the Old Men who forbid him to sing. Their own attitudes are continually being "compromised" and negated
by involuntary echoes of popular song in their speech.

In the passage quoted the actual events are lent still
more weight and attractiveness through the spontaneous
action of the Old Men's fantasy. This activity of the fantasy, even in this partly diseased form, is on the side of the
revolution and its propagation. Through it the core of what
is happening is highlighted and *poeticised,* i.e. the "magical" *transformation* of things, so that the customary and
accepted "laws" of being appear as repealed. (Compare
the role of the fantastic events in *Cock-a-doodle Dandy.*)
The elaborations of the Old Men's fantasy contribute—as
so often in Irish history—to raising the events to the level
and proportions of *legend.* In this case reality itself becomes
legendary and meets them at least half-way.

The impact of events produces a certain progressive development in the two superannuated old fellows. This
should not be exaggerated. The Birdlike Lad rightly calls
them "bastards" near the end. Nevertheless, they are, at
the last moment, able to do what at first they could not—
correctly interpret the evidence of their own senses, for they
finally recognise the Young Girl and the Young Man in
their festive splendour as the "silver apples of the moon"
(120) and the "golden apples of th' sun." (121)

343

In view of all this Manfred Pauli is surely missing the point when he writes, "In the jolly second part the old people are not only the victims but at the same time the ideologists of the unnatural set-up." [10] The truth is that they are, above all, propagandists against their own ideology. Failure to realise this leads the critic to a one-sided appreciation of the play: "The negative figures are laughed unmercifully to death. They are grotesques who offer very little of interest as regards human substance or a differentiated and contradictory character-structure. Their aesthetic appeal is entirely derived from the high degree of satirical intensity with which they are portrayed [. . .] Attempts at 'human enrichment' are not the way to endow these figures with theatrical life." [11]

Everything is entered into, nothing is left unaffected. There are no dead and hopeless things—except those in whom the human senses are dead. This is the case only with the Blind Man and the Deaf Man. They are in this scene not only as an ironical comparison and parallel to the two Old Men, but also, and this the beauty of it, to bring out the contrast. There is blindness and blindness, deafness and deafness. The *real* sensual deadness of the Blind Man and the Deaf Man is epitomised in the fact that they are *physically* blind and deaf. Despite their eagerness to "get in contact" there is no hope of these two corrupt journalists being touched as the Old Men are by the great renewal and coming to power of the whole sensual human being. At the moment when the revolution, in the form of the group of youths and girls, finally takes physical possession of the centre of the stage, the Birdlike Lad banishes the two cripples (but not the two old fellows) from the scene, as Ariel might do with evil spirits in that other play so reminiscent of this one—*The Tempest*.

This irresistible drive of the revolution from the centre (an urban centre) out into the uttermost and most intransigent extremities is generalised upon through the intervention of the Birdlike Lad. He is the personification of that union between man and nature which is consummated in the revolution. He is a typical O'Casey messenger, bringing news from the wider world and setting the apparently parochial events in context. The supporters of the status quo express a last hope in help from the North or from the bishops. The Lad dashes any such hopes–the Figuro has roused the North, and the Catholic hierarchy are sitting entranced in Maynooth singing "Comin' through the Rye," "Come and Kiss Me Sweet and Twenty," and other lusty love-lyrics! That subversion by song which lurks in and leaps out of all the old people has made itself manifest and moved into the highest seats of power–the old bishops.

The close of the play shows the revolution entering a new stage of consolidation. The first flash of passionate and tumultuous unleashing is passing. With the entry of the brilliantly dressed lads and lasses a new order and organisation is beginning to crystallise out of the chaos. As Brecht says, Communism is not chaos but order.[12] A new kind of order. In previous plays the festival which was being fought for sometimes took the "ordered" form of a processional march. Here now, the prevailing forces of life form up in ordered procession–not to stride to the music of a march, but to step to the music of the dance. Thus discipline and poetry merge and the march of life becomes an ordered, stately dance. That "music" which has been the moving spirit everywhere in this play has finally prevailed as one of the basic principles of all life.

This, then, is O'Casey's last word. The Blind Man in the play says, "When we heard the rumour, we guessed it was a hydrogen bomb." (108) To the 2nd Old Man the H-bomb is an "innocent thing" compared to the revolution. In point of fact, in the way O'Casey pictures the revolution in this play, it emerges as the fitting and adequate alternative and "replacement" for the nuclear bomb. His dynamic image of the revolution has a certain similarity to the immense force released by a nuclear explosion. The revolution is "nuclear fission" on the social plane. As with the neutron bomb (of which O'Casey of course knew nothing) the all-pervading radiation from the epicentre has no effect on material objects in themselves, but a tremendous effect on human beings—not destroying their life as the neutron bomb does, that "solution" of the international terrorists, but fanning the life that is in them into a flame. The radiation of the revolution is not an alien, murderous invader but something answering to the people's own inalienable human nature.

Notes

1. See "Rebel Orwell" in *Sunset and Evening Star*, op. cit., p. 540
2. See Karl Marx, *Economic and Philosophic Manuscripts of 1844*, Moscow, 1961, p. 101
3. See for instance Kosok, op. cit., p. 320; also Gabriel Fallon, *Sean O'Casey, the Man I Knew*, London and Boston, 1965, p. 196
4. "I go the high road" cp. song *Loch Lomond* ("I'll take the high road")
5. "And I go with you" cp. song *I know where I'm going* ("And I know who's going with me")
6. "No, John, no" cp. song *Oh, no John*
7. This is a line from the poem *My Garden* by T. E. Brown
8. Pauli, op. cit., p. 188
9. Hogan, "In Sean O'Casey's Golden Days," op. cit., p. 174
10. Pauli, op. cit., p. 188
11. Ibid.
12. Bertolt Brecht, *In Praise of Communism*